WORK THE ROOM

oe & b_books
CRITICAL READERS IN VISUAL CULTURES #8

WORK THE ROOM

A HANDBOOK OF PERFORMANCE STRATEGIES

EDITED BY / HERAUSGEGEBEN VON: ULRIKE MÜLLER

ACKNOWLEDGEMENTS:

This project was made possible by the enthusiasm, persistence, and hard work of all participants. I sincerely want to thank the artists, authors, and translators. Sara Marcus proofread the English texts, and Martin Gastl exceeded his role as German language corrector and translator, helping with editorial concerns. Katya Sander and Simon Sheikh invited me to publish this book in their series, OE; without their invitation, this book would not exist. Zach Formwalt was in charge of the design and the book production for OE and did an excellent job. My gratitude also goes to the Museum of Modern Art in Vienna, to Achim Hochdörfer, who invited me to organize the performance symposium, and to Dagmar Steyrer and Manuela Ammer for their perfect organization and care of the event.

Many conversations and experiences helped me formulate my understanding of performance as political acts. I am indebted to LTTR—especially to Ginger Brooks Takahashi, K8 Hardy, and Emily Roysdon—and to my brother Martin Müller, to Carola Platzek, and to all my friends in Vienna and New York. I cherish the continuous exchange I share with Barbara Schröder, and I am deeply grateful to Gregg Bordowitz for invaluable reading suggestions, thoughts, and for his generous support of my work.

Ulrike Müller

BUNDESKANZLERAMT KUNST

DANK:

Der Enthusiasmus, aber auch die Ausdauer und Arbeit aller Beteiligten haben dieses Projekt möglich gemacht. Ich möchte mich an dieser Stelle herzlich bei den KünstlerInnen, AutorInnen und ÜbersetzerInnen bedanken. Sara Marcus hat die englischen Texte korrigiert, und Martin Gastl hat nicht nur seine Rolle als deutschsprachiger Korrektor und Übersetzer ausgezeichnet erfüllt, sondern mich auch redaktionell unterstützt. Katya Sander und Simon Sheikh haben mich eingeladen, diese Publikation in ihrer Reihe OE zu veröffentlichen – ohne diese Einladung würde es dieses Buch nicht geben. Zach Formwalt hat für OE die Gestaltung und Produktion betreut und hervorragende Arbeit geleistet. Dank an das Museum Moderner Kunst Stiftung Ludwig Wien, an Achim Hochdörfer, der das Projekt angeregt hat, an Dagmar Steyrer und Manuela Ammer für die ausgezeichnete Organisation und Betreuung der Veranstaltung.

Zahlreiche Gespräche und Erlebnisse haben mir geholfen, mein Verständnis von Performance als politischem Handeln zu formulieren. Ich danke LTTR, insbesondere Ginger Brooks Takahashi, K8 Hardy und Emily Roysdon, meinem Bruder Martin Müller, Carola Platzek und all meinen Freundinnen und Freunden in Wien und New York. Mit Barbara Schröder teile ich einen kontinuierlichen Austausch, den ich sehr zu schätzen weiß, und Gregg Bordowitz danke ich von ganzem Herzen für wertvolle Lesetipps, Gedanken und für seine großzügige Unterstützung meiner Arbeit.

Ulrike Müller

WORK THE ROOM

EDITED BY / HERAUSGEGEBEN VON: ULRIKE MÜLLER

OE CRITICAL READERS IN VISUAL CULTURES #8
BERLIN: B_BOOKS, 2006

THIS BOOK IS PUBLISHED IN RELATION TO THE SYMPOSIUM PUBLIC AFFAIRS/ ÖFFENTLICHE ANGELEGENHEITEN AT THE MUSEUM OF MODERN ART LUDWIG FOUNDATION (MUMOK) IN VIENNA, AUSTRIA, SEPTEMBER 26-28, 2003.

THIS BOOK IS ONE IN A SERIES OF OE-READERS.
SERIES EDITORS: KATYA SANDER AND SIMON SHEIKH

COPY EDITOR: ZACH FORMWALT
GRAPHIC DESIGN / GESTALTUNG: ZACH FORMWALT

WWW.OE.DK

1st EDITION, BERLIN 2006

B_BOOKS, LÜBBENERSTRAßE 14, 10997 BERLIN
X@BBOOKSZ.DE

ISBN: 3-933557-70-4

CONTENTS

INHALT

Work the Room

by Ulrike Müller

"The scandal consists in the fact that the act cannot know what it is doing."
Shoshana Felman, *The Scandal of the Speaking Body*

In the fall of 2003 I invited thinkers, artists, and musicians for a symposium on performance and political acts at the Museum of Modern Art Ludwig Foundation in Vienna. I began this project with a question: "What does it mean to act critically?" Recalling performance works I had encountered in previous years, I followed a thread of political engagement and wanted to trace some shared concerns.

At this event, people seemed united more by emotions than by a shared perspective regarding political action. The war in Iraq had started several months earlier; questions of agency collided with the feelings of helplessness, depression, and despair that arose in response to the daily news. Gathered in a subterranean museum gallery equipped with a stage and rows of chairs, we did not seem to be able to do anything *against* what was bothering us. These feelings of political futility stood out in stark contrast to the enthusiasm of the participants and the intensity of sensations evoked by the performances and experienced by those present.

While working on the symposium and this book I recurrently felt a need for clarity. Historical and theoretical definitions of performance always seemed to fall short, entangling me in irresolvable contradictions. In the end, I had to accept the slippery and contradictory nature of performance as a part of its capacity. Using a term coined by the poet John Keats in a letter written in 1817, this capacity could be called "Negative Capability." As artists, we produce meaning without ever being able to fully understand the world or ourselves. Keats writes, "At once it struck me what quality went to form a Man of Achievement, especially in literature and which Shakespeare possessed so enormously—I mean Negative Capability, that is when a man is capable of being in uncertainties, mysteries, doubts, without any irritable reaching after fact and reason." Performance presents us with a realism rife with ambivalence and paradox. Irresolvable questions further creativity and stimulate the production of new meaning.

Performance belongs both to art and to the quotidian. On the stage or in everyday life, the performer—a person doing something—throws the question of an authentic subject into high relief. This is complicated by the psychological and cultural baggage accompanying public speaking and acting: The language we use is not our own, our acts are not original, and on a stage we drag with us the traditions of theater, performance art, art history and activism. The simultaneity of and tension between physical presence and representation, singularity and repetition, immediacy and reproduction, all link performance to performativity and the subversive potential of repetition. Performers and audiences can be aware of this, but they cannot predict with any certainty what its effects will be. Nevertheless, as Sharon Hayes points out in the conversation with Yvonne Rainer published in this book, the formal means of performance "allow for very precise examinations of the performative operations of subject formation."

Performance art mostly takes place in a specific and delineated setting. Yet, this Here and Now is transcended through the connection between performance and subject formation and the politics possible in a given situation, in a room among those present, gains a new dimension. As Gregg Bordowitz stated at the event in Vienna, the Here and Now can never be grasped and is always already over. Nevertheless the moment is significant as the instant in which decision-making takes place. From experience we know that in the end decisions are made impulsively and emotionally. The characteristic of a satisfactory decision is a feeling of relief. In decades of feminist practice and feminist thinking, the political has folded even more deeply into the personal to include unconscious, irrational, and affective realms. Thorough inspection of the Self dissolves the Self, our assumed stable point of reference in the world. This complicates the notion of agency and shifts it into a region between the no longer tenable categories of inside and outside, "I" and "You."

Live performances are shared by everybody present, and the people in the audience act as well as the performers do. The effects of these acts are real, while the intentions do not necessarily influence experienced reality: I had the intention to be entertained, but find myself bored, distressed, appalled, outraged, embarrassed, or ecstatic. Or: I had the intention to disturb the audience, but they, familiar with the techniques of the avant-garde, thought I was amusing (or boring). Performances create "situations" that include audience and performer, speaker and listeners. These situations are effective only when they become experiences and resonate with the personal and cultural history of those present. I am reminded of De Sade's Justine, the literary embodiment of the good girl falling prey to all evil. She is immune to art's transforming potential. Angela Carter writes that Justine's innocence devaluates experience and transforms it into mere events. Things happen to her, but cannot change her.

Performance creates spaces for shared experience while at the same time establishing hierarchies. Somebody does something. This doing something demands attention and needs the support of an audience. The audience is not an anonymous crowd. It consists of specific persons, each stepping out of an individualized everyday life and into a situation where he or she assumes the art-specific role of the spectator. What the performer does would not make sense without the personal effort and the mental presence of the audience. The London-based artist and musician Anat Ben-David told me that she finds it worst when her gigs are admiringly described as "absolutely crazy." This indicates that a person did not engage with the performance and kept her- or himself at a safe distance. Art arises in the moment of presentation. When an artwork addresses me personally, it gains meaning in the world. Performance short-circuits this function in time and space and creates opportunities for collective meaning production and conceptions of subjectivity. In this humble proposition lies the politics of performance, its potential to change us.

The contributions in this handbook do not document the event in Vienna; they are rather intended to outline a network of contemporary problems and to open perspectives for further doing and thinking. I asked the participants to find formats to describe their work with performance, and the results are collected here:

Sharon Hayes and Yvonne Rainer discuss, in an email conversation, the handling of historical references and repetition as a method.

Linda Bilda invented a patented technology and reports about her performance as a businesswoman for over two years, in which—as her management consultant advised—it was key to be "authentic," entirely herself in every situation.

Gregg Bordowitz gives an account of his ongoing research on volition and the mechanisms of deciding and acting.

Marie-Thérèse Escribano talks about historical facts and artistic considerations in relation to her critical interpretations of German popular songs from the 1920s and 1930s and the unmasking of their ideology.

In an image-text collage, Discoteca Flaming Star present the magical space opened up by their poetic hardcore performances. In addition, they invite Matthew Lyons to formulate his perspective on their project.

Christof Kurzmann contributes a personal statement about the concrete and emotional motivation for his album *The Air Between*.

Mattin asks about the political connotations of improvised music and about moments of productive insecurity.

The representational critique of Sabine Marte's work is presented in an image-text contribution by the artist and an analytical essay by Christa Benzer.

The transcript of Andrea Fraser's introduction to her video "Official Welcome" and of the discussion following it at the symposium in Vienna comments on the sources of her performative work and on her own involvement in the relationships she investigates in her project of institutional critique.

Stephan Dillemuth and Achim Hochdörfer talk about agitation and the potential of a self-organized art public.

The script of Xavier Le Roy's performance "Product of Circumstance" narrates how he developed from being a natural scientist to dancing and choreographing.

Using images from their film project "The Uninvited," Judith Hopf and Katrin Pesch exemplify how the media haunt the everyday with ghostly familiar appearances.

The title *Work the Room*[1] refers to the performer's desire to activate a space, to share it with the audience, and to give everything: To jolt the viewers into re-thinking their own position (Yvonne Rainer), to avoid simplistic or escapist entertainment without attacking or instrumentalizing the audience (Sharon Hayes), to produce an immediate experiential context (Linda Bilda), to conceive thinking and feeling as neither separate nor opposite (Gregg Bordowitz), to use laughter to make viewers feel understood (Marie-Thérèse Escribano), to share a space of artistic encounters (Discoteca Flaming Star), to broadcast one's own sadness (Christof Kurzmann), to overcome fear and to risk insecurity in order to discover novelties (Mattin), to interrupt the fantasies and viewing habits of TV consumers (Sabine Marte), to perceive oneself as part of the critically examined art system (Andrea Fraser), to define the stage as a social and experimental site (Stephan Dillemuth), to present the audience with different and contradictory facts about the body (Xavier Le Roy), and to investigate how our experience is determined by the mass media (Judith Hopf and Katrin Pesch).

Work the Room emphasizes the space shared by performer and audience—physical, emotional, and mental space. Simultaneously, the title directs attention to work and to art practice without falling into a rhetoric that assigns the role of activity to performers and a passive role to the members of the audience. The challenge for both spectators and performers lies in redistributing the roles time and again and in filling the space between subject and object with verbs.

In the past few years I have repeatedly experienced the political capacity of performance. Since the beginning of 2005 I have been working in the queer feminist collective LTTR with Ginger Brooks Takahashi, K8 Hardy, and Emily Roysdon. LTTR helped me build an understanding of a political art practice that does not exhaust itself as a protest movement against grievances and injustice. LTTR rather operates from within a queer community to temporarily activate spaces. It forms an open experimental field for the lived performance of alternative relations and self-conceptions and furthers the continuous production of meaning. Queer sexuality, creativity, and sensibility are the foundations on which we can shape the world with and for each other. Performance, as a mode of expression and a tool, is essential for this project, to which I feel enthusiastically committed.

Note:

1. The colloquial U.S.-American locution "to work the room" describes an active mode of address in social situations. Here are a few related dictionary entries:

   work the house *v.* [US] [Circus] to sell popcorn, peanuts, etc., to work up the audience's thirst before one produces trays of drinks and ices.

   —Jonathon Green. *Dictionary of Jargon.* London and New York, 1987.

   work a spot *v.* to sell drugs or sex in a certain location.

   —Geneva Smitherman. *Black Talk.* Boston, 2000.

   work the room *v.* [1950s +] to chatter to people at a party or meeting. [show business use, for an entertainer to move through the audience, chatting to people and involving them in the act]

   —Jonathon Green, ed. *Cassell's Dictionary of Slang*. London, 2005.

Literature:

Angela Carter. *The Sadeian Woman and the Ideology of Pornography*. New York, 1978.

Shoshana Felman. *The Scandal of the Speaking Body: Don Juan with J.L. Austin, or a seduction in two languages*. Stanford, California, 2002 (Paris, 1980).

Hyder Rollins, ed. *The Letters of John Keats*. Cambridge, Massachusetts, 1958.

Eckhard Schumacher, "Performativität und Performance." In Uwe Wirth, ed. *Performanz. Zwischen Sprachphilosophie und Kulturwissenschaften*. Frankfurt/Main, 2002

Work the Room

von Ulrike Müller

„Der Skandal besteht darin, dass der Akt nicht wissen kann, was er tut."
Shoshana Felman, *Le Scandale du corps parlant*

Im Herbst 2003 hatte ich DenkerInnen, KünstlerInnen und MusikerInnen zu einem Symposium über Performance und politisches Handeln ins Museum Moderner Kunst Stiftung Ludwig Wien eingeladen. Meine Ausgangsfrage lautete: Was heißt es, sich kritisch aufzuführen? Unter dem Eindruck von Performancearbeiten, die mir in den Jahren zuvor begegnet waren, war ich dem roten Faden politischen Engagements gefolgt und wollte dabei geteilten Anliegen nachspüren.

Emotionale Verfasstheiten schienen bei dieser Veranstaltung viel eher eine Klammer zu bilden als gemeinsame politische Perspektiven. Im selben Jahr hatte der Krieg im Irak begonnen, und die Frage nach politischer Handlungsfähigkeit stand im Widerspruch zu Gefühlen der Hilflosigkeit, Niedergeschlagenheit und Verzweiflung, die mich und andere angesichts der globalen und nationalen Nachrichten erfassten. Versammelt in einem Ausstellungsraum im unterirdischen Teil des Museums, der für den Anlass mit einer Bühne und mit Stuhlreihen ausgestattet worden war, schienen wir nichts *dagegen* zu vermögen. Der Enthusiasmus der Beteiligten und die Intensität der von den Performances hervorgerufenen kollektiven Gefühle bildeten jedoch einen Kontrast *dazu*.

Während meiner Arbeit an dem Symposium und an dem vorliegenden Buch verspürte ich immer wieder ein Bedürfnis nach Klarheit. Historische und theoretische Definitionen von Performance schienen stets zu kurz zu greifen oder mich in unauflösbare Widersprüche zu verwickeln. Schließlich musste ich Flüchtigkeit und Widersprüchlichkeit als Teil des Vermögens von Performance als gegenwärtiger Kunstpraxis akzeptieren. Der Dichter John Keats hat 1817 in einem Brief den Ausdruck „Negative Capability" verwendet. Als KünstlerInnen produzieren wir Bedeutung, ohne uns selbst oder die Welt jemals völlig verstehen zu können. Keats schreibt: „Plötzlich wurde mir bewusst, welche Eigenschaft eine Person bedeutender Errungenschaften ausmacht und was Shakespeare in solch großem Ausmaß besaß – ich meine negative Befähigung, wenn einer fähig ist, das Ungewisse, Mysteriöse, die Zweifel zu ertragen, ohne alles aufgeregte Greifen nach Fakten und Verstandesgründen." Performance fasziniert, weil sie eine realistische Kunstform darstellt und dabei Raum für Ambivalenz lässt. In einem scheinbaren Paradox sind es gerade die nicht lösbaren Fragen, die Kreativität befördern und die Produktion neuer Bedeutungen anregen.

Performance ist zugleich kunstspezifisch und alltäglich. Auf der Bühne oder im Alltag wirft die Performerin oder der Performer als handelnde Person die Frage nach einem authentischen Subjekt auf. Diese Annahme wird jedoch durch das psychologische und kulturelle Gepäck verkompliziert, das öffentliches Sprechen und Handeln begleitet: Die Sprache, die wir verwenden, ist nicht unsere eigene, die Handlungen, die wir setzen, sind nicht originell, und auf der Bühne haben wir zusätzlich die Traditionen von Theater, Performancekunst, Kunstgeschichte und Aktivismus im Schlepptau. Die Gleichzeitigkeit und Spannung von körperlicher Anwesenheit und Darstellung, Einzigartigkeit und Wiederholung, Unmittelbarkeit und Reproduktion docken Performance an Performativität und das subversive Potenzial von Wiederholung an. Diese Verbindung kann zwar mitgedacht, zugleich aber weder von PerformerInnen noch vom Publikum als Effekt vorausgesetzt werden. Dennoch eignen sich die formalen Mittel der Performance, wie Sharon Hayes in ihrem E-Mail-Wechsel mit Yvonne Rainer betont, „für sehr genaue Untersuchungen der performativen Mechanismen von Subjektformierung".

Performancekunst findet zumeist in einem spezifischen und begrenzten Rahmen statt. Im Zusammenhang von Performance und Subjektformierung wird dieses Hier und Jetzt jedoch überschritten, und die Politik, die in einer gegebenen Situation, in einem Raum und zwischen den anwesenden Personen möglich ist, erhält eine neue Dimension. Wie Gregg Bordowitz bei der Veranstaltung in Wien feststellte, ist das Hier und Jetzt niemals greifbar und immer schon vorbei. Dennoch ist der Augenblick bedeutend als der Moment, in dem Entscheidungen getroffen werden. Aus Erfahrung wissen wir, dass Entscheidungen schlussendlich impulsiv und emotional getroffen werden und dass das Merkmal einer zufrieden stellenden Entscheidung ein Gefühl der Erleichterung ist. In Jahrzehnten feministischer Praxis und feministischen Denkens hat sich das Politische noch tiefer in das Persönliche gefaltet und umfasst das Unbewusste, Irrationale und Affektive. Bei genauer Betrachtung löst sich das Selbst auf, das unseren vermeintlich stabilen Bezugspunkt in der Welt bietet. Dies verkompliziert den Begriff von Handlungsfähigkeit und verschiebt ihn in einen Bereich zwischen den nicht länger haltbaren Kategorien von Innen und Außen, „Ich" und „Du".

Liveperformances werden von allen Anwesenden geteilt, die Personen im Publikum handeln ebenso wie die Auftretenden. Die Effekte des Handelns sind real, während Intentionen nicht unbedingt Einfluss auf die erlebte Realität nehmen: Ich hatte die Absicht, mich zu unterhalten, bin aber gelangweilt, erschüttert, verschreckt, empört, peinlich berührt oder ekstatisch entzückt. Oder: Ich hatte die Absicht, das Publikum zu verstören, aber dieses, mit den Techniken der Avantgarde vertraut, fand mich amüsant (oder langweilig). Performances schaffen „Situationen", die Publikum und PerformerIn, SprecherIn und Zuhörende involvieren. Diese Situationen sind nur dann effektiv, wenn sie zu Erlebnissen werden und die persönliche und kulturelle Geschichte der Anwesenden zum Schwingen bringen. An de Sades Justine, dem literarischen Inbegriff des „guten Mädchens", das allem Bösen zum Opfer fällt, ginge dieses verändernde Potenzial von Kunst verloren. Angela Carter schreibt, dass Justines Unschuld Erfahrung entwerte und in bloße *Ereignisse* verwandle, Dinge, die ihr zustoßen, die sie aber nicht verändern können.

Performance schafft Erfahrungsräume und etabliert zugleich Hierarchien. Jemand tut etwas. Dieses Tun verlangt nach Aufmerksamkeit und wird vom Publikum getragen, das jedoch keine anonymisierte Masse ist. Einzelne Personen treten aus ihrem individuellen Alltag in eine Situation, in der sie die kunstspezifische Rolle von ZuseherInnen annehmen. Ohne den persönlichen Einsatz und die mentale Präsenz des Publikums würde das, was die Performerin oder der Performer tut, keinen Sinn machen. Die in London lebende Künstlerin und Musikerin Anat Ben-David hat mir gesagt, dass sie es am allerschlimmsten finde, wenn ihre Auftritte bewundernd als „absolut verrückt" bezeichnet würden, weil das darauf hinweise, dass sich jemand nicht auf die Performance eingelassen und sich auf sicherer Distanz gehalten habe. Kunst entsteht in einem Prozess der Veröffentlichung. Wenn eine künstlerische Arbeit mich persönlich anspricht, gewinnt sie Bedeutung in der Welt. Performance schließt diese Funktion in Raum und Zeit kurz und bietet Gelegenheiten für kollektive Bedeutungsproduktion und Subjektentwürfe. In diesem bescheidenen Angebot liegt die Politik von Performance, ihr Potenzial, verändernd zu wirken.

Die in diesem Handbuch versammelten Beiträge sind keine Dokumentation der Wiener Veranstaltung, sie sollen vielmehr ein Netz gegenwärtiger Fragestellungen spannen und damit Perspektiven für weiteres Tun und Denken eröffnen. Ich habe die Beteiligten gebeten, Formate zu finden, um ihre Arbeit mit Performance darzustellen:

Sharon Hayes and Yvonne Rainer erörtern in einem E-Mail-Wechsel den Umgang mit historischen Referenzen und Wiederholung als Methode.

Linda Bilda hat eine patentierte Technologie erfunden. Sie berichtet von ihrer mehr als zwei Jahre dauernden Performance als Geschäftsfrau, bei der es – wie ihr Unternehmensberater sagt – vor allem darum gehe, „authentisch" zu sein, in jeder Situation ganz man selbst.

Gregg Bordowitz veröffentlicht einen Zwischenbericht seiner laufenden Recherche über Willenskraft und die Mechanismen von Entscheiden und Handeln.

Marie-Thérèse Escribano erläutert historische Hintergründe und künstlerische Überlegungen zu ihren ideologiekritischen Interpretationen deutscher Schlager der 1920er- und 1930er-Jahre.

Discoteca Flaming Star präsentieren in einem Text-Bild-Beitrag den magischen Raum, den ihre poetischen Hardcore-Performances eröffnen. Ergänzend dazu, haben sie Matthew Lyons eingeladen, seine Perspektive auf ihr Projekt zu formulieren.

Christof Kurzmann veröffentlicht ein persönliches Statement über die konkrete und emotionale Motivation seines Albums *The Air Between*.

Mattin fragt nach den politischen Konnotationen improvisierter Musik und nach Momenten produktiver Unsicherheit.

Sabine Martes repräsentationskritische Arbeit wird in einem Bild-Text-Beitrag der Künstlerin und einem analytischen Text von Christa Benzer vorgestellt.

Das Transkript der Einleitung zu Andrea Frasers Video *Official Welcome* und der folgenden Diskussion erläutert den Hintergrund ihrer Arbeit mit Performance und ihre eigene Verwicklung in Verhältnisse, die sie in ihrem institutionskritischen Projekt untersucht.

Stephan Dillemuth unterhält sich mit Achim Hochdörfer über agitatorische Ansätze und das Potenzial einer selbst organisierten Kunstöffentlichkeit.

Das Skript von Xavier Le Roys Performance *Product of Circumstances* behandelt seinen Weg vom Naturwissenschaftler zum Tänzer und Choreografen.

Katrin Pesch hat einen Bildbeitrag zu dem von Judith Hopf und ihr realisierten Film *The Uninvited* gestaltet, der das gespenstische Wiedererkennen von aus den Medien vertrauten Gesichtern behandelt.

Die Wahl des Titels *Work the Room*[1] bezieht sich auf den Wunsch, als PerformerIn einen Raum zu aktivieren und mit dem Publikum zu teilen, sowie auf die Bereitschaft, alles zu geben: die ZuseherInnen aufzurütteln (Yvonne Rainer); der allzu einfachen und eskapistischen Unterhaltung zu entgehen, ohne die Anwesenden anzugreifen oder zu vereinnahmen (Sharon Hayes); einen Zusammenhang unmittelbarer Erfahrung zu erzeugen (Linda Bilda); Denken und Fühlen nicht getrennt oder gegenläufig zu fassen (Gregg Bordowitz); den ZuseherInnen im Lachen das Gefühl zu geben, verstanden zu sein (Marie-Thérèse Escribano); einen künstlerischen Begegnungsraum zu teilen (Discoteca Flaming Star); die eigene Trauer zu veröffentlichen (Christof Kurzmann); Angst zu überwinden und Unsicherheit zu riskieren, um Neues zu entdecken (Mattin); die Fantasien und Sehgewohnheiten von FernsehkonsumentInnen zu stören (Sabine Marte); sich selbst als Teil des kritisierten Kunstsystems zu begreifen (Andrea Fraser); die Bühne als sozialen und experimentellen Raum zu sehen (Stephan Dillemuth); dem Publikum widersprüchliche Tatsachen über den Körper zu präsentieren (Xavier Le Roy); zu untersuchen, wie unser Erleben von Massenmedien bestimmt ist (Judith Hopf und Katrin Pesch).

Work the Room betont den von PerformerIn und Publikum geteilten Raum – physischen, emotionalen und mentalen Raum. Zugleich lenkt der Titel die Aufmerksamkeit auf den Aspekt der Arbeit und künstlerischen Praxis, ohne dabei in eine Rhetorik zu verfallen, die PerformerInnen eine aktive und Publikumsmitgliedern eine passive Rolle zuschreiben würde. Die Herausforderung besteht für ZuseherInnen und PerformerInnen darin, die Rollen immer wieder neu zu verteilen und den Raum zwischen Subjekt und Objekt mit Verben zu füllen.

In zahlreichen Diskussionen, Veranstaltungen und anderen geteilten Momenten habe ich in den vergangenen Jahren immer wieder das politische Vermögen von Performance erfahren. Seit Anfang 2005 arbeite ich mit Ginger Brooks Takahashi, K8 Hardy und Emily Roysdon im queer feministischen Kollektiv LTTR. LTTR hat mir zu einem Verständnis politischer Kunstpraxis verholfen, die sich nicht als Protestbewegung an Missständen und Ungerechtigkeiten abarbeitet, sondern aus einer queeren Community heraus temporär Räume aktiviert und ein offenes Experimentierfeld für die gelebte Performance alternativer Beziehungsformen, Selbstverständnisse und für kontinuierliche Bedeutungsproduktion schafft. Queere Sexualität, Kreativität und Sensibilität bilden die Grundlagen dafür, miteinander und füreinander die Welt zu gestalten. Performance – als Ausdrucksmittel und als Werkzeug – ist von zentraler Bedeutung für dieses Projekt, dem ich mich begeistert verpflichte.

Anmerkung:

1. Die umgangssprachliche US-amerikanische Redewendung „to work the room" beschreibt einen aktiven Modus der Ansprache in sozialen Situationen. Hier einige Wörterbucheinträge dazu:

   work the house *v.* [US] [Circus] to sell popcorn, peanuts, etc., to work up the audience's thirst before one produces trays of drinks and ices.

   – Jonathon Green, *Dictionary of Jargon*. London, New York 1987.

   work a spot *v.* to sell drugs or sex in a certain location.

   – Geneva Smitherman, *Black Talk*. Boston 2000.

   work the room *v.* [1950s +] to chatter to people at a party or meeting. [show business use, for an entertainer to move through the audience, chatting to people and involving them in the act]

   – Jonathon Green (Hg.), *Cassell's Dictionary of Slang*. London 2005.

Referenzliteratur:

Angela Carter, *The Sadeian Woman and the Ideology of Pornography*. New York 1978.

Shoshana Felman, *Le scandale du corps parlant : Don Juan avec Austin, ou, la séduction en deux langues*. Paris 1980.

Hyder Rollins (Hg.), *The Letters of John Keats*. Cambridge/MA 1958.

Eckhard Schumacher, „Performativität und Performance", in: Uwe Wirth (Hg.), *Performanz. Zwischen Sprachphilosophie und Kulturwissenschaften*. Frankfurt/M. 2002, S. 383–402.

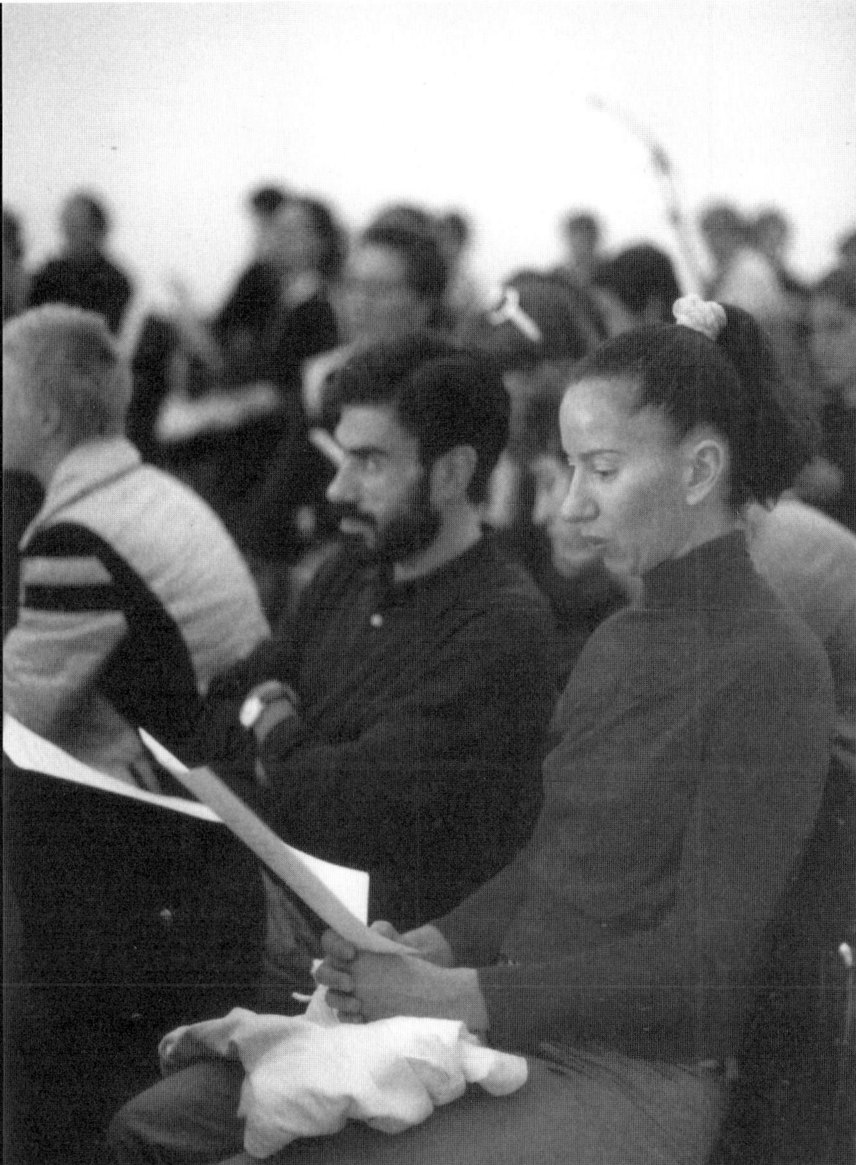

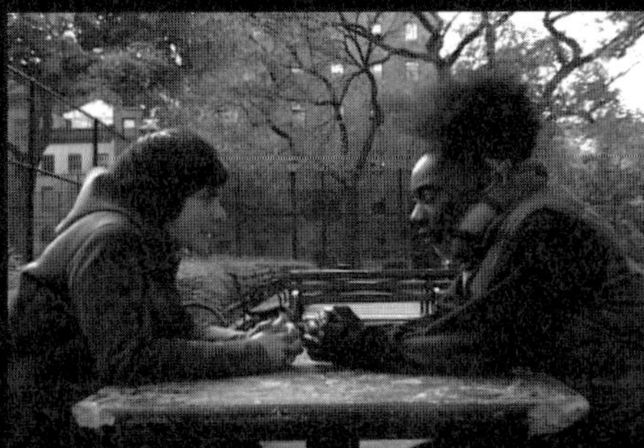

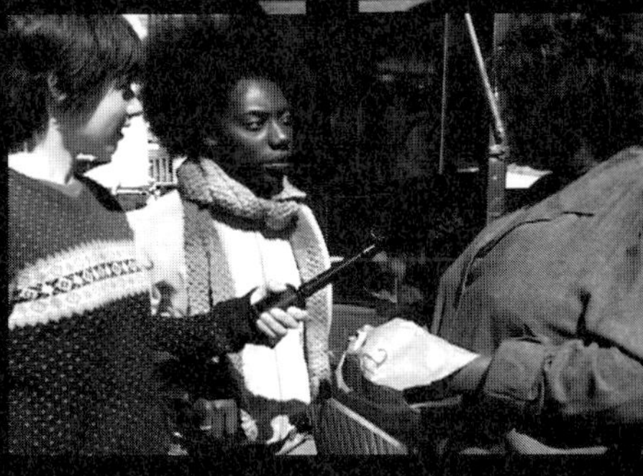

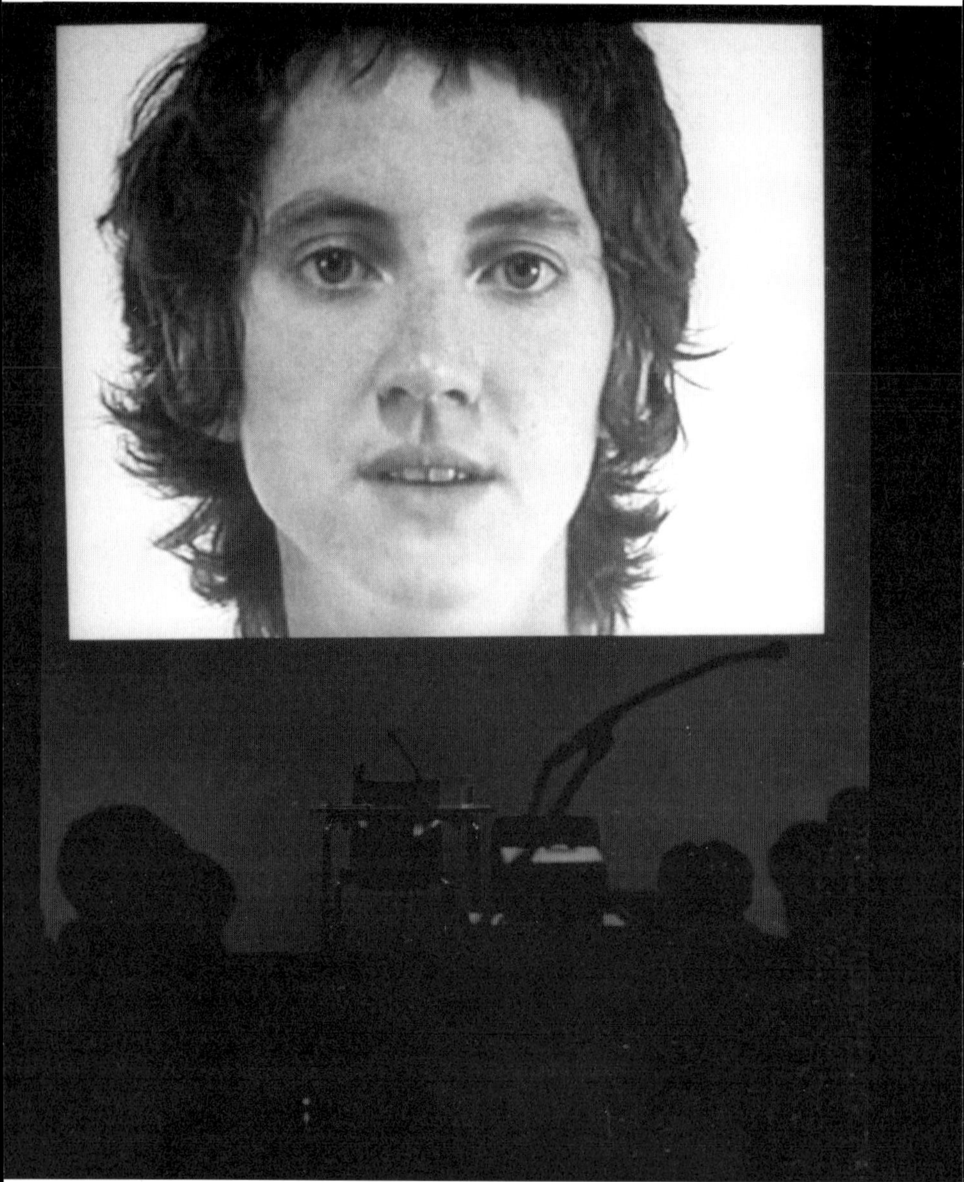

Familiarity, irony, ambivalence

(and love, hate, envy, attraction, revulsion, hubris as byproducts of the "performative" act)

An email conversation between Sharon Hayes and Yvonne Rainer

In 2003, with her performance/talk at *Public Affairs*, Sharon Hayes launched an experimental research project to survey the current political moment in the U.S. While being fascinated by the collective constructions of democracy, Hayes wanted to disrupt the curious temporality intrinsic in the singular moment of an election. In her quasi-fictional, quasi-documentary video project *After Before* (2005), two central figures (Kemba Bloodworth and Ewa Einhorn) examine the production of "public opinion" by interviewing people on the streets of New York City throughout the month of September 2004, two months before the 2004 U.S. presidential elections. In its performative staging of "the interview," *After Before* investigates the relation between individual opinion and the mythic construction of "the public." In summer 2005, while editing that material, Sharon Hayes initiated the following email conversation with Yvonne Rainer.

Yvonne Rainer started out as a choreographer in 1960, switched to filmmaking in 1972, and returned to dance in 2000. In the spring of 2005, Dance Theater Workshop in New York invited her to participate in *Stravinsky Project*, a program consisting of choreographic and musical takes on Igor Stravinsky by five artists. She immediately thought of *Agon*, the collaboration between Balanchine and Stravinsky premiered in 1957 by the New York City Ballet. *Agon* is a plotless, abstract ballet for eight female and four male dancers, which Rainer saw a number of times in the following years. The conversation with

Sharon Hayes took place during the period in which she was rehearsing her reworking of the Balanchine dance (which, as she points out, is "certainly not a remaking or reconstruction, though perhaps an appropriation"), this time for four women, one of them *en pointe*.

Yvonne Rainer: What do you see as the difference between performance and "the performative"? Or does that matter? Is performance only about framing? Re-contextualizing? Re-speaking? Combinative? i.e., about jolting the audience into re-thinking their position of looking and listening?

Sharon Hayes: More and more I think my work has become something like an enactment of a series of performatives rather than performance. This perhaps reveals that although I was greatly relieved to abandon (by moving out of the performance and theatrical venue) the demand to be entertaining, I nevertheless have a bit of discomfort that most of the work I do in front of an audience now involves just standing in front of them and speaking.

I've been doing a series of works that engage a strategy of respeaking which is related, for me, to the speech act of the "performative." Here by "performative" I mean Austin's term, an utterance, which does rather than says. For the last several years, I've been interested in extending this to the notion of a "performative copy": an utterance which does something in its repetition. By performative copy, I am thinking of any or all of Gertrude Stein's writing. But I also mean a performative copy as it functions in certain literal acts of performance: Ron Vawter's performance in *Roy Cohn/Jack Smith* of Jack Smith's *What's Underground About Marshmallows* for instance. In the Vawter there is something akin to what I am most interested in about and around the performative copy: the collision and collapse of two temporal moments, two instances of speech. What I like about Vawter's piece is that his repetition of Smith's performance references the theatrical convention of repeatedly enacting a script, but exposes an important distinction between theater and performance: the difference between the "performer" and the "character." The character is a device specifically constructed to be "filled" by multiple actors across multiple geographic, ethnic, and temporal affiliations. One actor can be seen as better than another but there is, most often, no sense of an "original." The performer on the other hand, if you allow me this somewhat ungrounded distinction, is singularly attached to the performance that they enact. Such that Ron Vawter cannot "perform" Jack Smith without carrying Jack Smith along with him. I don't mean to assert that performance contains an authentic subject who is the performer/author but that it invokes the very problem of an authentic subject. That is what makes it interesting.

Y. R.: First off, who's Austin? Next, Ron Vawter's impersonation of Jack Smith was ever so powerful for me for my having seen the original. Of course, most people in that downtown audience would have seen or heard of the original. I always try to have my cake and eat it. Meaning, the ideal situation for me as both producer and spectator is to have the original, or reference to it, and the copy, however imperfect, running simultaneously. One of my schtiks when I was a member of the Grand Union in the early '70s was to go to a microphone and claim I was Martha Graham, then make all kinds of inappropriate statements that of course distanced me from the legendary icon. Very unlike Richard Move, who does a much more credible "copy" or imitation.

S. H.: Austin is J.L. Austin, the linguist who named the "performative utterance." But your questioning of him, of course, shows the term "performative" has circulated far from its origin.

In my work, I return to specific political texts to very specifically reinsert them into a present discourse, making a separation between myself as a biographical speaking subject and the words that I speak. In some instances, my gesture is one of affiliation and in others one of radical distinction such as when I read all 36 of Ronald Reagan's Address to the Nation speeches.

The performance was research but it was research for which I needed precisely the form of a live address. I don't think I could've understood how the speeches operated if I had read them to myself over the course of several weeks. In this Reagan reading it became clear to me that performance offers a very particular site for working through a set of political questions. While I find this terrain exciting, my only hesitation with this employment of performance, which was quite different from my other work, is that the one who "benefited the most" from this exercise was me. I'm not sure it had the same layered depth for an audience.

So perhaps I am not answering the question about performance and the performative. I don't think they are the same, but for me, performance, as a form, allows for certain very precise examinations of the performative operations of subject formation.

I am wondering if you see this as related to your use of quotation. I remember that you once said something like (I'm paraphrasing and probably also mis-remembering) one of the reasons you moved from dance to film is that you can't quote in dance. Much of your film work does seem to employ performance as a quotation. Like the multiple instances of "a performance within a film" in *Lives of Performers, MURDER and murder, Journeys from Berlin/1971*, etc. Part of what this quotation of performance seems to do, in addition to grounding and elaborating the characters, is engage the audience in the contemplation of multiple forms of address. I guess what I mean is that in these moments of quotation, the audience recognizes that they are sitting watching a film but that they could also be another audience in that case one watching a performance—moving them, as you offer in your question, into re-thinking their position. Do you see these things as distinct: citation, quotation? Does this use of quotation affect how you think about live performance now in your return to making dance work?

Y. R.: I'm working on a dance that spins off of Balanchine's *Agon*. At first I thought I'd just have my four dancers perform *traces* of the original, but more and more I'm thinking of having a monitor onstage *showing* a 1982 performance of *Agon* while my dance proceeds. In fact I would like to be there to fast forward the parts I'm not using. Which immediately brings up a copyright infringement can of worms. But it reminds me of your record-scratch performance. Hearing Eleanor Roosevelt's voice in the middle of your intense "reworking," re-contextualizing all that original material was what made it work for me.[1]

We're both involved in some kind of re-positioning or dislocation. In *MURDER and murder*, I put Mildred and Doris's domestic travails on a stage, or put my tuxedoed rant in a monitor frame that is observed by one of my characters. Why not just face the camera full-frame? So I can have two things going at once, culminating in the punch line "Is that PBS?!" And about "you can't quote in dance," you *can* quote in dance, but only to the cognoscenti. Not that I want to get into populism. Rather, I'm interested in "bad" acting and "bad" dancing, and these can more readily be understood in relation, if not to an "original," then to something more familiar, like Lawrence Olivier or Maria Tallchief or Ronald Reagan, people who embody standards, taste, and/or celebrity.[2] *Or* they can be understood in terms of "staginess," self-consciousness, incongruity, perversity, "abnormality." Irony is the key to re-speaking, re-staging. Dances are always reconstructed in all seriousness. There are many many versions of *Agon*, danced by different ballet companies. Of what interest is it to engage three middle-aged dancers, one of whom has never taken a ballet class in her life, and one young ballet-trained dancer who actually danced with the New York City Ballet, to perform parts of *Agon*? How to prevent the audience—and the dancers themselves—from recoiling with "They/I can't do the steps, they're/I'm terrible?" I'm going to find out as soon as I get back to New York and start rehearsals.

Maybe the name of the game is the destruction/re-making of revered icons. Following my presentation with Taisha for the squalors, one sharp squalor described it as an "autopsy."[3] Certainly my aged presence lent an aura of mortality, but beyond that I would hope that some kind of analysis took place, a liberation of *Agon* from its sanctified status, a re-investment in the original's complexity via my re-enactment. I didn't want to kill it, just make it lighter, more intelligible. A bit of hubris, perhaps, considering how many luminaries have danced it and written about it.

S. H.: I appreciate your reference to the term "familiar" because it reminds me that many of these strategies of remaking or re-speaking do turn on the notion of the familiar. They invoke a viewer's attachment to the familiar BUT then continue by *not* fulfilling that familiarity. Instead, to varying degrees, they produce something frustrating, strange, bad, perverse, or just not quite the same. And this new thing has to be contended with, it has to be considered in a way that the familiar object/event does not. *This* is why it's not the repetition of theater or, in your *Agon* case, the repetition of a repertory ballet company.

But is this an ironic gesture? I think irony is facile. Irony folds effortlessly into reverence for the replicated icons. It seems to me it's a safe cover for something else (perhaps something quite a bit more earnest) that is going on. The kind of re-speaking or copying that I'm interested in is not exclusive of reverence but it includes more complicated relations as well: love, hate, envy, attraction, revulsion, yes, hubris for sure.

I think the copy, the re-speaking, the re-make can't help but bring a certain death to the original. (Your reference to copyright infringement makes that clear in hard, cold economic facts.) In a sense I think you kill it and can't kill it all at the same time and this death of the original *combined* with the desire not to kill it (or the impossibility of killing it) is what creates such an interesting tension. And I think this tension is present to an audience whether they've seen the original or not. It's the constant concern you have as an audience to a production that has some clearly defined referent. The way you always have to qualify what you say by admitting to either having seen or not having seen the original from which the remake was done, having read or not having read the book on which the film was based, etc. For that reason, I like that you'll show *Agon* on a monitor on the side of the stage...like bringing the elephant into the room.

It seems to me that re-making is a bit like translation. When it is good—smooth and seamless, etc.—we can forget that it is lined with all of this complication. But when it is bad, and a translator can't find the word or has to struggle through various options, then we remember how precarious the whole enterprise is in the first place.

Y. R.: What's in it for me, the spectator? YOU understood Reagan's machinations better by reading him aloud, but would I have?

S. H.: When I first started making performance work, I fell into the very available trap of wanting to please the audience which I dealt with in the only way I knew how, which was to make it part of the content of the work. I've moved a long way from that point and I'm no longer afraid of boring large groups of people. Your initial question about jolting an audience into rethinking their position is interesting to consider here. Does "jolting" suggest an antagonistic or instrumental position toward the spectator? While I am deeply committed to provoking an idea of audience as an actively constructed position, I'm still uncomfortable with the idea that my work would invade their experience in such a way as to jolt, shock, or actively alarm them. Perhaps this is a problem. Too easy on the eyes and ears. On the other hand, I've found something quite interesting in the space of less spectacular maneuvers, which is to work with various notions of a phantom audience. This manifests itself in different ways, in different works. In *The Lesbian* (the last work I made in/for a theatrical venue), the "Audience" was one among seven characters: The Audience, The Lesbian, The Researcher, The Girlfriend, The Interviewer, The Choreographer, and The Tour Guide. So the character of The Audience existed not exactly in an imaginary space, but in an imagined one. It marked the audience as a participant but didn't ask for audience participation. Any audience participation was already scripted into the performance as the character of the audience was invoked every now and again as having laughed or as having been confused. The actual viewing audience knew that they weren't the character "The Audience" but they also knew they could be, that the actions and reactions were plausible, at times iterating or portending a reaction that the "real" audience actually expressed or at the very least thought about expressing. Thus the audience was enveloped in the frame of the performance even while they were quite assured that they were also sitting there, in their actual seats, outside of that frame.

My sense of your work is that you have actively resisted certain traps of placating the conventions of viewership. (I think here of the "NO! manifesto" but also your commitment to long takes, to fragmented narratives, to having more than one thing happening at once, etc.) Did you notice any differences in your relation to or considerations of audience when you re-entered the field of live performance?

Y. R.: The answer is a definite "No." Between my "performative" inclinations and the spectator there lies a predictable area ("chasm" some might call it) of ambiguity. Keep them on the edge of their seats with a series of questions or "moves": Where is this going? Is it funny or serious? Unexpected whammo between the eyes. Formal dance vs. "hanging out"/doing "nothing." Replicate the act of looking and being looked at.

There is a climactic moment in *Agon* where, following a pirouette, the ballerina wraps her leg around her partner's neck. An utterly reckless and amazing moment. I have my three postmodern choreographers (Pat Catterson, Patricia Hoffbauer, Sally Silvers) rush in at the same moment to establish a tableau replicating that moment (with ballerina Emily Coates) but also adding two "bathing beauty" cheese-cake poses on either side. Without my bidding they all plastered grins on their faces. My immediate impulse was to wipe them off. The configuration is hilarious without their "gilding the lily." On being confronted by their understandably anxious questions as to what it looked like, I came up with "hilarious, serious, poignant" in that order.

As I continue working (we're in the second week of rehearsals), I am finding that my ham-fisted replications are indeed creating something new and fascinating, if for no other reason than that the mechanics of hauling a body around—no matter that the body in question is a superbly ballet-trained machine—creates its own logic and dynamics when the "haulers" come from an entirely different sphere of operations. This new sphere is affected not only by differences in training, but by the inescapable difference of gender. My postmodern female choreographers simply lack the muscle mass and finesse of their idealized male original. And in adjusting and accommodating their specific limits—and wit, I must add—to the act of replication, we arrive at an unexpected end point. It's very gratifying, because I had no idea when I started out—even though I knew the *process* would be interesting—what the results would be.

S. H.: Your description of hauling a superbly ballet-trained body around makes me linger over the way in which you employ "task" as a way to disrupt or maybe just to refuse or alter certain conventions of performance. Similarly, I see my various re-speakings as the execution of a task rather than as the acting out (in the interpretive sense) of a text or a role. As you are pointing out in the anecdote from your rehearsals, the particular body/speaker who executes this task is relevant because of the questions that are raised by/in their doing of the task: for you in the *Agon* reenactments these might be questions around gender, or for me it is questions of authenticity. But the emphasis here is not on these bodies as a specific personality, as it is when marking a particular performance personality, as when Sandy Duncan is celebrated (or trashed) for her portrayal of Peter Pan, for instance. This seems quite significant.

The other thing I find compelling about the way in which you use task is that it seems to me that you use it to foreground, rather than hide, the effort of the repetition of performance. Try as any performer might, a task can never be performed precisely the same way night after night. Traditional theater and dance companies allow for and even enjoy slight nightly variation but the structure of the discipline is geared toward preventing too much fluctuation. So the dancers and actors are trained to be "up to the task" of doing the same set of actions and saying the same script of words night after night with energy, enthusiasm, and conviction. Even in "downtown" or "alternative" theater, performance and dance venues, this is often adopted as a goal (unless they are specifically using improvisation or some kind of variable structure that changes from night to night).

The way that you employ task in your work disrupts this aim. Do you think I'm off here? What you're describing about your "ham-fisted replications" of *Agon* seems to set up a situation in which the task is more difficult to repeat from night to night.

I've been trying to be quite specific in my attention to this relationship between task and repetition in another way. In certain pieces I won't perform the task twice—because the task of the speaking was only to generate a video recording, for instance. This isn't a rigid rule but something that I am trying to be intentional about from piece to piece. This has been a significant aspect of my shift from "doing" to "using" performance.

Y. R.: Regarding task and (professional) repetition: Oddly enough, I find myself "drilling" my motley group of dancers (no pejorative intended here; perhaps "unlikely" would be more accurate) as though their lives depended on it. I must push each to the limit of her particular skill. It is the differences in these skills that will hopefully foreground task and effort. Facility is at once gained, accomplished, broken down, analyzed, deconstructed, at some moments destroyed altogether. The question occurs to me: How is this different from the amateur dance company of Edith Stephen in which I danced as a rank beginner in 1958? The members of Edith's group might be said to have shared a comparable "spread" of skills as my current group. The comparison is off the mark—for one thing, there being no "rank beginner" among my *Agon* dancers—except for the factor of the "original." The original looms behind my dancers at every step, the balletic standard is the ground they traverse, the template of training and idealized bodies is the all-encompassing surround. There is something comforting about all this. These values are so ubiquitous, so endemic in Western culture that they provide me just as enduringly with a wall against which to beat my head. (I think you know John Cage's story about his deciding to spend his life beating his head against Schoenberg's valorizing of harmony, for which Cage admitted to having no "feeling.") Resistance needs, if not a hard, then a stable and well-worn surface.

Notes:

1. Yvonne Rainer refers to Sharon Hayes's DJ performance at the LTTR Explosion in July 2004 at Art in General, New York, in which Hayes spun a wide variety of spoken-word records.
2. The ballerina Maria Tallchief was the foremost exponent of Balanchine's choreography. They were married from 1946 to 1951 and together formed what eventually became the New York City Ballet.
3. Taisha Paggett is a dancer, who assisted Yvonne Rainer when she was a resident "squalor" (scholar) at the Getty Research Institute in spring 2005.

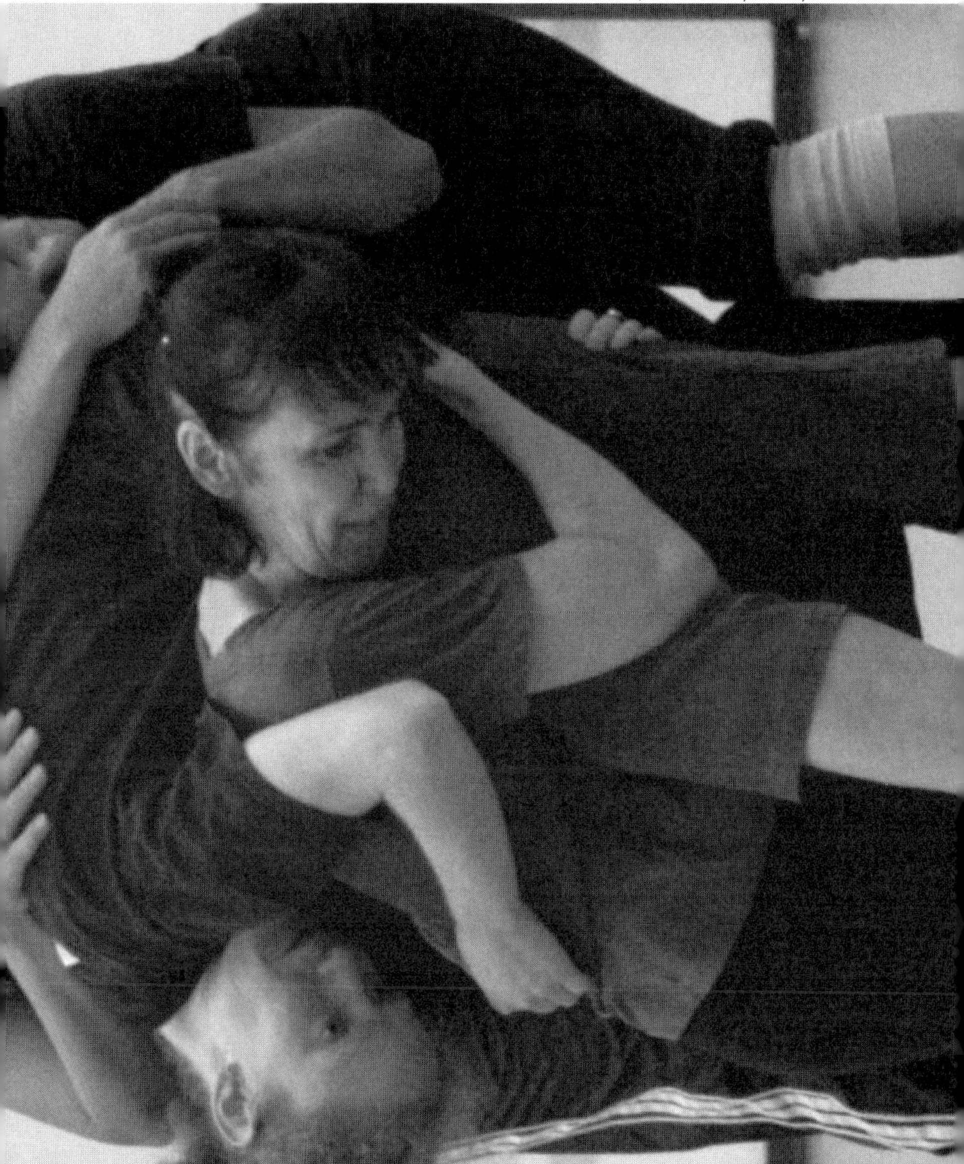

pp. 45, 47, and 48: *AG Indexical, with a little help from H.M.*, choreographed by Yvonne Rainer (after George Balanchine's Agon). Performed by Pat Catterson, Emily Coates, Patricia Hoffbauer, and Sally Silvers.

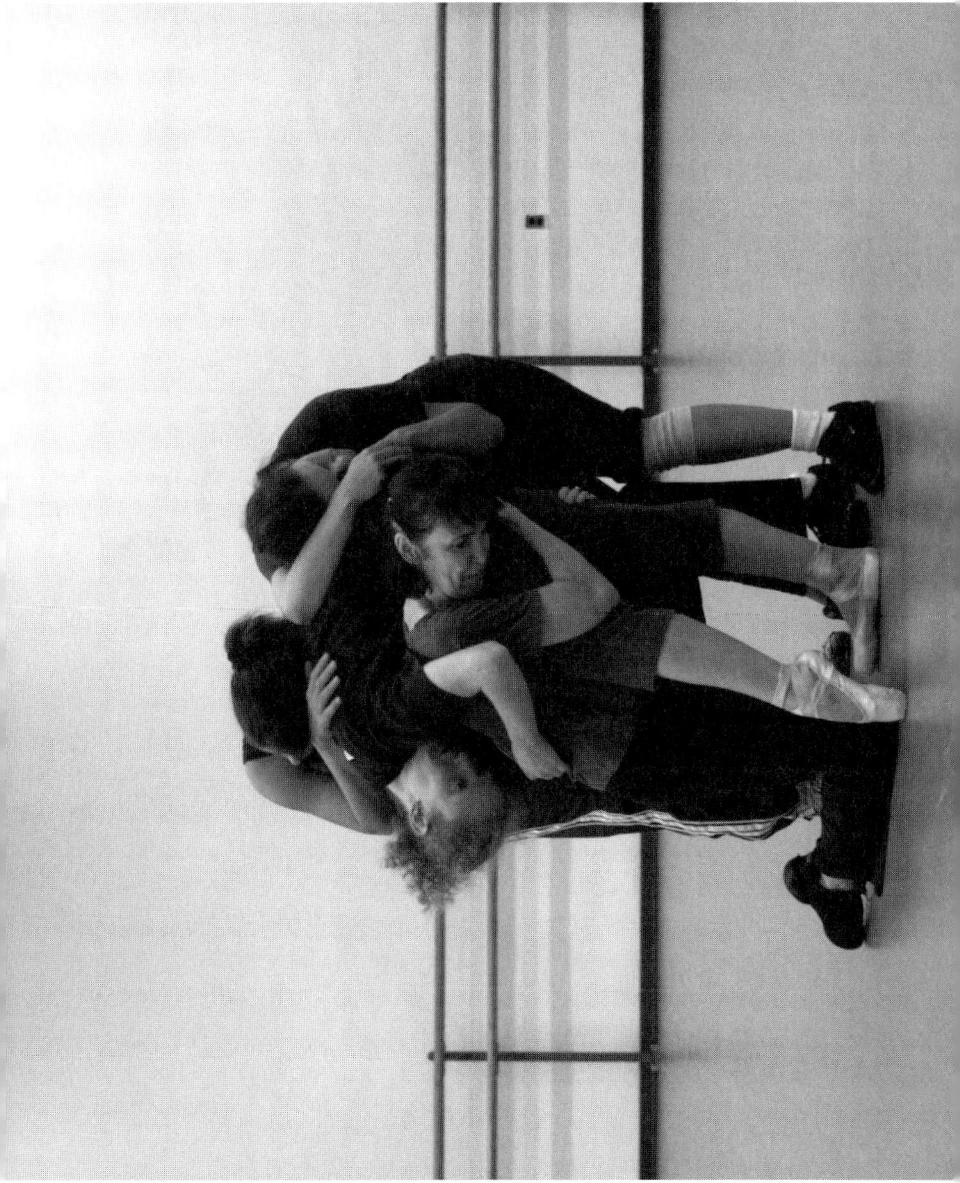

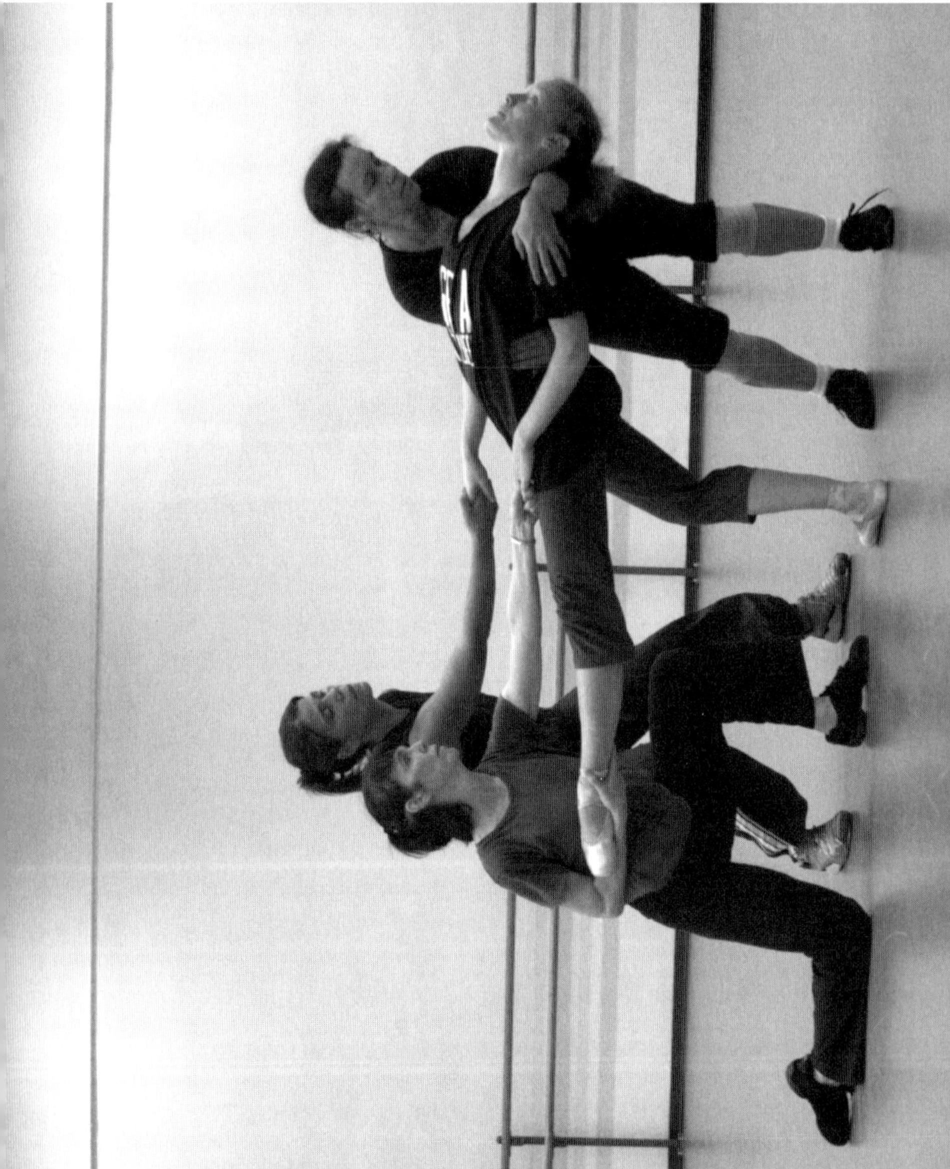

Vertrautheit, Ironie, Ambivalenz
(und Liebe, Hass, Neid, Anziehungskraft, Abscheu, Überheblichkeit als Nebenprodukte des „performativen" Akts)

Eine E-Mail-Konversation zwischen Sharon Hayes und Yvonne Rainer

Mit ihrem Auftritt/Vortrag bei *Öffentliche Angelegenheiten* begann Sharon Hayes 2003 ein experimentelles Forschungsprojekt, das die gegenwärtige politische Situation in den Vereinigten Staaten untersucht. Fasziniert von den kollektiven Konstruktionen von Demokratie, wollte Hayes in die seltsame, dem singulären Augenblick von Wahlen eigene Zeitlichkeit intervenieren. In ihrem quasifiktionalen, quasidokumentarischen Videoprojekt *After Before* (2005) untersuchen zwei zentrale Figuren (Kemba Bloodworth und Eva Einhorn) die Produktion von „öffentlicher Meinung", indem sie im September 2004, zwei Monate vor den Präsidentschaftswahlen in den Vereinigten Staaten, auf den Straßen von New York PassantInnen befragen. In performativ inszenierten Interviews hinterfragt *After Before*, wie individuelle Meinung und die Konstruktion des Mythos „Öffentlichkeit" zusammenhängen. Während der Arbeit mit den gesammelten Videointerviews initiierte Sharon Hayes im Sommer 2005 die folgende E-Mail-Konversation mit Yvonne Rainer.

Yvonne Rainer begann 1960 als Choreografin, wechselte 1972 zum Filmemachen und kehrte 2000 zum Tanz zurück. Im Frühjahr 2005 wurde sie vom Dance Theater Workshop New York zur Teilnahme am *Stravinsky Project* eingeladen, einem Programm, das aus choreografischen und musikalischen Beiträgen von fünf KünstlerInnen besteht. Ihr erster Gedanke galt *Agon*, einer 1957 vom New York City Ballet uraufgeführten Kooperation von George Balanchine und Igor Strawinsky. *Agon* ist ein abstraktes Ballett ohne Handlung für acht männliche und vier weibliche TänzerInnen, das Rainer in den Jahren nach der Uraufführung einige Male gesehen hat. Die Konversation mit Sharon Hayes fand im zeitlichen Umfeld der Proben zu ihrer Version von Balanchines Tanz statt (die, darauf weist sie hin, „natürlich keine Neubearbeitung oder Rekonstruktion, vielleicht aber eine Aneignung ist") diesmal mit vier Frauen, eine von ihnen *en pointe*.

Yvonne Rainer: Worin siehst du den Unterschied zwischen Performance und „dem Performativen"? Ist er überhaupt von Bedeutung? Geht es bei Performance lediglich um Rahmung? Rekontextualisierung? Wiederholung? Eine Kombination davon? Das heißt: Geht es darum, das Publikum wachzurütteln, damit es die einmal eingenommene BetrachterInnen- und HörerInnenhaltung überdenkt?

Sharon Hayes: Ich denke, meine Arbeit hat sich mehr zu einer Art der reihenhaften Darstellung performativer Akte entwickelt, weg von Performance im engeren Sinn. Obwohl ich ganz schön erleichtert war, den Unterhaltungsanspruch aufzugeben (indem ich die Bühne hinter mir ließ), verrät diese Entwicklung ein gewisses Unbehagen damit, dass der Großteil meiner Arbeit vor Publikum nun darin besteht, einfach nur vor ihm zu stehen und zu sprechen.

In einer Reihe von Arbeiten verwende ich eine Methode des Nachsprechens, die für mich mit performativen Sprechakten zusammenhängt. Mit „performativ" meine ich hier Austins Begriff einer Äußerung, die nicht etwas feststellt, sondern eher tut, was sie sagt. Die letzten paar Jahre war ich damit beschäftigt, dieses Konzept performativer Äußerungen zu einer „performativen Kopie" hin auszuweiten: eine Äußerung, die in ihrer Wiederholung etwas tut. Dabei denke ich an einige, wenn nicht sogar an alle Texte von Gertrude Stein. Ich meine aber auch jene performative Nachahmung, die in der Performance manchmal ganz direkt stattfindet: Ein Beispiel dafür wäre Ron Vawters Darstellung von Jack Smiths *What's Underground About Marshmallows* in

Roy Cohn/Jack Smith. Bei Vawter sehe ich eine Parallele zu dem, was mich an der performativen Kopie am meisten interessiert: der Konflikt und Zusammenfall zweier zeitlicher Momente, zweier sprachlicher Ereignisse. Ich mag an Vawters Stück, wie sich seine Wiederholung von Smiths Performance auf die Konvention des Theaters bezieht, einen Text immer wieder aufzuführen, dabei aber einen bedeutenden Unterschied zwischen Theater und Performance enthüllt: den Unterschied zwischen „DarstellerIn" und „Rolle". Die Rolle ist ein eigens entwickelter Kunstgriff, der es den unterschiedlichsten SchauspielerInnen vielfältigster geografischer, ethnischer und zeitlicher Anbindung ermöglicht, sie „auszufüllen". Die SchauspielerInnen können zwar als besser oder schlechter wahrgenommen werden, meistens gibt es aber keine Vorstellung von einem „Original". Auf der anderen Seite ist in der Performance, wenn du mir eine nicht ganz haltbare Unterscheidung gestattest, der Performer oder die Performerin auf einzigartige Weise mit dem Aufgeführten verbunden. Und zwar so, dass Ron Vawter Jack Smith nicht darstellen kann, ohne dabei Jack Smith mit sich herumzutragen. Ich möchte damit nicht behaupten, dass Performance ein authentisches Subjekt impliziert, das mit DarstellerIn oder AutorIn identifizierbar wäre, sondern dass Performance die akute Problematik eines authentischen Subjekts anspricht. Das macht Performance so interessant.

Y. R.: Zunächst: Wer ist Austin? Und dann: Ron Vawters Verkörperung von Jack Smith war für mich umso eindrucksvoller, weil ich das Original gesehen hatte. Klar, die meisten Leute in dem Downtown-Publikum hatten damals wohl das Original gesehen oder zumindest davon gehört. Ich will immer alles auf einmal haben. Das heißt: Für mich als Produzierende und Zuschauerin ist es optimal, wenn das Original beziehungsweise Verweise darauf und die wie auch immer unzulängliche Kopie gleichzeitig ablaufen. In den frühen Siebzigern, als Mitglied von Grand Union, war es eines meiner „shtiks", mir ein Mikrofon zu schnappen, zu behaupten, ich sei Martha Graham, und dann jede Menge unpassender Bemerkungen zu machen, die mich deutlich vom legendären Vorbild unterschieden. Ganz anders als Richard Move, dessen „Kopie" oder Nachahmung von Martha Graham sehr viel glaubwürdiger ist.

S. H.: Austin ist J. L. Austin, der Sprachwissenschaftler, der die Wendung „performative Äußerung" geprägt hat. Deine Frage zeigt allerdings, dass der Begriff „performativ" inzwischen weitab von seinem Ursprung verwendet wird.

In meiner Arbeit verwende ich spezifische historisch-politische Texte, die ich gezielt in den aktuellen Diskurs einfüge, wobei ich eine Trennung zwischen mir als biografischem, sprechendem Subjekt und meinen Äußerungen einführe. Manchmal entspricht mein Gestus eher einer Annäherung, in anderen Fällen einer radikalen Abgrenzung, wenn ich zum Beispiel alle von Ronald Reagans 36 Reden an die Nation vorlese.

Diese Performance war eine Art von Recherche, eine Untersuchung, für die ich genau den formalen Rahmen eines Live-Auftritts brauchte. Ich glaube nicht, dass ich die Funktionsweise der Reden verstanden hätte, wenn ich sie über Wochen verstreut nur für mich gelesen hätte. Während dieser Reagan-Lesung ist mir klar geworden, dass Performance eine sehr spezielle Möglichkeit bietet, gewisse politische Fragestellungen aufzuarbeiten. Ich finde dieses Feld spannend, mein einziger Vorbehalt gegenüber dieser Verwendung von Performance, die sich ziemlich von meinen anderen Arbeiten unterscheidet, ist, dass ich selbst von dieser Übung „am meisten profitierte". Ich bin mir nicht sicher, ob es für das Publikum die gleiche Komplexität und Tiefe hatte.

Mir scheint, ich antworte nicht auf die Frage nach dem Unterschied von Performance und dem Performativen. Ich würde sie nicht gleichsetzen, aber meiner Meinung nach eignen sich die formalen Mittel der Performance für sehr genaue Untersuchungen der performativen Mechanismen von Subjektformierung.

Ich frage mich, ob du hier eine Verbindung zu deinem Gebrauch von Zitaten siehst. Ich erinnere mich, dass du einmal gesagt hast, einer deiner Beweggründe, vom

Tanz zum Film zu wechseln, war, dass man im Tanz nicht mit Zitaten arbeiten kann (ich versuche, das zu paraphrasieren, irre mich aber möglicherweise). Ein Großteil deiner filmischen Arbeit scheint sich mit zitathafter Darstellung zu beschäftigen. Wie etwa die vielfältigen Beispiele „einer Performance im Film" in *Lives of Performers*, *MURDER and murder*, *Journeys from Berlin/1971* et cetera. Neben der Einführung und Ausformulierung von Charakteren scheint dieses Zitieren von Performance das Publikum zum Nachdenken aufzufordern, indem es auf vielfältige Weisen der Ansprache verweist. Ich will damit sagen, dass dem Publikum in diesen zitathaften Sequenzen bewusst wird, dass es zwar dort sitzt und einen Film sieht, genauso gut aber auch ein anderes Publikum sein könnte, eines, das in diesem Fall eine Performance sieht – also, wie in deiner Frage bereits angeklungen ist, das Publikum dazu bewegen, seine Position zu überdenken. Siehst du da einen Unterschied: Zitathaftigkeit, Zitat? Hat dieser Gebrauch von Zitaten deine Einstellung zu Liveperformances verändert, jetzt, da du wieder mit Tanz arbeitest?

Y. R.: Ich arbeite an einem Tanzstück, das sich aus Balanchines *Agon* entwickelt. Zuerst dachte ich, ich würde meine vier Tänzerinnen einfach nur „Spuren" des Originals vortragen lassen. Inzwischen denke ich immer mehr darüber nach, einen Monitor auf die Bühne zu stellen, der parallel zu meiner Version eine Aufführung von *Agon* aus 1982 zeigt. Tatsächlich wäre ich gerne anwesend, um die Teile, die ich nicht verwende, schnell vorzuspulen. Was sofort einen ganzen Rattenschwanz an UrheberInnenrechtsverletzungen nach sich ziehen würde. Das erinnert mich an deine „Scratch-Performance". Eleanor Roosevelts Stimme zu hören inmitten deiner „Umarbeitung", deiner Rekontextualisierung dieses ganzen Materials, hat für mich den Erfolg des Ganzen ausgemacht.[1]

Wir sind beide mit einer Art Umordnung oder Verschiebung beschäftigt. In *MURDER and murder* stellte ich etwa Mildreds und Doris' häusliche Mühsal auf die Bühne oder zeigte meine im Frack gehaltene Schimpftirade auf einem Monitor, der von einer der Darstellerinnen beobachtet wurde. Warum mich nicht einfach direkt vor die Kamera stellen? Damit zwei Dinge gleichzeitig passieren, die in der Pointe: „Soll das öffentliches Fernsehen sein?!", kulminieren. Und was die Aussage: „Man kann im Tanz nicht zitieren", betrifft: Man kann im Tanz zitieren, aber nur für die KennerInnen. Nicht dass ich populistisch werden wollte. Genauer gesagt, mich interessieren „schlechte" Schauspielerei und „schlechter" Tanz, und beides kann leichter verstanden werden, wenn man es in Bezug setzt, vielleicht nicht zu einem „Original", aber doch zu etwas Vertrautem, nämlich zu Leuten, die Normen, Geschmack und/oder Berühmtheit verkörpern wie Laurence Olivier oder Maria Tallchief oder Ronald Reagan.[2] Oder sie können über Begriffe wie „Theatralik", Selbstbewusstheit, Deplatziertheit, Verrücktheit, „Abnormalität" verstanden werden. Ironie ist der Schlüssel beim Nachsprechen, beim Wiederaufführen. Tanz wird immer mit sehr viel Ernst rekonstruiert. Es gibt so viele von unterschiedlichen Balletttruppen getanzte Versionen von *Agon*. Worin besteht also das Interesse, drei Tänzerinnen mittleren Alters zu engagieren, von denen eine noch nie in ihrem Leben Ballettunterricht hatte, und dazu eine junge, ausgebildete Balletttänzerin, die mit dem New York City Ballet schon in Teilen von *Agon* getanzt hat? Wie verhindert man, dass das Publikum und auch die Tänzerinnen selbst zurückschrecken: „Sie/ich bringe/n die Schritte nicht auf die Reihe, sie sind/ich bin fürchterlich schlecht." Sobald ich zurück in New York bin und mit den Proben beginne, werde ich das wohl herausfinden.

Vielleicht ist die Zerstörung/Wiederzusammensetzung verehrter Ikonen der springende Punkt. Im Anschluss an meine und Taishas Präsentation für die StipendiatInnen beschrieb einer diese Methode scharfsinnig als „Autopsie".[3] Bestimmt hat meine gealterte Erscheinung eine Aura von Sterblichkeit verbreitet, darüber hinaus hat aber, wie ich hoffe, eine genauere Analyse stattgefunden, eine Befreiung von *Agon* aus seiner sakrosankten Stellung und ein Wiederbeleben der Komplexität des Originals durch meine Neuinszenierung. Ich wollte es nicht zerstören, nur etwas lockerer damit umgehen, es verständlicher machen. Das ist vielleicht ein wenig überheblich, wenn man bedenkt, wie viele Koryphäen *Agon* schon getanzt oder darüber geschrieben haben.

S. H.: Gut, dass du den Begriff „vertraut" aufbringst. Das erinnert mich daran, wie viele dieser Strategien des Nachmachens oder Nachsprechens um diese Idee des Vertrauten kreisen. Diese Strategien appellieren an die Verbundenheit der BetrachterInnen mit dem Vertrauten, aber sie lösen diese Vertrautheit in der Folge gerade nicht ein. Stattdessen erzeugen sie – in unterschiedlichem Ausmaß – etwas Frustrierendes, Befremdliches, Böses und Perverses, vielleicht auch nur etwas ein klein wenig Abweichendes. Und mit diesem neuen Ding muss man sich dann herumschlagen, darüber muss auf eine Art nachgedacht werden, die für das schon vertraute Objekt/Ereignis nicht nötig war. Deswegen handelt es sich nicht um eine Wiederaufführung von Theater oder – im Falle von *Agon* – eine Wiederaufführung durch eine Repertoiretanztruppe.

Aber ist das eine ironische Geste? Ich denke, Ironie ist zu einfach. Sie fügt sich mühelos in die Verehrung für die replizierten Ikonen ein. Sie scheint mir ein Schutzschild gegen etwas anderes (vielleicht gegen etwas weitaus Ernsthafteres) zu sein, das sich dahinter abspielt. Die Art des Nachsprechens oder Kopierens, die mich interessiert, schließt Verehrung nicht aus, sie beinhaltet aber auch kompliziertere Beziehungen: Liebe, Hass, Neid, Anziehung, Abscheu und natürlich Überheblichkeit.

Ich denke, die Kopie, das Nachsprechen und Nachmachen bedeuten – gewollt oder nicht – den sicheren Tod für das Original. (Dein Hinweis auf UrheberInnenrechtsverletzungen macht das an harten und kalten ökonomischen Tatsachen fest.) Ich denke, in gewisser Weise tötet man es und kann es aber auch nicht wirklich töten, und dieser Tod des Originals, der mit dem Verlangen, es nicht zu töten, verbunden ist (oder mit der Unmöglichkeit, es zu töten), erzeugt eine interessante Spannung. Diese Spannung ist für das Publikum spürbar, denke ich, egal, ob man das Original nun gesehen hat oder nicht. Als Publikum hat man das ständig im Kopf angesichts einer

Produktion, die einen klar ausgewiesenen Bezug auf ein Original hat. Man muss die Qualifikation der eigenen Meinung ja auch ständig deklarieren, indem man bekennt, das Original zum Remake entweder gesehen zu haben oder nicht, das Buch, auf dem der Film basiert, gelesen zu haben oder nicht, et cetera. Deswegen finde ich es gut, dass du *Agon* auf einem Monitor am Rand der Bühne zeigen wirst ... und damit das Unausgesprochene mit hereinholst.

Reinszenierungen scheinen mir ein wenig wie Übersetzungen zu funktionieren. Wenn sie gut gemacht sind – fließend und bruchlos et cetera –, können wir die mitgeschleppten Komplikationen vergessen. Sind sie aber schlecht gemacht und ein Übersetzer oder eine Übersetzerin konnte das passende Wort nicht finden oder musste mit zahlreichen Alternativen kämpfen, werden wir daran erinnert, wie heikel das ganze Unterfangen grundsätzlich ist.

Y. R.: Was ist für mich drinnen, für mich als Zuseherin? Du hast Reagans Machenschaften durch das Vorlesen besser verstanden – aber wäre es mir genauso ergangen?

S.H.: Als ich begann, Performance zu machen, bin ich in die erstbeste Falle getappt, nämlich dem Publikum gefallen zu wollen. Damit ging ich auf die einzige mir mögliche Art um und machte es auf inhaltlicher Ebene zu einem Teil der Arbeit. Davon bin ich inzwischen weit entfernt. Ich habe auch keine Angst mehr, größere Gruppen von Leuten zu langweilen. In diesem Zusammenhang wird deine Eingangsfrage zum Aufrütteln des Publikums wieder bedeutend und wie man es dazu bringt, seine Position zu überdenken. Impliziert dieses „Aufrütteln" eine antagonistische oder instrumentalisierende Haltung gegenüber den ZuschauerInnen? Mir liegt zwar sehr daran, die Position des Publikums als bewusst konstruiert zu zeigen, der Gedanke aber, in sein Erleben einzugreifen, indem es durch meine Arbeit aufgerüttelt, schockiert oder stark verunsichert wird, ist mir nach wie vor unbehaglich. Möglicherweise ist das ein Problem. Es den Augen und Ohren zu leicht zu machen. Andererseits bin ich im weiten

Feld der weniger spektakulären Aktionen auf etwas durchaus Interessantes gestoßen, und zwar auf die Arbeit mit verschiedenen Entwürfen eines Phantompublikums. In unterschiedlichen Arbeiten zeigt sich das auf unterschiedliche Art und Weise. In *The Lesbian* (der letzten Arbeit, die ich fürs Theater gemacht habe) war „das Publikum" eine von sieben Rollen: das Publikum, die Lesbe, der Forscher, die Freundin, der Interviewer, der Choreograf und der Reiseführer. Die Rolle des Publikums gehörte also nicht unbedingt einem imaginären, sondern eher einem fiktional entworfenen Bereich an. Sie zeichnete das Publikum als TeilnehmerIn aus, ohne jedoch zu einer aktiven Publikumsbeteiligung aufzufordern. Die Beteiligung des Publikums war in der Performance bereits angelegt, weil ja das Publikum als Figur immer wieder angesprochen wurde, mal lachend, mal verwirrt. Die tatsächlichen ZuschauerInnen wussten, dass nicht sie die Figur „das Publikum" waren, sie wussten aber auch, dass sie es sein könnten, weil die Handlungen und Reaktionen schlüssig waren und manchmal sogar eine Reaktion wiederholten oder ankündigten, die das „wirkliche" Publikum tatsächlich zum Ausdruck brachte oder zumindest in Erwägung zog. Auf diese Weise wurde das Publikum in den Rahmen der Performance integriert, obwohl es wusste, dass es gleichzeitig außerhalb dieses Rahmens in seinen realen Sesseln saß.

In deiner Arbeit habe ich den Eindruck, dass du der Verlockung, konventionelle Sehgewohnheiten zu befriedigen, ganz entschieden widerstanden hast. (Ich denke dabei an das „NO! Manifest", aber auch an dein Bekenntnis zu langen Einstellungen, zu fragmentarischen Erzählstrukturen, dazu, mehrere Dinge gleichzeitig geschehen zu lassen, et cetera.) Hast du nach deiner Rückkehr zur Liveperformance irgendwelche Unterschiede in deinem Verhältnis oder deiner Einstellung zum Publikum bemerkt?

Y. R.: Die Antwort ist ein klares Nein. Zwischen meinen „performativen" Vorlieben und den BetrachterInnen liegt ein voraussehbarer Bereich (manche würden sagen: „Abgrund") von Mehrdeutigkeit. Halte sie mit Fragen oder „Schachzügen" in Atem:

Wo führt das hin? Ist das komisch oder ernst gemeint? Unerwartete Wummen zwischen die Augen. Traditioneller Tanz versus „Herumhängen"/„Nichtstun". Den Akt des Sehens und Angesehenwerdens nachbilden.

In *Agon* gibt es einen Höhepunkt, an dem die Ballerina nach einer Pirouette ihrem Partner das Bein um den Hals legt. Ein hinreißend kühner und verblüffender Moment. Ich lasse im gleichen Moment meine drei postmodernen Choreografinnen (Pat Catterson, Patricia Hoffbauer, Sally Silvers) hereinstürmen, um diese Szene in einem Tableau (mit Emily Coates als Ballerina) nachzustellen und ihr noch zwei „badende Schönheiten" in koketten Posen an die Seite zu stellen. Ohne dass ich sie aufgefordert hätte, setzten alle ein breites Grinsen auf. Meine unmittelbare Reaktion war: „Weg damit!" Die Anordnung ist komisch genug, auch ohne „Zuckerguss". Angesichts der durchaus verständlichen besorgten Nachfrage, wie es denn aussähe, kamen mir „urkomisch", „ernsthaft", „ergreifend" in genau dieser Reihenfolge in den Sinn.

Im Verlauf der Arbeit (wir proben jetzt die zweite Woche) stelle ich fest, dass aus meinen groben Nachbildungen tatsächlich etwas Neues und Faszinierendes entsteht, zumindest insofern, als die Mechanik, die mit dem Transportieren eines Körpers verbunden ist – egal, ob dieser Körper eine erstklassig ausgebildete Ballettmaschine ist –, eine eigene Logik und Dynamik entwickelt, weil ja die „Transporteure" aus völlig anderen Handlungszusammenhängen kommen. In dem neuen Zusammenhang wirken sich nicht nur die Unterschiede in der Ausbildung aus, sondern auch die unhintergehbare Differenz der Geschlechter. Meine postmodernen Choreografinnen haben einfach nicht die Muskelmasse und die Finesse des idealisierten männlichen Originals. Indem sie aber ihre spezifischen Grenzen – und ich muss hinzufügen: ihren Verstand – in den Vorgang des Nachbildens einbringen und an ihn anpassen, kommen wir zu einem unerwarteten Ergebnis. Das ist sehr befriedigend, denn anfangs hatte ich überhaupt keine Vorstellung von den Resultaten – wenn ich auch wusste, dass der Prozess interessant werden würde.

S. H.: Deine Beschreibung eines bestens ausgebildeten Ballettkörpers, der herumtransportiert wird, bringt mich darauf, wie du „Aufgaben" verwendest, um bestimmte Konventionen von Performance zu durchbrechen, ihnen Widerstand entgegenzuhalten oder sie zu verändern. Ich sehe meine unterschiedlichen Akte des Nachsprechens ganz ähnlich: nämlich eher als Erfüllen einer Aufgabe denn als (im interpretativen Sinn) Aufführen eines Texts oder einer Rolle. Wie in deiner Anekdote von den Proben deutlich wird, erhält jeder einzelne Körper oder jede Sprecherin, die eine Aufgabe ausführen, Bedeutung durch die Fragen, die sich in und durch die Ausführung der Aufgaben stellen: In deinem Fall der *Agon*-Wiederaufführungen könnten das Fragen über Geschlechtsidentität, für mich Fragen der Authentizität sein. Das Augenmerk liegt hier aber nicht auf den Körpern als eigenständigen Persönlichkeiten, wie sie eine spezielle DarstellerInnenpersönlichkeit kennzeichnen, wenn zum Beispiel Sandy Duncan für ihre Verkörperung des Peter Pan gefeiert (oder verrissen) wird. Das erscheint mir ziemlich bedeutsam.

Mir erscheint auch die Art überzeugend, wie du Aufgaben einsetzt, um die Mühsal des Wiederholens einer Performance auszustellen, und nicht etwa, um sie zu verdecken. So sehr sich KünstlerInnen auch anstrengen, eine Aufgabe kann niemals Abend für Abend in genau der gleichen Weise erfüllt werden. Traditionelle Theater- und Tanztruppen lassen allabendlich leichte Abweichungen zu und finden daran auch Gefallen; die Anforderungen des Genres sind aber darauf ausgerichtet, allzu deutliche Schwankungen zu verhindern. Dafür sind TänzerInnen und SchauspielerInnen ausgebildet – „der Aufgabe gerecht zu werden", indem sie Abend für Abend mit Energie, Enthusiasmus und Überzeugung die gleiche Abfolge von Handlungen ausführen und die immer gleichen, vorgeschriebenen Worte sagen. Sogar in Theatern und Veranstaltungsorten für Performance und Tanz, die „downtown" oder „alternativ" sind, wird diese Erwartungshaltung oft übernommen (so sie nicht ausdrücklich improvisieren oder sich einer variablen Struktur bedienen, die sich Abend für Abend verändert).

Das Verwenden von Aufgaben in deiner Arbeit unterläuft diese Absicht. Liege ich damit jetzt falsch? Was du hinsichtlich deiner „plumpen Nachbildungen" von *Agon* beschreibst, scheint mir eine Situation zu schaffen, in der die Aufgabe von Abend zu Abend schwerer zu wiederholen ist.

Ich habe noch in anderer Hinsicht versucht, meine Aufmerksamkeit sehr gezielt auf diese Beziehung zwischen Aufgabe und Wiederholung zu richten. In einigen Stücken führe ich die Aufgabe nicht zweimal aus – wenn die Aufgabe des Sprechens zum Beispiel nur darin bestand, eine Videoaufnahme zu machen. Dabei gibt es keine feste Regel, sondern ich versuche, das von Stück zu Stück bewusst zu entscheiden. Das war ein wichtiger Punkt, als ich vom „Machen" der Performance zur „Verwendung" von Performance übergegangen bin.

Y. R.: Was Aufgaben und (professionelle) Wiederholung betrifft: Seltsamerweise ertappe ich mich dabei, wie ich meine zusammengewürfelte Tanztruppe (das ist nicht abwertend gemeint; „unerwartet" wäre wohl treffender) „drille", als ginge es um ihr Leben. Ich fühle mich genötigt, jede Einzelne an die Grenzen ihrer individuellen Fähigkeiten zu treiben. Denn genau die Unterschiede in den Fähigkeiten lassen hoffentlich Aufgabe und Anstrengung hervortreten. Leichtigkeit wird gleichzeitig errungen, erfüllt, niedergerissen, auseinander genommen, dekonstruiert und manchmal auch völlig zerstört. Natürlich stellt sich die Frage: Wie unterscheidet sich das von einer AmateurInnentanzgruppe wie jener von Edith Stephen, mit der ich 1958 als völlig blanke Anfängerin getanzt habe? Man könnte sagen, die Mitglieder von Ediths Gruppe hatten eine vergleichbare „Bandbreite" an Fähigkeiten wie meine jetzige Gruppe. Der Vergleich hinkt – zumal unter den *Agon*-Tänzerinnen keine „völlig blanken Anfängerinnen" sind –, er hinkt also, außer was den Aspekt des „Originals" betrifft. Hinter meinen Tänzerinnen lauert auf Schritt und Tritt das Original; die Standards des Balletts sind der Boden, auf dem sie stehen; die Vorgaben von Ausbildung und körperlichen Idealen sind allumfassend. Darin liegt etwas Beruhigendes. Diese

Werte sind in der westlichen Kultur so allgegenwärtig, so einzementiert, dass sie eine dauerhafte Wand bilden, gegen die ich mit dem Kopf anrennen kann. (Ich glaube, du kennst die Geschichte von John Cage, der beschlossen hatte, sein Leben lang gegen Schönbergs Überbewertung der Harmonie anzurennen, für die Cage eingestandenermaßen nichts „empfand".) Widerstand braucht, wenn schon keine harte, so doch eine dauerhafte, gut etablierte Reibefläche.

Übersetzt von Jutta Braidt

Anmerkungen:

1. Yvonne Rainer bezieht sich hier auf Sharon Hayes' DJ-Performance bei *LTTR Explosion*, einer Serie von Performances im Juli 2004 bei Art in General, New York, bei der Hayes Schallplatten mit verschiedensten Sprechaufnahmen mixte.
2. Die Ballerina Maria Tallchief war die bedeutendste Interpretin der Choreografien Balanchines. Die beiden waren von 1946 bis 1951 verheiratet und gründeten gemeinsam das spätere New York City Ballet.
3. Taisha Paggett ist eine Tänzerin, die Yvonne Rainer während ihres Gaststipendiums am Getty Research Institute im Frühjahr 2005 assistierte.

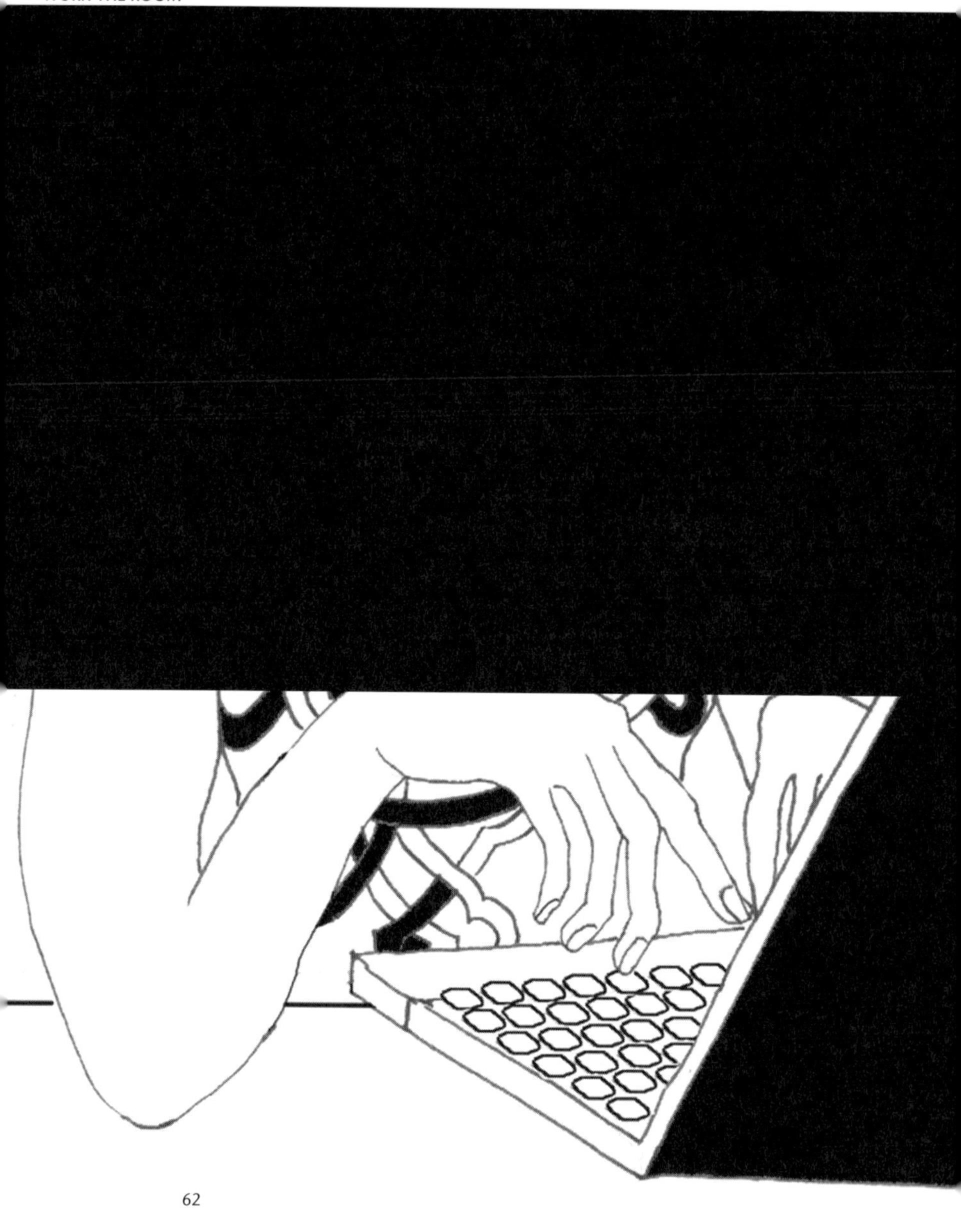

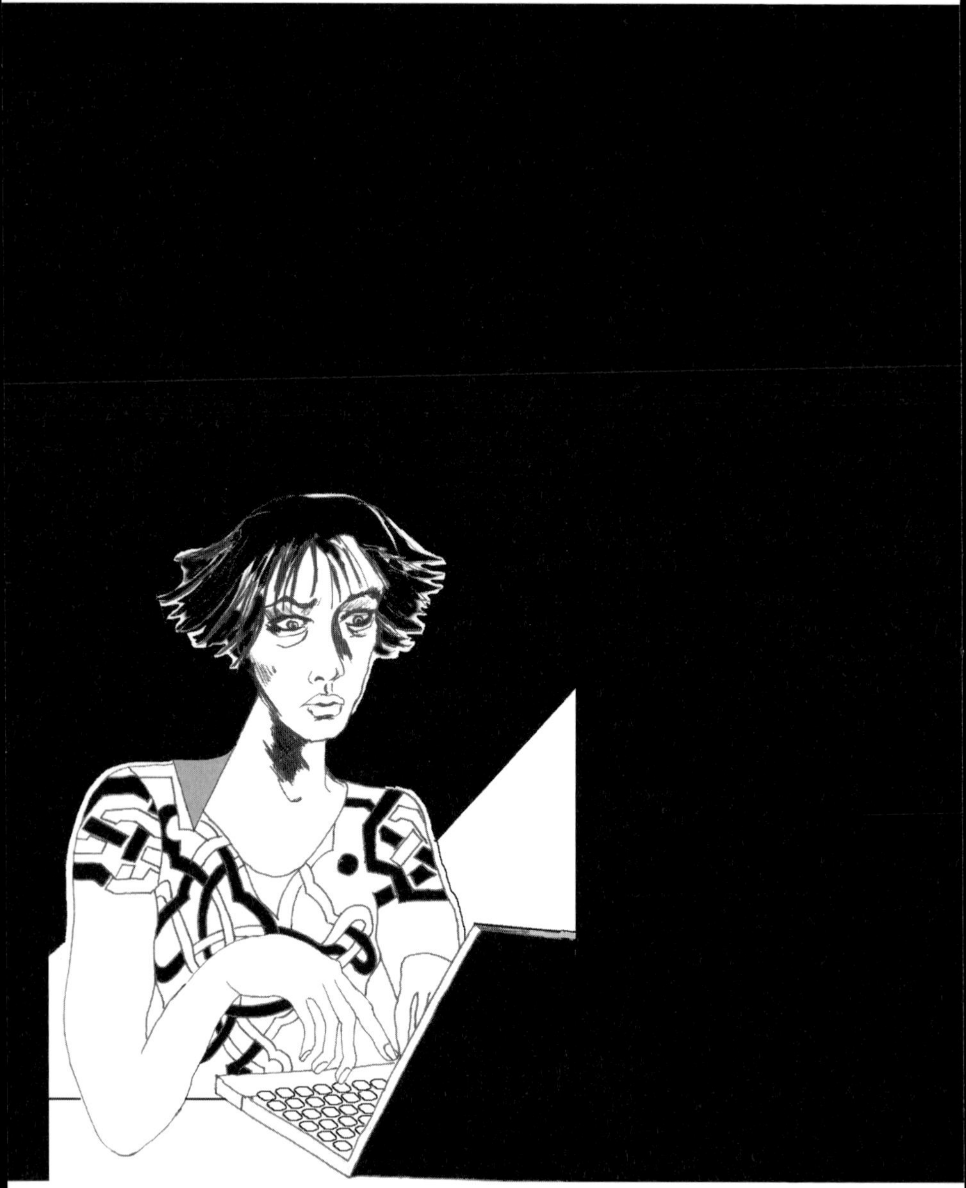

Linda in Action or Business as Usual

by Linda Bilda

My performance at MUMOK on September 28, 2003 had actually begun way earlier than that, in December 2001, when I filed a patent for colored glass in buildings.

I had gained a certain visiblity as an avant-garde artist and editor of comic books, when, in the course of my engagement with sculpture for a public art project, I developed a technology that offered entirely new design possibilities. Reactions were immediately so positive that I decided to market the technology internationally, thereby creating a financial future for myself.

The LIGHTGLASS technology inserts one or more colored plexiglass segments between the two panes of insulating glass units. A narrow spacer holds the plexiglass in place. For a perfect fit, the colored elements are precisely cut to form with a laser's accuracy and inlaid like a jigsaw puzzle. Minimal distances between the pieces of glass ensure the stability of the system, and prevent any disturbances due to expansion or contraction of the acrylic elements.

LIGHTGLASS can be used in interior design to create eye-catching colorful accents in glass or to insert colored content (texts, images). It can optically enclose an area, create orientation systems in office buildings and public spaces, and add color to glass furniture, staircases, elevator shafts, display showcases, etc.

The factors: Price advantage over colored glass, material can be tooled with highest precision, even for parts as small as 1 cm^2, very lightweight, available in large sheets, up to 3 x 5 m, 100% transparency.

So far. So good.

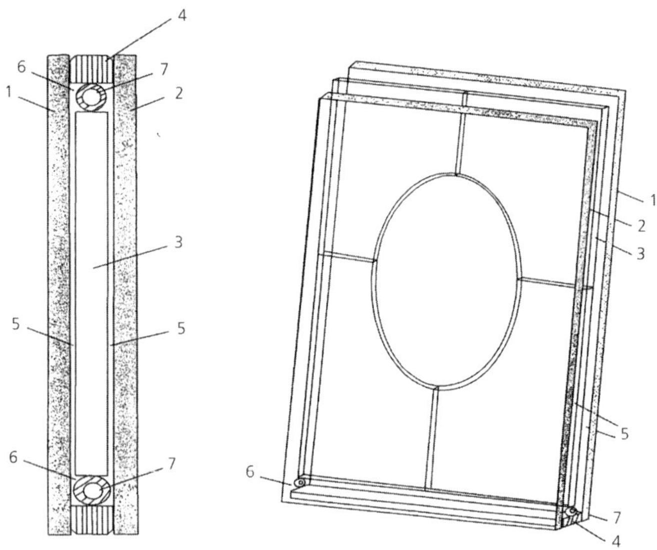

1,2 Glass

3 Plexiglas (Acrylic)

4 Spacer

To describe the extent of my performance—and I insist on using that word—I will now make a little digression into patent law. Patent law was not written to protect the intellectual property of individual inventors, but rather for large corporations that have money and law departments. In order to take out a national patent (e.g., in Austria), one has to expect costs of about 200 Euros; it is, however, mandatory to employ a patent lawyer, as it is otherwise as good as impossible to correctly formulate the patent claim, which serves to protect the invention from knock-offs and to sell licenses. This produces costs in the range of 4000 Euros. As fundless inventor I was offered a pro bono patent lawyer by the patent lawyers' association. After the registration process, an annual fee has to be paid for the national patent. It starts at about 100 Euros and incrementally goes up to some 2000 Euros at the end of the 20-year duration of the patent.

Within one year from the patent registration, it is possible to file the national patent in other countries using notarized translations. This time limit can be expanded for another 18 months with a PCT registration, which costs about 3500 Euros. A worldwide registration in countries that allow patents costs at least 100,000 Euros.

In order to generate this amount in the prescribed time period, I immediately began a very intense marketing campaign for licenses.

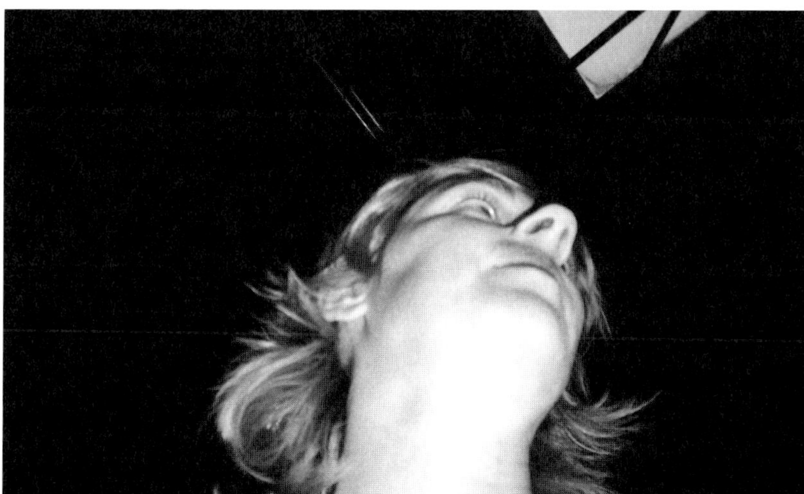

Linda Bilda

My experience with performance proved to be very helpful. In a performance the goal is not to play a role—like in the theater—but to create and communicate an immediate experiential context. My management consultant kept telling me: "Stay authentic!" e.g., the aim was not to take on a new role, but rather to deal with the situation, my own abilities and the unknown counterpart (entrepreneurs and business people from Asia, the U.S., and Europe) and thus develop a good performance.

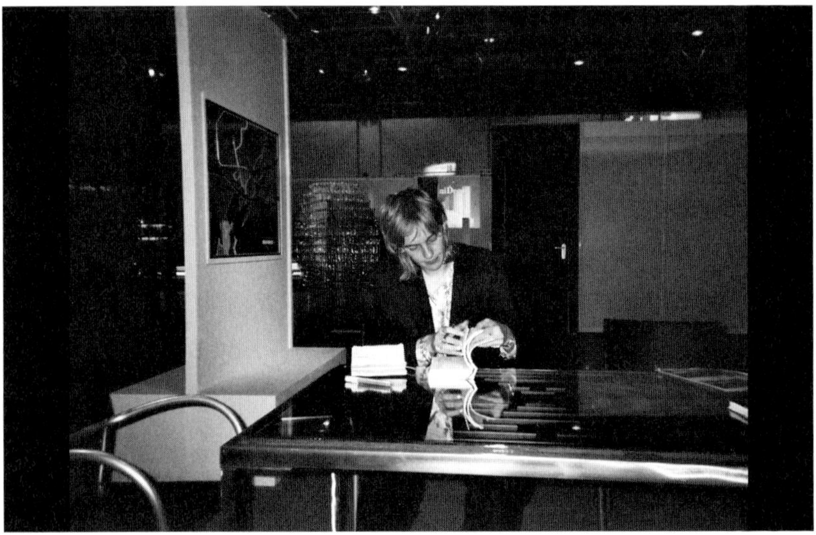

Glass Tech, Düsseldorf, 2002

Everybody who has been to a trade fair before knows that it is hard work—communicating, presenting, etc. As I could not afford to pay somebody, I was mostly alone. Sometimes I could not even go and eat or take a pee.
How strenuous!

The results: some contacts, and concrete interest from a Korean businessman, who wanted to sign a licensing agreement immediately. Know-how-Con? I don't know. I didn't even have any contract sheets in English on me. I simply hadn't expected something like that.

Every performance needs and defines a space. Concentration and the production of an immediate space-time-experience make a good performance.

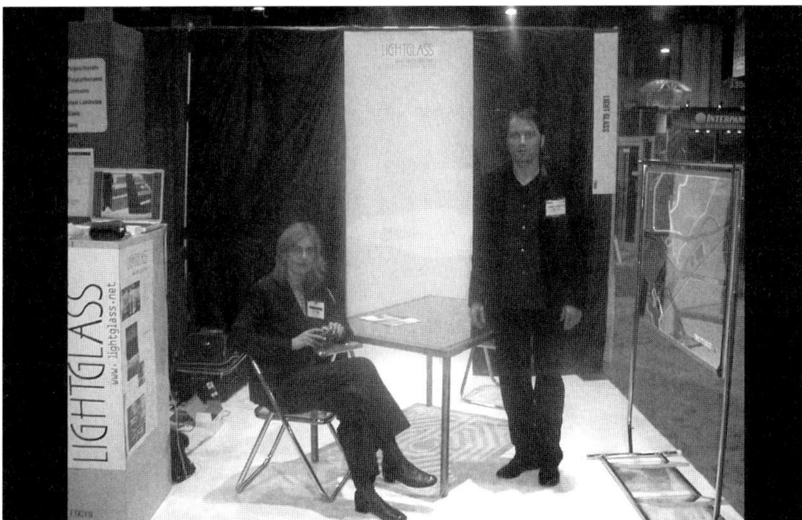

Glass Build Atlanta, with Thomas Sandbichler, 2003

Translated by Ulrike Müller

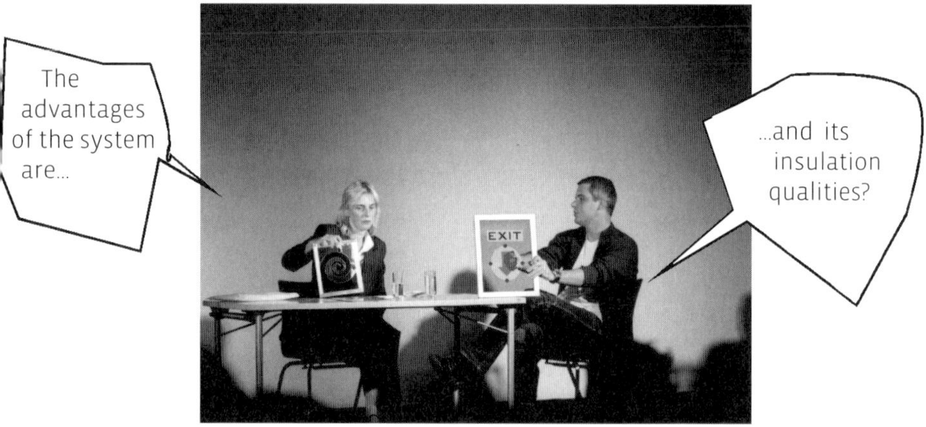

Performance Business as Usual *with Peter Döllmann, MUMOK, September 28, 2003*

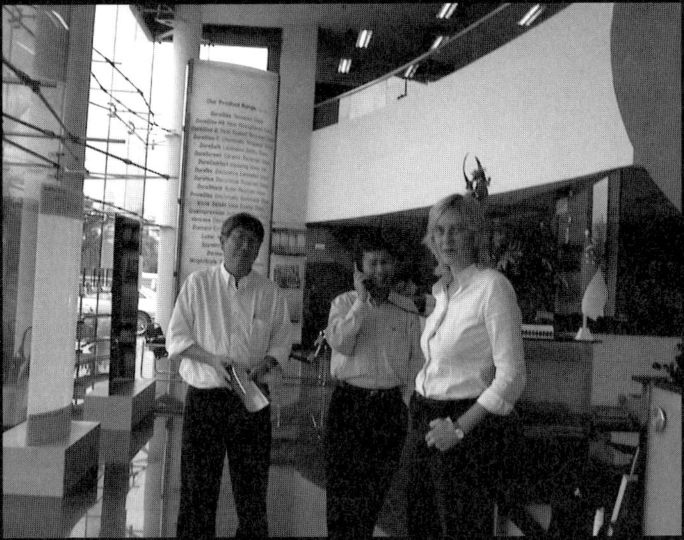

In Singapore, 2003, with Mark Chiang and Gan Chua von SSG

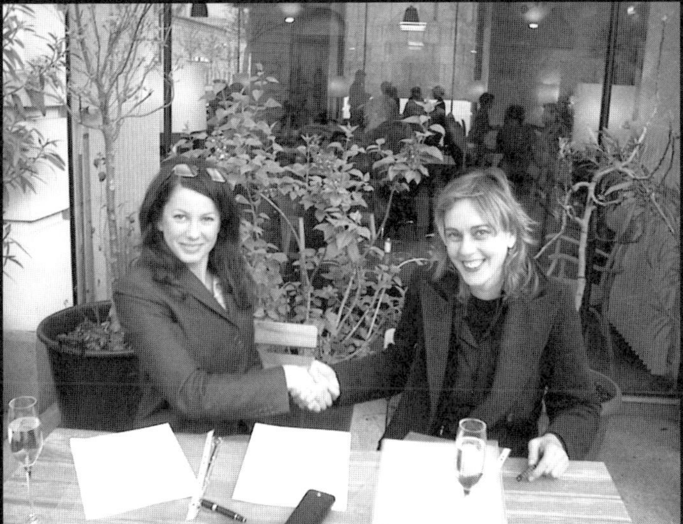

March 2004: Signing of the license contract for Europe with Iris Sageder

LIGHTGLASS Performance

December 7, 2001: Patent Application

2002

February: Beginning of the marketing campaign in Austria	
concrete negotiations on a licensing partnership with an Austrian company, Vienna	no agreement reached about the payment for the license
Mailing 1: 20 addresses	
German manufacturers of insulated glass, facades, and building materials	
contact with and visits to five companies—interest in marketing the technology	
negotiations on a licensing partnership with an internationally active, medium-sized company in Würzburg	no agreement reached about the payment for the license
March: Presence at the Frontale trade fair in Nürnberg	
contact with large German concern	technology does not fit into their profile, no priority
contact with large Swiss concern	contact person is no longer with the company
Mailing 2: 15 addresses	
Interior and store fittings, glass processing companies in Germany	
contact with several companies	not maintained from our side—company too small
contact with architecture firm in Berlin	interested in using in their own offices
Mailing 3: ca. 20 addresses (including Austria)	
contact with German company	not maintained from our side—company too small
April: Presence at the Austroglas trade fair in Salzburg	
contact with Austrian glass processing company, interested in marketing the technology	not maintained from our side—company doesn't seem very trustworthy
Mailing 4: 6 addresses	
Follow-up from Glass Tech trade fair Düsseldorf	no results
P.R. activities:	
published in "Intelligente Architektur"—ca. 15 inquiries	no projects
published in "Architektur aktuell"—ca. 8 inquiries	no projects
published in "Plexipoint"	
published in "Glaswelt"	
Other:	
presence at Glass Tech trade fair, Düsseldorf, 10/28–11/1	no concrete results
participation in a business competition, among the first 25 of 120 entries	discontinued for lack of time
participation in the "Creative Industries Call" of the City of Vienna	grant from the business development fund

2003

Contacts with companies in Europe, America, Asia

Trade Fairs	
January 13–18, Bau Munich	Low interest in colored glass in Germany (chromophobia)
booth, March 12–14, Glass Build, Atlanta	financed by a "business angel"
licensing negotiations with US glass concern	unable to launch the project on a higher management level (lack of travel funds)
project cooperation with US glass company that does very interesting projects	follow-up insufficient
booth, June 25–28, Vitrum, Milan	
licensing negotiations with glass company in Malaysia	fails after one and a half years of insufficient communication. (lack of travel funds)
licensing negotiations, Yurinara, Korea	fails due to a misunderstanding (loss of face)
cooperation with agents for LIGHTGLASS, Singapore and France	not enough samples (costs)
booth, October 8-10, Glass Tech, Singapore	presentation material does not arrive in time!
licensing partnership with company in Malaysia	compensation payment never received
cooperation with agents for LIGHTGLASS, New Zealand, Australia	not enough samples (costs)

P.R. activities:
published in "Schöner Wohnen," Germany
published in "Vidrio Technology," Brazil
published in "Glass," U.S.A.
published in "Vetro," Italy
published in "South East Glass Technology," Asia

Further development of the technology, search for investment partners and cooperative arrangements.

In March 2004, two licensing contracts on license duration were signed with licensees for Europe and the U.S.A. In Asia the patent could not be maintained.

In May 2006, the license contract for Europe was cancelled due to lack of sales. Instead marketing of individual licenses.

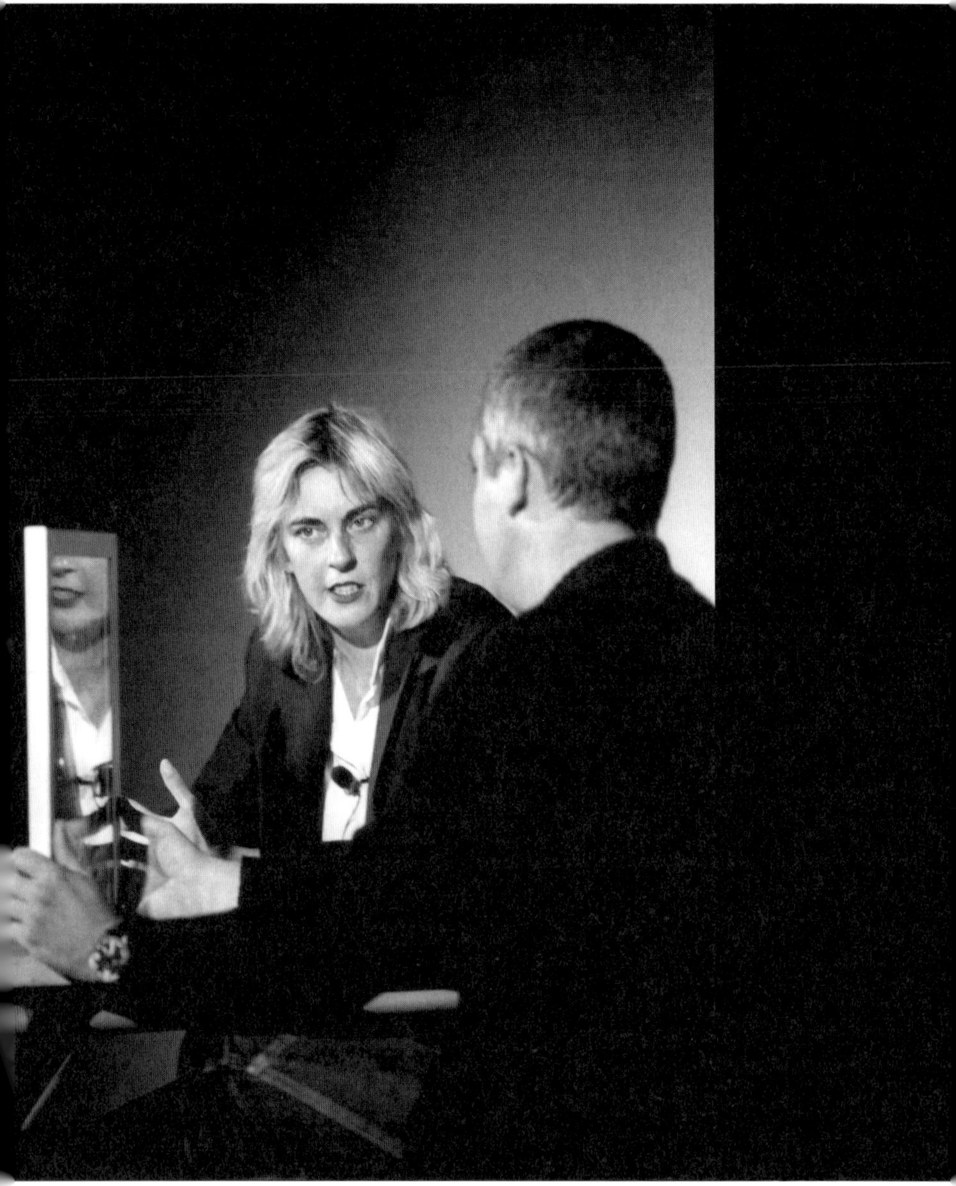

Linda in Aktion oder Business as Usual

von Linda Bilda

Meine Performance, die im MUMOK am 28. September 2003 stattfand, begann eigentlich viel früher, nämlich im Dezember 2001, als ich ein Patent für farbige Glasgestaltung anmeldete.

Zuvor war ich als Avantgardekünstlerin und Herausgeberin von Comics und Kunstzeitschriften in Erscheinung getreten und hatte durch meine Beschäftigung als Bildhauerin im Zuge eines „Kunst am Bau"-Projekts ein Verfahren mit Acrylglas entwickelt, das vollkommen neue Gestaltungsmöglichkeiten bot. Die Reaktionen waren spontan so positiv, dass ich beschloss, das Verfahren international zu vermarkten, um mir eine finanzielle Zukunft zu schaffen.

Bei LIGHTGLASS werden in einen handelsüblichen Isolierglasverbund mit schmalem Abstandhalter farbige ein- oder mehrteilige Acrylglasplatten frei hineingestellt. Exakt mit Laser zugeschnitten, erreichen die Plattenteile höchste Passgenauigkeit, sodass sie ohne Klebung – wie Intarsien – ein Ganzes (Puzzle) bilden. Knappe Abstände der Acrylglaselemente zu den Glasscheiben bewirken die Stabilität des Systems.

Verwendung im Innenbereich überall, wo auffallende farbliche Akzentuierung in Glas gewünscht wird oder Inhalte (Texte, Bilder) farbig sein sollen, wie bei Geschäftseinrichtungen, Liftanlagen, optischer Abschirmung von Räumen, Orientierungshilfen in Bürogebäuden, Glasmöbeln und Glastreppen usw.

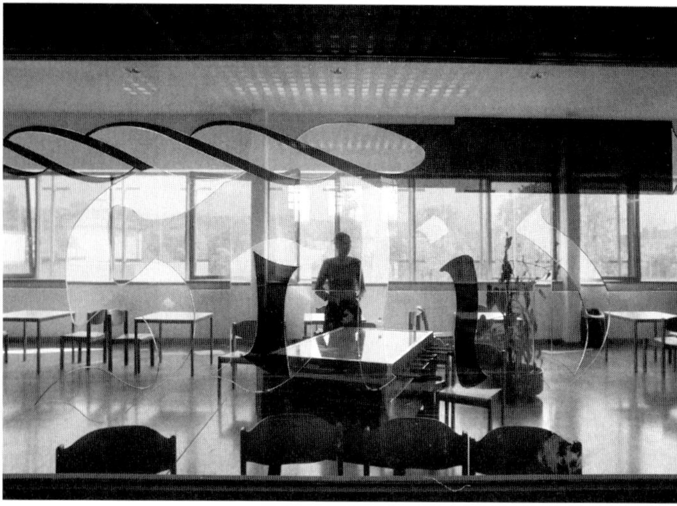

LIGHTGLASS-Anwendung in der HTL Lastenstraße, Klagenfurt, Kärnten

Die Faktoren: Preisvorteil gegenüber Farbglas, auch mit kleinen Entwurfsteilen ab 1 cm^2 exakt zu bearbeiten, geringes Gewicht, in sehr großen Abmessungen bis zu 3 x 5 m erhältlich, vollkommen transparent.

So weit. So gut.

Um den Umfang meiner Performance zu beschreiben – und ich bestehe darauf, sie so zu nennen –, mache ich nun einen kleinen Exkurs ins Patentrecht. Das Patentrecht wurde nicht dafür geschaffen, das geistige Eigentum von EinzelerfinderInnen zu schützen, sondern das von Konzernen, die über Geld oder eigene Rechtsabteilungen verfügen.

Um ein Patent national (z. B. in Österreich) anzumelden, ist mit ca. 200 Euro zu rechnen; es ist aber unbedingt notwendig, einen Patentanwalt beizuziehen, da es sonst kaum möglich ist, den Patentanspruch korrekt zu formulieren, um ihn vor Nachahmungen zu schützen oder Lizenzen zu verkaufen, wobei mit Kosten von ca. 4000 Euro zu rechnen ist. Als mittelloser Erfinderin wurde mir für die Anmeldung ein Patentanwalt von der Patentanwaltskammer kostenlos zur Seite gestellt. Danach sind für das z. B. in Österreich angemeldete Patent jährlich tangential ansteigende Jahresgebühren zu zahlen, die bei ca. 100 Euro beginnen und bei ca. 2000 Euro am Ende der Patentlaufzeit von 20 Jahren enden.

Diese Anmeldung gibt die Möglichkeit, das nationale Patent innerhalb eines Jahres auch in anderen Ländern mit beglaubigten Übersetzungen anzumelden, bzw. kann diese Frist mittels einer PCT-Anmeldung nochmals um 18 Monate verlängert werden, was ca. 3500 Euro kostet. Eine weltweite Anmeldung in Ländern, die Patente erlauben, kostet mindestens 100.000 Euro.

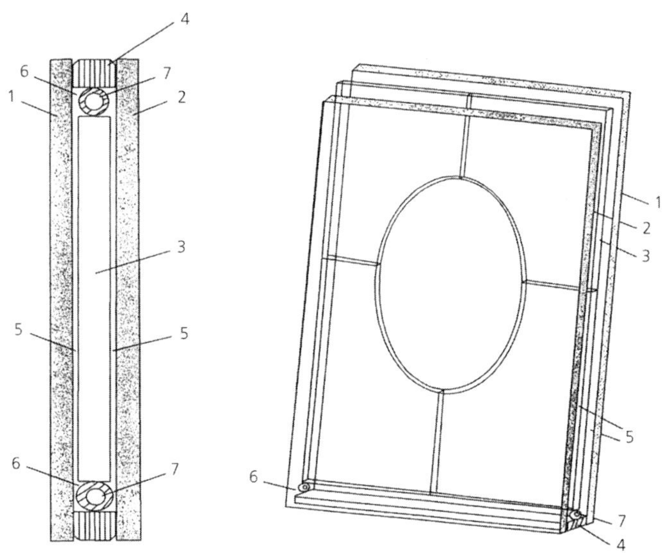

1, 2 Glas

3 Acrylglas

4 Abstandhalter

Um diese Summe in der vorgesehenen Zeit zu erwirtschaften, begann ich sehr rasch mit einer sehr intensiven Marketingtätigkeit für Lizenzen.

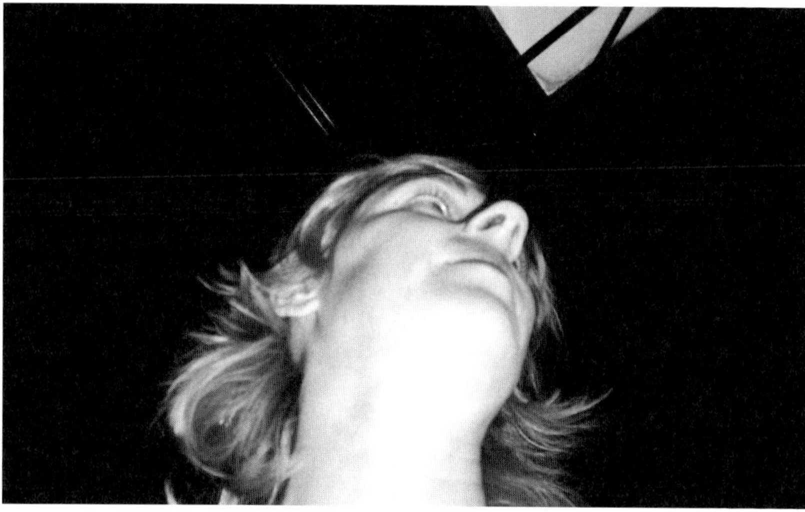

Dabei kam mir meine Erfahrung mit Performance zugute. Bei einer Performance geht es nicht darum, eine Rolle zu spielen – wie im Theater –, sondern einen unmittelbaren Erfahrungszusammenhang zu erzeugen und zu kommunizieren. Mein Unternehmensberater sagte mir ständig: „Bleiben Sie authentisch!", d. h., es ging darum, keine neue Rolle anzunehmen, sondern mit der Situation, den eigenen Möglichkeiten und dem unbekannten Gegenüber (UnternehmerInnen, Geschäftsleute aus Asien, den USA, Europa) umzugehen und eine gute Performance zu entwickeln.

Wer schon mal auf einer Messe war, weiß, dass das schwere Arbeit ist – kommunizieren, präsentieren usw. Da ich niemanden bezahlen konnte, war ich die meiste Zeit allein – manchmal konnte ich z. B. nicht mal essen oder pinkeln gehen.

Anstrengend!

Ergebnis: einige Kontakte, ein konkreter Interessent aus Korea, der sofort einen Lizenzvertrag abschließen wollte. Know-how-Klau? Ich weiß nicht. Ich hatte gar keine Vertragsunterlagen auf Englisch mit, hatte damit einfach nicht gerechnet.

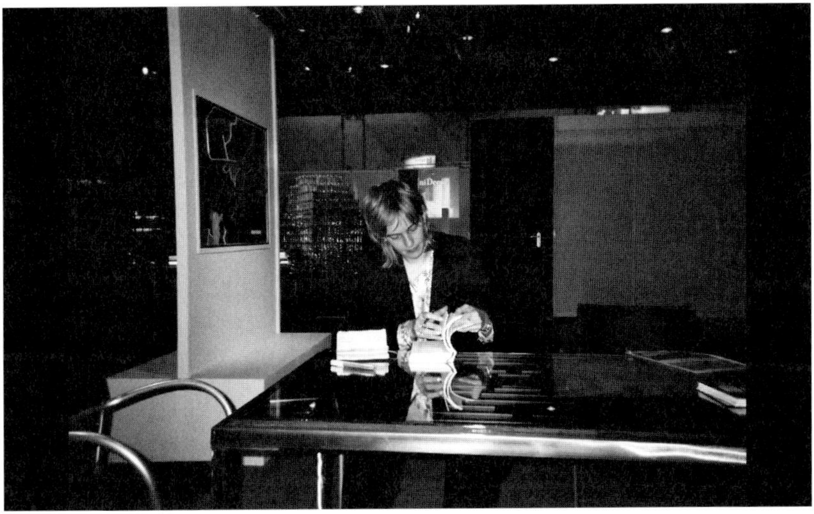

Glass Tech, Düsseldorf, 2002

Jede Performance braucht Raum, der durch sie erst definiert wird. Konzentration und das Erzeugen einer unmittelbaren Raum-Zeit-Erfahrung machen eine gute Performance aus.

LIGHTGLASS Performance

7. Dezember 2001: Anmeldung des Patents

2002

Februar: Beginn der Vermarktungstätigkeit in Österreich	
Konkrete Verhandlungen über eine Lizenzpartnerschaft mit einer österreichischen Firma, Wien	scheitert an der Höhe der Abstandszahlung f. d. Lizenz
Mailing 1: 20 Adressen	
deutsche Isolierglashersteller, Fassaden, Glasbau	
Kontakt und Besuch von 5 Firmen – möchten das System vertreiben	
Verhandlungen über eine Lizenzpartnerschaft mit einem international tätigen, mittelständischen Unternehmen in Würzburg	scheitert an der Höhe der Abstandszahlung f. d. Lizenz
März: Besuch der Frontale-Messe in Nürnberg	
Kontakt dt. Großunternehmen	System passt nicht in ihre Identität, keine Priorität
Kontakt Schweizer Großunternehmen	Ansprechpartner ist nicht mehr in der Firma
Mailing 2: 15 Adressen	
Innen-, Ladenbau, Glasveredelung Deutschland	
Kontakt mit mehreren Unternehmen	Kontakt von unserer Seite nicht aufrecht – zu kleine Firma
Kontakt Berliner Architekturbüro	an Anwendung im eigenen Büro interessiert
Mailing 3: ca. 20 Adressen (auch Österreich)	
Kontakt dt. Unternehmen	Kontakt von unserer Seite nicht aufrecht, zu klein
April: Besuch der Austroglas-Messe in Salzburg	
Kontakt österr. Glasverarbeitungsbetrieb, möchte das System vertreiben	Kontakt von unserer Seite nicht aufrecht, scheinen nicht sehr seriös
Mailing 4: 6 Adressen	
Nacharbeit Glass Tech Düsseldorf	keine Ergebnisse
PR-Tätigkeit:	
Veröffentlichung in „Intelligente Architektur" – ca. 15 Rückfragen	keine Projekte
Veröffentlichung in „Architektur aktuell" – ca. 8 Rückfragen	keine Projekte
Veröffentlichung in „Plexipoint"	
Veröffentlichung in „Glaswelt"	
weiters:	
Messeauftritt, Glass Tech, Düsseldorf, 28.10.–1.11.2002	keine konkreten Ergebnisse
Teilnahme an einem Businesswettbewerb – unter den ersten 25 von 120 Einreichungen	aus Zeitmangel abgebrochen
Teilnahme am „Creative Industries Call" der Stadt Wien	Förderung der Wirtschaftsförderung

2003

Kontaktaufnahme mit Firmen in Europa, Amerika, Asien

Messebesuche

13.–18. Jänner, Bau München	Deutschland will kaum farbiges Glas (Chromophobie)
Stand, 12.–14. März, Glass Build, Atlanta	wird von einem „business angel" finanziert
Lizenzverhandlung amerik. Glaskonzern	wir schaffen es nicht, das Projekt in einer höheren Managementebene zu lancieren (Reisekostenmangel)
Projektkooperation amerik. Glasfirma, die sehr interessante Projekte macht	Nacharbeit ungenügend
Standteilnahme, 25.–28. Juni, Vitrum, Mailand	
Lizenzverhandlung Glasfirma Malaysia	scheitert nach eineinhalb Jahren an ungenügender Kommunikation (Reisekostenmangel)
Lizenzverhandlung Yurinara, Korea	scheitert an einem Missverständnis (Gesichtsverlust)
Kooperation mit AgentInnen für LIGHTGLASS Singapur und Frankreich	nicht genügend Muster (Kosten)
Stand, 8.–10. Oktober, Glass Tech, Singapur	Ausstellungsstücke kommen nicht rechtzeitig an!
Lizenzpartnerschaft mit Firma in Malaysia	zahlt nie die Abstandszahlung
Kooperation mit Agenten für Neuseeland, Australien	nicht genügend Muster (Kosten)

Öffentlichkeitsarbeit
veröffentlicht in „Schöner Wohnen", Deutschland
veröffentlicht in „Vidrio Technology", Brasilien
veröffentlicht in „Glass", USA
veröffentlicht in „Vetro", Italien
veröffentlicht in „South East Glass Technology", Asien

Außerdem Weiterentwicklungen des Systems, Suche nach InvestmentpartnerInnen und Kooperationen

Im März 2004 kam es zum Abschluss von 2 Lizenzverträgen mit LizenznehmerInnen für Europa und die USA auf Patentlaufzeit, für Asien konnte das Patent nicht aufrechterhalten werden.

Im Mai 2006 wurde der europäische Lizenzvertrag wegen mangelnden Umsatzes gekündigt. Stattdessen Vermarktung von Einfachlizenzen.

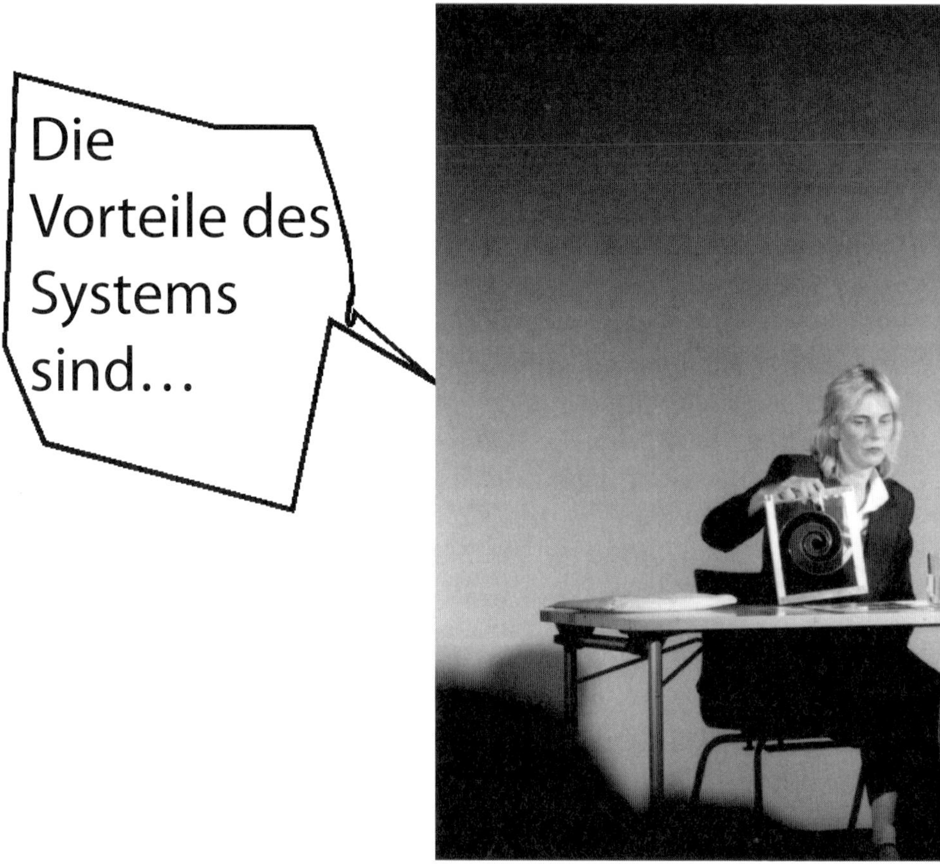
Die Vorteile des Systems sind…

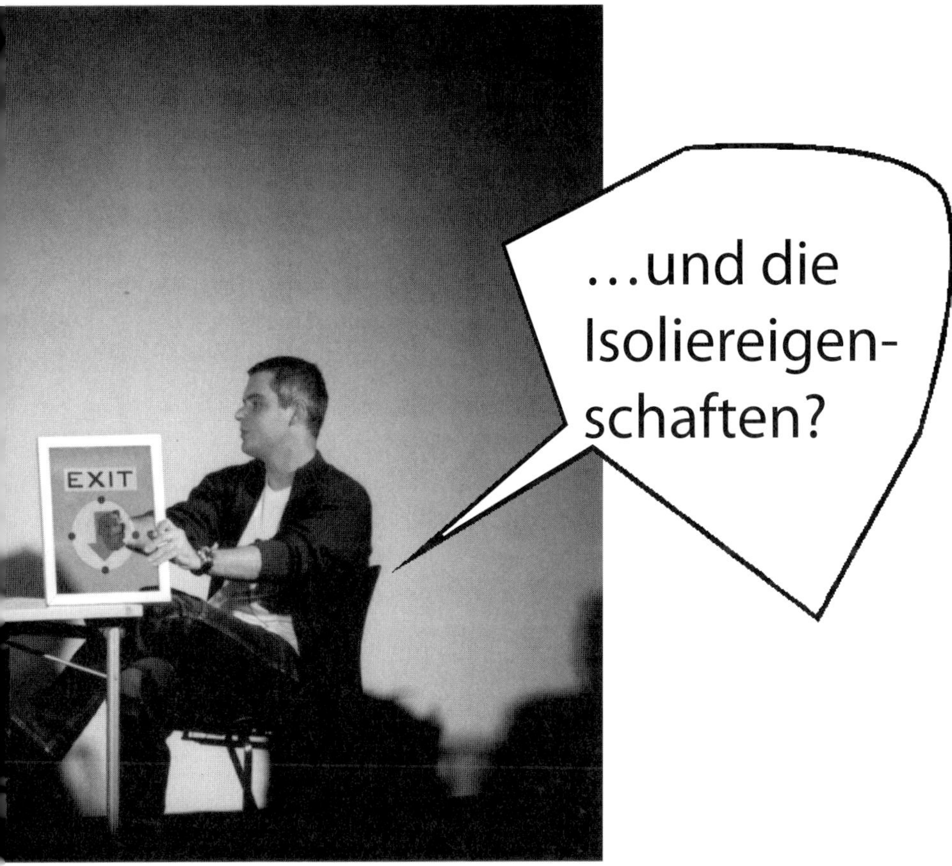
EXIT
…und die Isoliereigen-schaften?

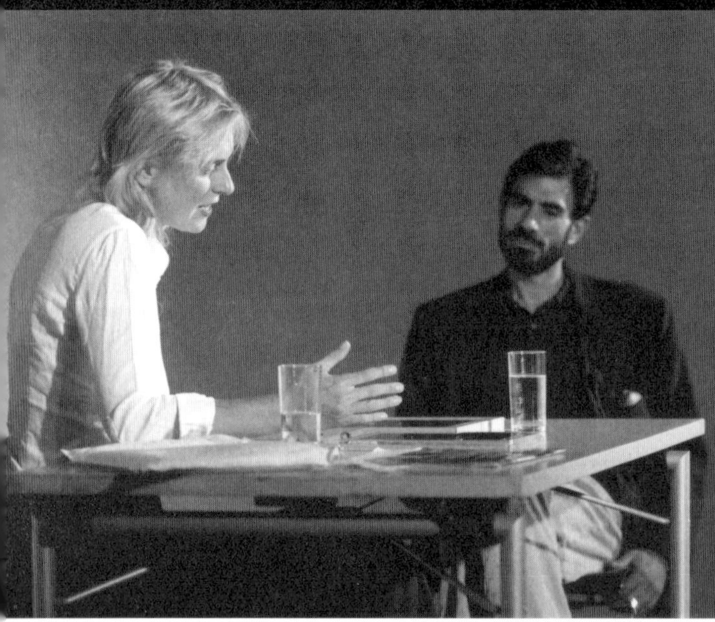

Abstract for You

by Gregg Bordowitz

The material for creative work is a largely unseen but intensely felt substance that connects people, things, and signs. This substance is most clearly comprehended in our moods, emotions, and affects.

Thinking and feeling are two movements within the same composition. To think it I first must sense it. To be aware that I sense it I must have it as an idea. I can feel my thoughts and think my feelings. That I distinguish between feelings and thoughts is largely a matter of the mind's conventions. The mind is only able to discuss itself as something other than itself. Language is the means of this discussion. Language differentiates between thought and feeling as a matter of daily habit. The truth of the matter is revealed to us anytime the distinction is immolated by passion.

Reason and imagination arise together. To reason about anything I must imagine it from all sides: as it has been, as it is, how it will be—to myself and to others. When I imagine anything I must reason about its features, its qualities, and ultimately whether it exists or not.

Thought and feeling, reason and imagination, thinking and doing are all as inseparable as sleeping and breathing, dreaming and waking, walking and standing upright.

"What does it mean?" "Why does she do that?" These questions never lead to definitive resolutions. "How does it work?" "What is she doing?" These questions yield workable resolutions. Effects are registered and weighed by the senses. Intentions are never discoverable, even by the individual contemplating her own actions.

Thinking and doing are not causally related. They have no necessary relation. Thinking and doing often coincide as a matter of chance opportunity.

We can judge actions, not beliefs; consequences, not thoughts. Actions follow from beliefs, and consequences follow from thoughts, though one cannot predict what follows from either beliefs or thoughts. We barely know what we believe until our beliefs are tested. We are only dimly aware of our thoughts until we face their consequences. Circumstances in our daily lives confer recognition and value on our ideas. The worth of our ideas is set as a matter of custom.

Habit solidifies morale. Wave upon wave of generations' collective emotional experiences accrete to form the criteria of what is right or wrong, appropriate or inappropriate. The prevalent feelings of a historical period shape that period's behaviors: what makes us proud and what brings us shame. Each period has a character with dominant moods and subordinate states. Fashion, beauty, manners, conduct, style, etc.—Aesthetics variously affect the forms of the most forceful feelings and the least acknowledged ones. Culture is the affective embodiment of order.

There are no dilemmas presented here. No decisions to make. One cannot choose between the active life or the contemplative life. Simply do more. Think more. Feel more. Don't be fooled. Doing more certainly includes the possibility of doing nothing. For me doing less means reading more.

The following question once again asserts an urgent claim on our attention: How can I lead a life of contentment, both ethical and pleasurable?

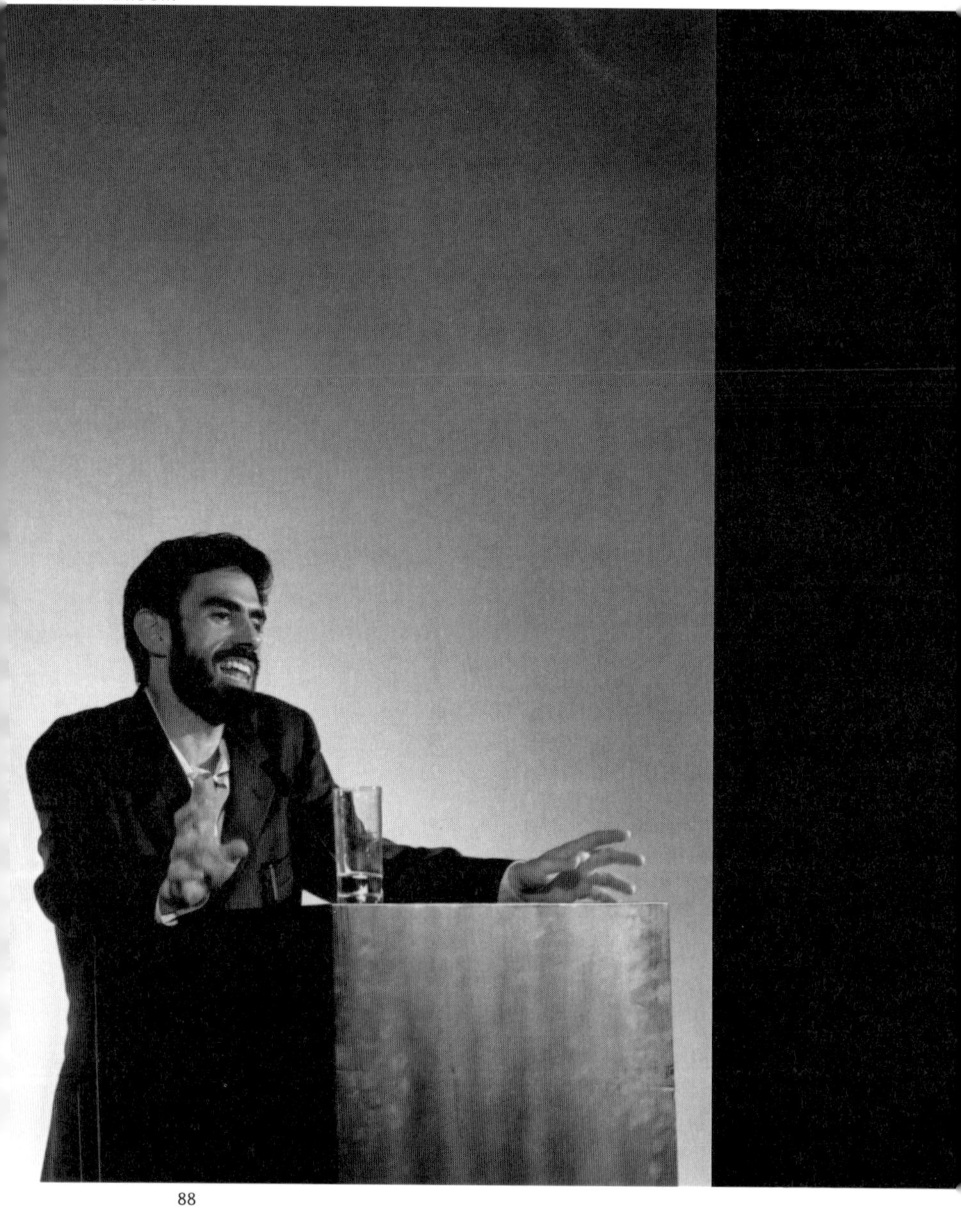

Für dich: rein begrifflich. Ein Abriss

von Gregg Bordowitz

Der schöpferische Grundstoff ist eine großenteils ungesehene, jedoch eindringlich gefühlte Substanz, die Menschen, Dinge und Zeichen verbindet. Diese Substanz wird am klarsten erfasst in unseren Stimmungen, Gefühlen und Affekten.

Denken und Fühlen sind zwei Bewegungen innerhalb derselben Komposition. Um etwas zu denken, muss ich es zuerst fühlen. Um mir bewusst zu sein, dass ich etwas fühle, muss ich es als eine Idee haben. Ich kann meine Gedanken fühlen und meine Gefühle denken. Dass ich zwischen Gefühlen und Gedanken unterscheide, ist hauptsächlich den Konventionen des Geistes geschuldet. Der Geist kann sich selbst nur diskutieren als etwas anderes als er selbst. Sprache ist das Mittel dieser Diskussion. Sprache unterscheidet zwischen Gedanke und Gefühl als eine Sache der täglichen Gewohnheit. Die Wahrheit der Sache wird uns immer dann offenbart, wenn die Unterscheidung der Leidenschaft zum Opfer fällt.

Vernunft und Vorstellung erheben sich gemeinsam. Um irgendetwas vernunftgemäß zu erfassen, muss ich es mir von allen Seiten vorstellen: wie es gewesen ist, wie es ist, wie es sein wird – für mich und für andere. Wenn ich mir etwas vorstelle, muss ich mittels meiner Vernunft dessen Merkmale und Eigenschaften sowie letztlich dessen Existenz oder Nichtexistenz ergründen.

Gedanke und Gefühl, Vernunft und Vorstellung, Denken und Tun sind ebenso wenig voneinander zu trennen wie Schlafen und Atmen, Träumen und Wachen, Gehen und aufrecht Stehen.

„Was bedeutet das?" – „Warum tut sie das?" Diese Fragen führen nie zu eindeutigen Entschlüssen. „Wie funktioniert das?" – „Was macht sie gerade?" Diese Fragen lassen Schlüsse zu, mit denen etwas anzufangen ist. Wirkungen werden von den Sinnen registriert und abgewogen. Absichten können nie entdeckt werden, nicht einmal vom Individuum, das seine eigenen Handlungen betrachtet.

Denken und Tun sind nicht ursächlich verwandt. Sie weisen keine notwendige Verwandtschaft auf. Das Aufeinandertreffen von Denken und Tun ist oft eine zufällige Angelegenheit.

Wir können Taten beurteilen, nicht Überzeugungen; Konsequenzen, nicht Gedanken. Taten folgen aus Überzeugungen, und Konsequenzen folgen aus Gedanken, obwohl man nicht vorhersagen kann, was aus Überzeugungen oder aus Gedanken folgt. Wir wissen kaum, wovon wir überzeugt sind, bevor unsere Überzeugungen geprüft werden. Wir sind uns unserer Gedanken nur undeutlich bewusst, bis wir ihre Konsequenzen zu gewärtigen haben. Gegebenheiten in unseren täglichen Leben verleihen unseren Ideen Bestätigung und Wert. Die Geltung unserer Ideen ist bestimmt durch Sitten und Gebräuche.

Gewohnheit festigt Moral. Welle um Welle der kollektiven emotionalen Erfahrungen von Generationen schlägt zusammen, um die Kriterien zu bilden, was richtig oder falsch, angemessen oder unangemessen ist. Die vorherrschenden Gefühle einer historischen Periode formen die Verhaltensweisen dieser Periode: was uns stolz macht und was uns Schande bringt. Jede Zeit hat einen Charakter mit dominanten Stimmungen und untergeordneten Zuständen. Mode, Schönheit, Benehmen, Verhalten, Stil et cetera: Ästhetik beeinflusst verschiedentlich die Formen der stärksten Gefühle – und der am wenigsten eingestandenen. Kultur ist die affektive Verkörperung von Ordnung.

Hier sind keine Dilemmata vorgelegt. Keine Entscheidungen zu treffen. Man kann nicht wählen zwischen dem aktiven Leben und dem kontemplativen Leben. Tu einfach mehr. Denke mehr. Fühle mehr. Lass dich nicht täuschen. Mehr zu tun beinhaltet gewiss die Möglichkeit, nichts zu tun. Für mich bedeutet weniger zu tun mehr zu lesen.

Die folgende Frage erfordert ein weiteres Mal dringlich unsere Aufmerksamkeit: Wie kann ich ein Leben in Zufriedenheit führen, gleichermaßen ethisch und lustvoll?

Übersetzt von Martin Gastl und Markus Schmitt

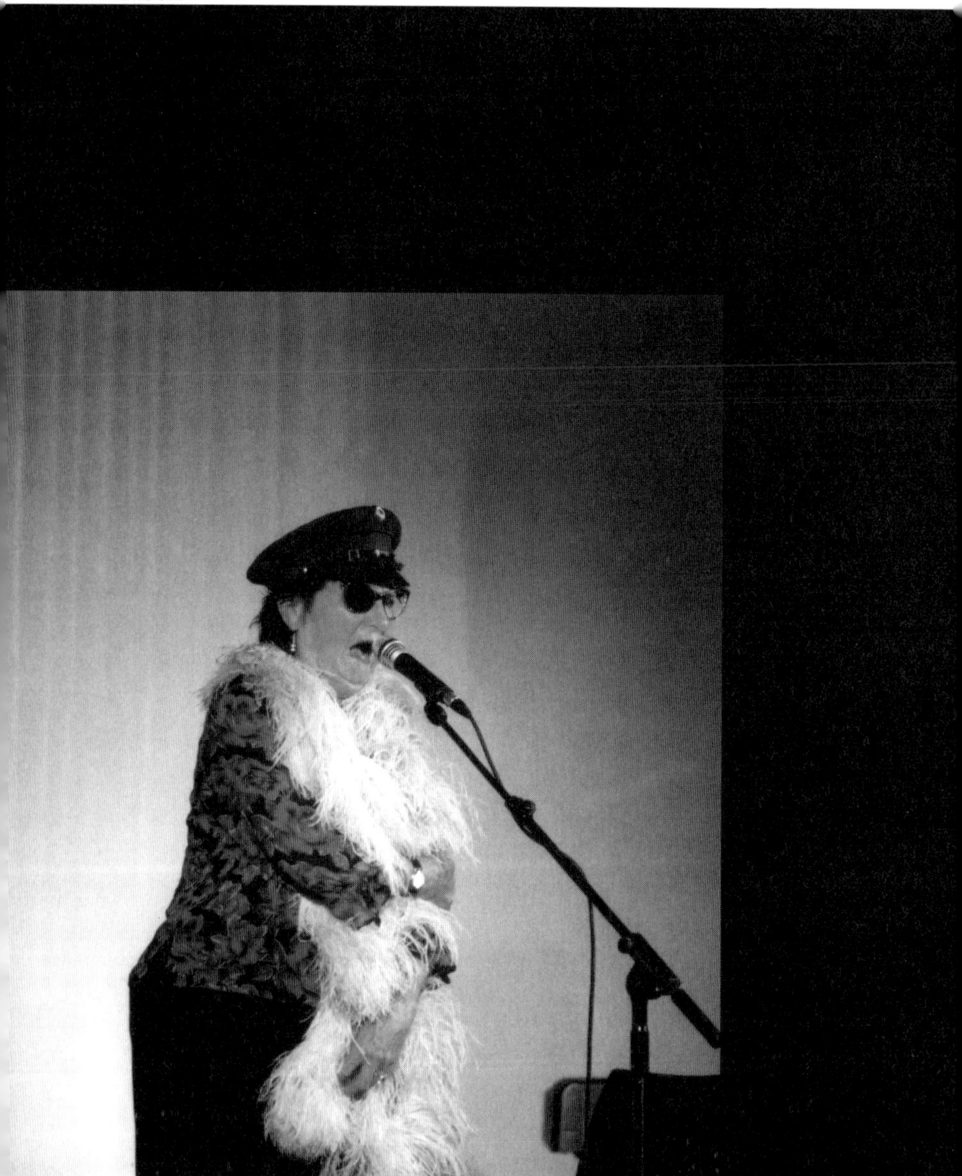

"I Don't Know Who I Belong To"

Marie-Thérèse Escribano Answers Questions from Ulrike Müller

Ulrike Müller: In your interpretations of German popular music of the 1920s and '30s, you expose the ideological content of songs whose political context is all too easily forgotten. And you do that in a very entertaining way. Although I was born more than a quarter of a century after the Second World War, I am familiar with this genre and know a few of the songs you present onstage from my childhood. During the regime of National Socialism in Germany and Austria, you lived in Spain...

Marie-Thérèse Escribano: I lived with my parents in Madrid. The Spanish Civil War (from 1936 to 1939) was hardly over when the Second World War began. Nazi propaganda was raging. A pro-German military group called *Divisón Azul* emerged. This volunteer legion, mind you, encountered no sympathy with the population. The legionnaires had an arrogant, even downright brazen air about them, and more than that, the Spanish had had enough of everything that reminded them of war. We were aware that Franco was on the side of Fascist Germany, and feared that he would get involved in the new war.

U. M.: The National Socialists' propaganda recognized the potential of popular music and appropriated it to their ends. In 1933 Goebbels had already recognized that politics had to be communicated to a broad public in a modern and accessible fashion. The regime of National Socialism also had an active interest in the proliferation of radio. In your program of popular songs you point to the ideological content of the songs, and show that politics and culture cannot be separated from one another. You make use of the feminist insight that the personal is political for your critique of Fascism. When did you begin working with popular music?

M-T. E.: I remember a scene that I experienced in Madrid. My parents went to a café to hear the news on a radio. When it was announced that the government had decided to remain neutral, all the people in the café stood up and applauded. Despite this neutrality, the media's sympathies were clearly on one side, and German songs were very popular. They were sold on cheap shellac records. We had them at home too, and I continually cranked up the gramophone in order to hear "*Adieu, mein kleiner Gardeoffizier*" (Farewell, My Little Officer of the Guard).[1] I learned the melody quickly. As far as the text was concerned, I only understood "Farewell, farewell, la-la-la officer, farewell, operituitui, operituitui..."[2] Like my parents, I had no political consciousness and did not think of anything while listening to it. The image of the young man who was drawn into war was in fact euphemistically conveyed by entertainment music. "What would he have looked like?" I asked myself—"Blond and blue-eyed?" After my childhood was over, I did not sing that song any more. I had lost any interest in popular music. At the age of 17 I began to study so-called serious music. Only 30 years later, when I was about to leave serious music behind, I presented a few verses (*Gstanzln*[3]) at a birthday party. And that was fun. It in fact proved to be successful in terms of entertainment. Perhaps I should pick up on this? However, I quickly found myself confronted with a dilemma: Most of these songs represented an ideology that I in no way wanted to support with my voice.

U. M.: The melodies are so catchy that often the text's content doesn't even register on a conscious level. In your interpretation, this is altered. The texts and their messages are brought to the fore. According to which criteria did you put together your program of popular songs? Can you give a few examples of pieces that you perform?

M-T. E.: In the case of "*Adieu mein kleiner Gardeoffizier*," I try to expose the untruthfulness and lulling quality of the last verse. I do not change the couplet, but fashion the major—who is taking leave of his old comrades after the war—as a wreck, so he is in no sense heroic. He can hardly move around, his hands shake, and he is in constant pain.

Catchy tunes get stuck in your head, and they can function like a contagious illness. One repeats a song without thinking about it, and yet something of it clings to the unconscious. That is true not only of the fascistic side, but also of the machoistic. Let's take, for example, the song "*Ich hab' das Fräul'n Helen baden seh'n*" (I Saw Miss Helen Bathing).[4] In it, a man relates how he fell in love when he accidentally saw Helen in the bath. In the first line he enthuses about Helen's legs, and finally he marries her. Nowadays it is amusing that Helen's nakedness or her legs could bring about such passion, even leading up to marriage. So far so good. But then comes the third verse: Helen has in the meantime aged, and her legs (so "sweet" at that time) are now "as fat as the legs of a piano." Friedrich, the husband, remembers her earlier legs with nostalgia.[5]

In my version of this song I don't sing this third verse, but rather narrate the text to the audience. Then I say that I also like men who have beautiful legs, but I would not marry them because of that. The laughter takes on a certain quality, one is no longer laughing at Helen, but rather at the poet who wrote this stupid text.

U. M.: When you sing "faithfulness makes no sense at all" and speak of love, you appeal to the passions and wishes of your listeners. At the same time, this song—as light and frivolous as it may sound—conceals some explosives. Do you see a possibility for intervening in a feminist way, to work toward something like a revolution within one's own emotional economy? What kind of reactions do you want from your public?

M-T. E.: The song "Ich weiß nicht, zu wem ich gehöre" (I Don't Know Who I Belong To), from which the line "faithfulness makes no sense at all" comes, was written by Friedrich Hollaender,[6] Marlene Dietrich's favorite composer. Certainly he was being serious in some place at the bottom of his heart. Women love this song, because it takes them out of the humdrum petit-bourgeois existence within which many of them live and for which I guess they are also responsible. The woman on the stage offers a little illusion, but it is not dangerous, since after the performance everyone quickly goes back to their sweet homes.

I hope that a few sharp people are sitting in my audience who will understand my irony. Then I get the sense that I'm communicating. I do not believe that I can change human beings. But I have often heard from women that they felt understood—and then, perhaps they were no longer alone. There is one thing that I enjoy very much: standing on the stage, and hearing the laughter.

Translated by Julia Bernard

Notes:

1. Popular song by Robert Stolz (music) and Walter Reisch (lyrics), from the film *The Song Is Ended* (director Géza von Bováry, Germany, 1930), sung by Liane Haid.
2. The refrain goes like this: "Farewell, my little officer of the guard, farewell, farewell/And forget me not/And forget me not/Farewell, my little officer of the guard, farewell, farewell/May good luck be yours/May good luck be yours."
3. A Bavarian and Austrian term for a song with four- or eight-line lyrics (sometimes longer). In Viennese dialect "*Gstanzl*" is also used to refer in general to a short catchy song.
4. By Fred Raymond (music) and Fritz Grünbaum (lyrics), 1925.
5. The third verse goes like this: "Our friend, he took Helen as his wife, but her calves which were once so beautiful, slim and soft and sweet, would later become awful and as fat as the legs of a piano. When the wife goes into the bathroom today, her husband does not look at the ruins any more, but wisely closes the door on her gently, and plays on the out-of-tune piano."
6. The text is by Friedrich Hollaender and Robert Liebmann, 1932.

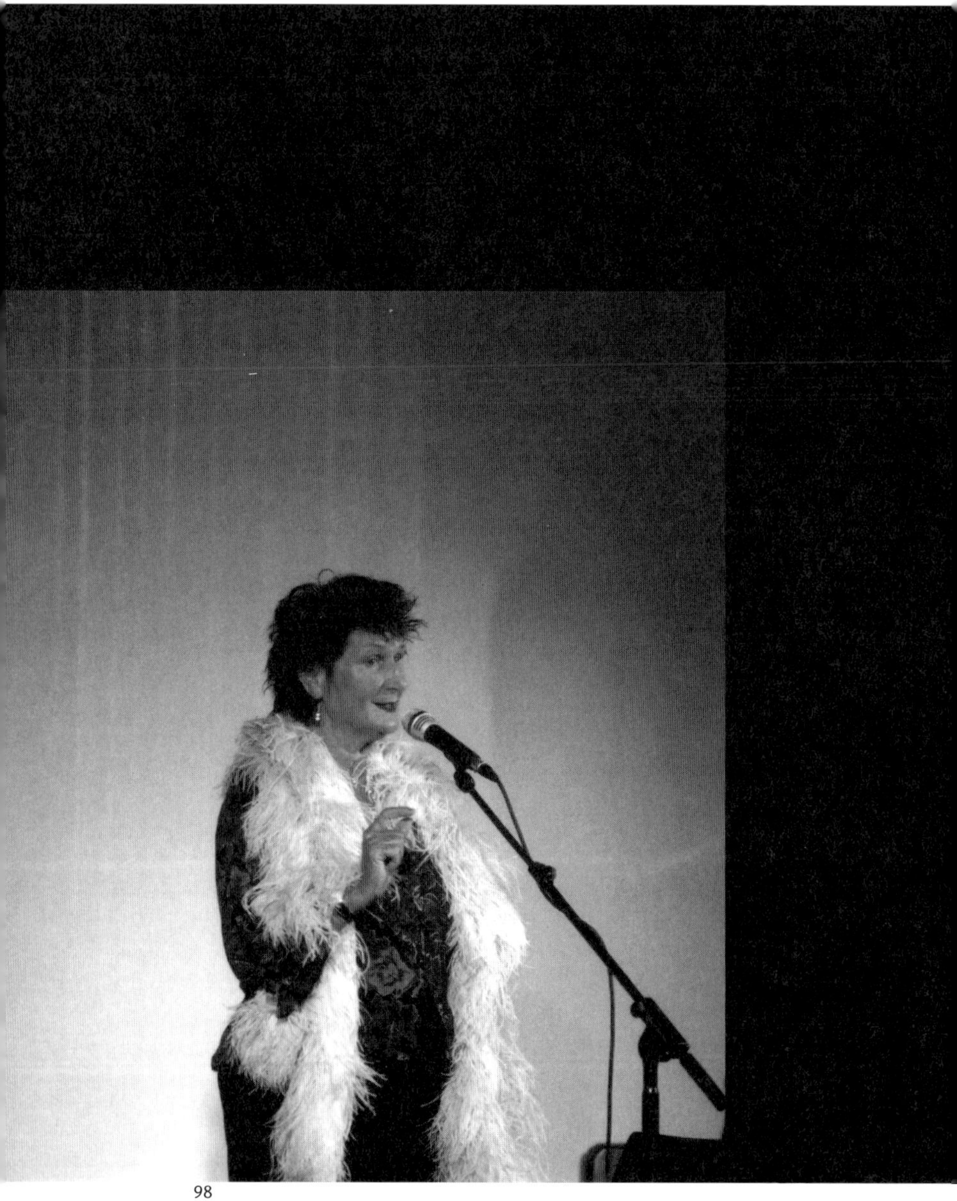

„Ich weiß nicht, zu wem ich gehöre"

Marie-Thérèse Escribano antwortet auf Fragen von Ulrike Müller

Ulrike Müller: In deinen Interpretationen von deutschen Schlagern der 1920er und 1930er legst du auf äußerst unterhaltsame Weise den ideologischen Gehalt von Liedern offen, deren politischer Kontext allzu leicht vergessen wird. Obwohl ich mehr als ein Vierteljahrhundert nach dem Zweiten Weltkrieg geboren wurde, bin ich mit dem Genre vertraut und kenne einige der Lieder, die du auf die Bühne bringst, aus meiner Kindheit. Während des nationalsozialistischen Regimes in Deutschland und Österreich hast du in Spanien gelebt ...

Marie-Thérèse Escribano: Ich lebte mit meinen Eltern in Madrid. Kaum war der spanische Bürgerkrieg – 1936 bis 1939 – beendet, begann der Zweite Weltkrieg. Um uns tobte die Nazipropaganda. Eine prodeutsche militärische Gruppierung, „División Azul" genannt, entstand. Diese Freiwilligenlegion fand, wohlgemerkt, innerhalb der Bevölkerung keine Sympathie. Die Legionäre hatten arrogante, ja geradezu unverschämte Allüren – und überhaupt, die Spanier hatten genug von allem, was an Krieg erinnerte. Man wusste, dass Franco auf der Seite des faschistischen Deutschland war, und fürchtete, er würde sich in den neuen Krieg einmischen.

U. M.: Nationalsozialistische Propaganda hatte das Potenzial von Schlagermusik erkannt und für ihre Zwecke vereinnahmt. Schon 1933 stellte Goebbels fest, dass Politik der breiten Bevölkerung auf modernere und eingängigere Weise vermittelt werden muss. Das nationalsozialistische Regime hat sich ja auch sehr für die Verbreitung des Radios eingesetzt. In deinem Schlagerprogramm verweist du auf die ideologischen Inhalte populärer Songs und darauf, dass Politik und Kultur nicht getrennt werden können. Du setzt die feministische Erkenntnis, dass das Private politisch ist, für deine Faschismuskritik ein. Wann hast du begonnen, mit Schlagern zu arbeiten?

M.-T. E.: Ich erinnere mich an eine Szene, die ich in Madrid erlebte. Meine Eltern gingen ins Kaffeehaus, um Nachrichten im Radio zu hören. Als verkündet wurde, dass die Regierung beschlossen hatte, neutral zu bleiben, standen alle Menschen in dem Etablissement auf und applaudierten. Trotz dieser Neutralität war die Sympathie der Medien deutlich auf einer Seite, und deutsche Schlager waren sehr populär. Sie wurden auf billigen Schellacks verkauft. Wir hatten sie auch zu Hause, und ich kurbelte ununterbrochen am Grammofon, um „Adieu, mein kleiner Gardeoffizier"[1] zu hören. Ich lernte bald die Melodie. Was den Text betrifft, verstand ich nur: „Adieu, adieu, la-la-la Offizier, adieu, opterituitui-opterituitui ..."[2] Wie meine Eltern hatte ich kein politisches Bewusstsein und dachte mir nichts dabei: Das Bild des jungen Mannes, der in den Krieg zieht, wurde durch die süßliche Unterhaltungsmusik tatsächlich euphemistisch vermittelt. „Wie mag er wohl ausgesehen haben?", dachte ich mir. „Blond und blauäugig?" Nach meiner Kindheit habe ich das Lied dann nie mehr gesungen. Mit 17 Jahren begann ich das Studium der so genannten ernsten Musik. Schlager haben mich nicht mehr interessiert. Erst 30 Jahre später, als ich aus der ernsten Musik ausstieg, habe ich zufällig bei einem Geburtstagsfest ein paar Gstanzln[3] offeriert, und es hat mir Spaß gemacht. Es war tatsächlich eine gelungene Unterhaltung. Vielleicht sollte ich da anknüpfen? Bald aber stand ich vor einem Dilemma: Ein Großteil der Schlager vertritt eine Ideologie, die ich keineswegs mit meiner Stimme unterstützen wollte.

U. M.: Die Melodien sind so eingängig, dass der Inhalt der Texte beim Zuhören oft gar nicht richtig bewusst wird. In deiner Interpretation ändert sich das. Die Texte und ihre Botschaften treten in den Vordergrund. Nach welchen Kriterien hast du dein Schlagerprogramm zusammengestellt? Kannst du ein paar Beispiele geben für Lieder, die du aufführst?

M.-T. E.: Im Fall von „Adieu, mein kleiner Gardeoffizier“ versuche ich, das Verlogene und Einlullende des Schlagers in der letzten Strophe zu entlarven. Ich verändere das Couplet nicht, gestalte aber den Major, der sich nach dem Krieg von den alten Kameraden verabschiedet, als Wrack – keinesfalls heldenhaft. Er kann sich kaum noch bewegen, seine Hände zittern, und er hat fortwährend Schmerzen.

Ohrwürmer können wie eine ansteckende Krankheit wirken. Man wiederholt ein Lied, ohne sich etwas dabei zu denken, und etwas bleibt im Unterbewusstsein hängen. Das betrifft nicht nur die faschistische Seite, sondern auch die machistische. Nehmen wir den Schlager „Ich hab' das Fräul'n Helen baden seh'n“[4]: Da wird erzählt, dass ein Mann sich verliebt, als er die Helen zufällig im Bad sieht. Er schwärmt in erster Linie für die Beine der Helen, und schließlich heiratet er sie. Heutzutage amüsiert, dass die Nacktheit oder Beine der Helen zu einer derartigen Leidenschaft führen können, ja sogar zur Heirat. So weit alles in Ordnung. Aber dann kommt die dritte Strophe: Helene ist inzwischen älter, und ihre Beine, damals „so süß“, sind „so dick wie vom Klavier die Füß'“. Friedrich, der Ehemann, erinnert sich mit Nostalgie an die früheren Beine.[5]

In meiner Interpretation singe ich diese dritte Strophe nicht, sondern erzähle den Text. Ich sage dann, dass auch ich es gerne habe, wenn ein Mann schöne Beine hat, aber deswegen würde ich ihn nicht heiraten. Das Lachen bekommt hier eine Qualität, man lacht nicht mehr Helene aus, sondern den Dichter, der diesen dummen Text geschrieben hat.

U. M.: Wenn du singst: „Treue hat gar keinen Sinn“, und dabei von Liebe sprichst, appellierst du an die Leidenschaften und Wünsche deiner Zuhörerinnen und Zuhörer.

Zugleich birgt das Lied, so leicht und frivol es auch klingt, einigen Sprengstoff. Siehst du hier eine Möglichkeit, feministisch zu intervenieren, quasi an einer Revolution im eigenen Gefühlshaushalt zu arbeiten? Welche Reaktionen wünschst du dir von deinem Publikum?

M.-T. E.: Das Lied „Ich weiß nicht, zu wem ich gehöre", aus dem die Zeile „Treue hat gar keinen Sinn" kommt, ist von Friedrich Hollaender geschrieben worden,[6] dem Lieblingskomponisten von Marlene Dietrich. Ganz sicher hat er die Komposition in einem Winkel seines Herzens ernst gemeint. Frauen lieben dieses Lied, weil es sie aus der Spießigkeit herausholt, in der manche leben und für die sie wohl auch verantwortlich sind. Die Frau auf der Bühne vermittelt ihnen ein wenig Illusion, aber das ist nicht gefährlich, denn nach der Vorstellung geht es schnell wieder zurück ins traute Heim.

Von meinem Publikum erhoffe ich mir, dass ein paar gescheite Leute dort sitzen, die meine Ironie verstehen. Dann habe ich das Gefühl von Kommunikation. Ich glaube nicht, dass ich Menschen verändern kann. Ich habe aber öfters von Frauen gehört, dass sie sich verstanden gefühlt haben – da waren sie vielleicht nicht mehr allein. Eines genieße ich sehr: auf der Bühne zu stehen und das Lachen zu hören.

Anmerkungen:

1. Schlager von Robert Stolz (Musik) und Walter Reisch (Text) aus dem Film *Das Lied ist aus* (Regie: Géza von Bolváry, Deutschland 1930), gesungen von Liane Haid.
2. Der Refrain lautet: „Adieu, mein kleiner Gardeoffizier, adieu, adieu/Und vergiss mich nicht/Und vergiss mich nicht/Adieu, mein kleiner Gardeoffizier, adieu, adieu/Sei das Glück mit dir/Sei das Glück mit dir."
3. Bayrisches und österreichisches Wort für einen gesungenen Vier- oder Achtzeiler (manchmal mehr Zeilen). Im Wienerischen wird mit „Gstanzl" auch allgemein eine kurze, publikumswirksame Gesangseinlage bezeichnet.
4. Von Fred Raymond (Musik) und Fritz Grünbaum (Text), 1925.
5. Die dritte Strophe lautet: „Unser Freund, der nahm zur Frau Helene, doch die Waden, welche erst so schöne, schlank und zart und süß, wurden später mies und so dick wie vom Klavier die Füß'! Die Füß', die Füß', die Füß'. Geht die Gattin heut' ins Badezimmer, schaut der Mann sich nicht mehr an die Trümmer, sondern weise schließt er leise ihr die Tür und spielt am verstimmten Klavier."
6. Der Text stammt von Friedrich Hollaender und Robert Liebmann, 1932.

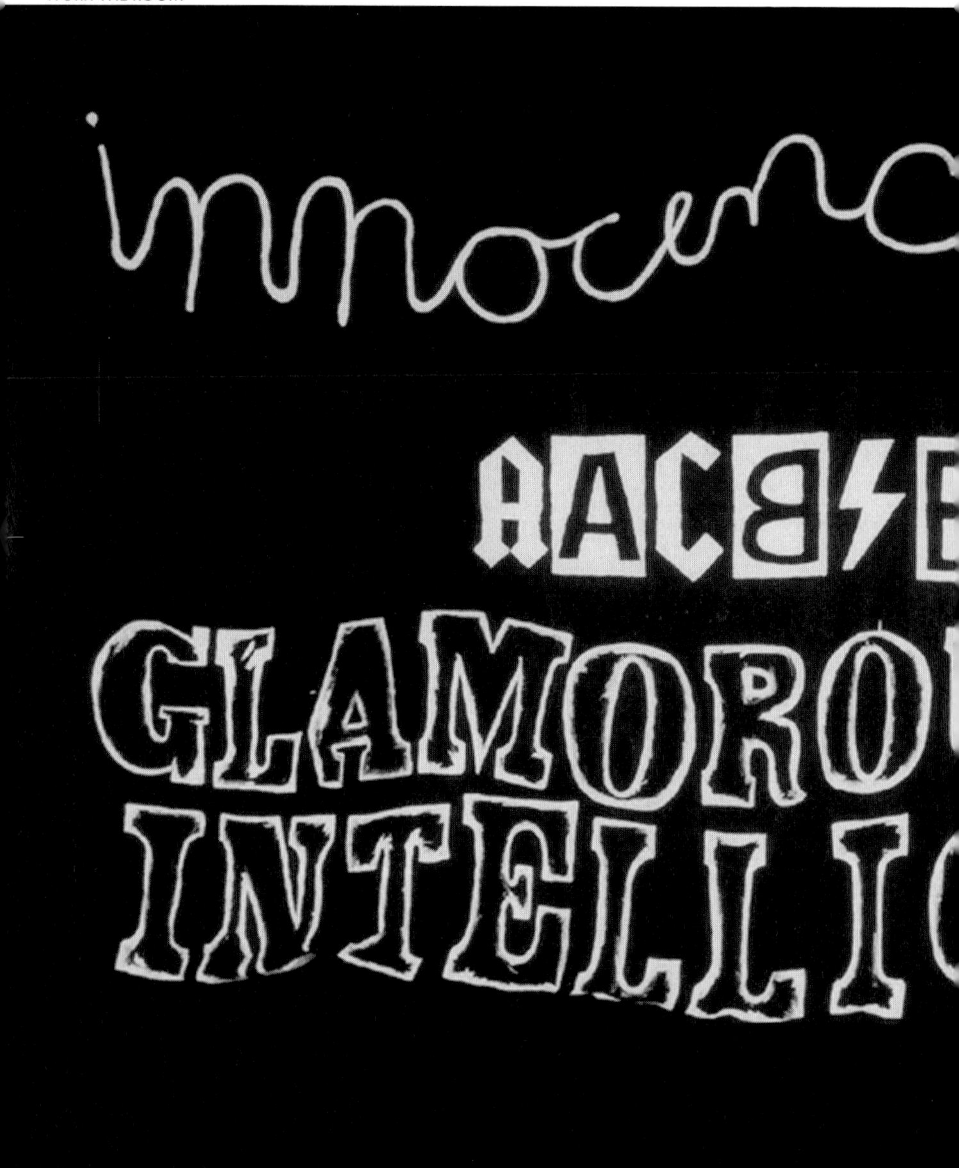

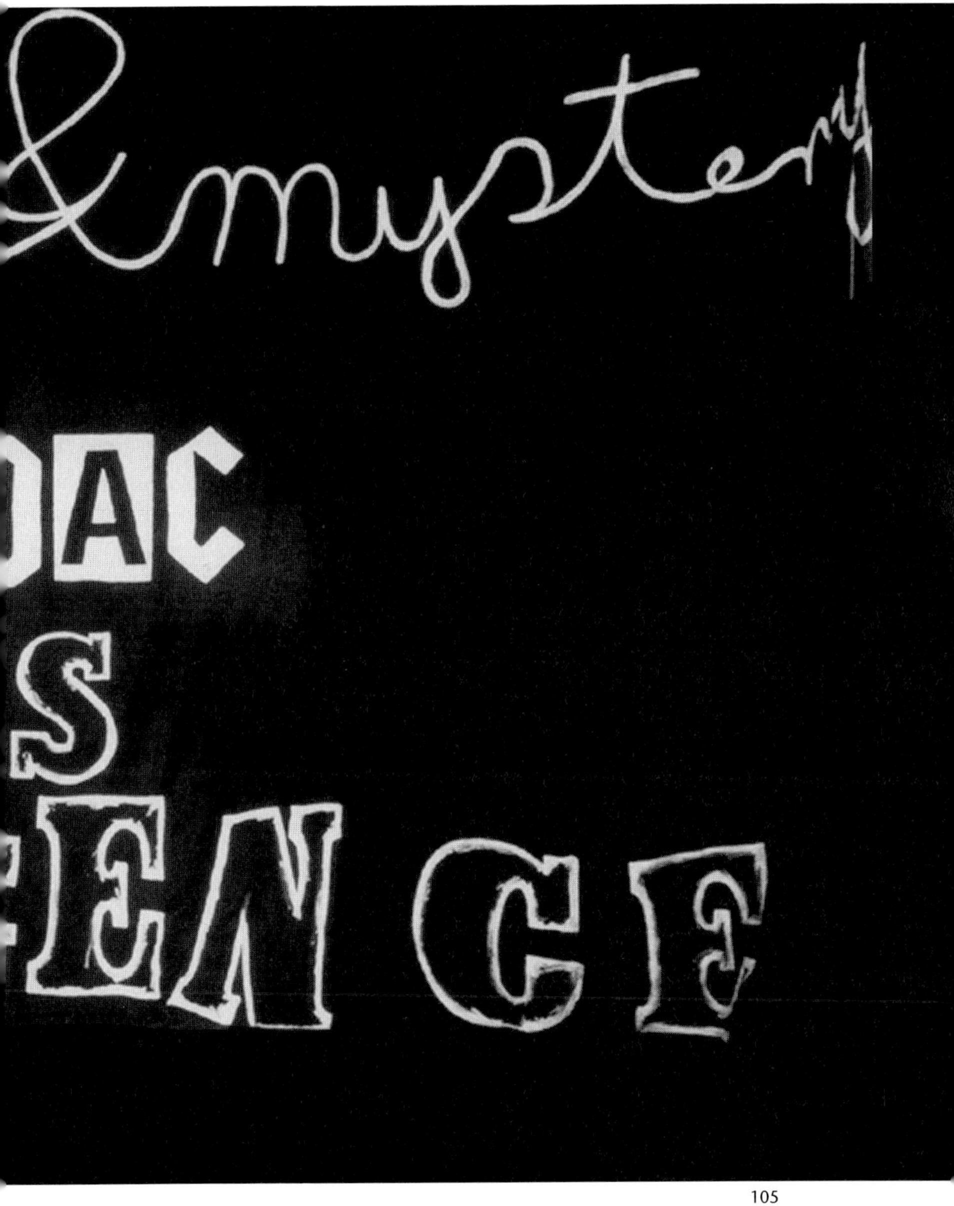
mystery
AC
S
EN CF

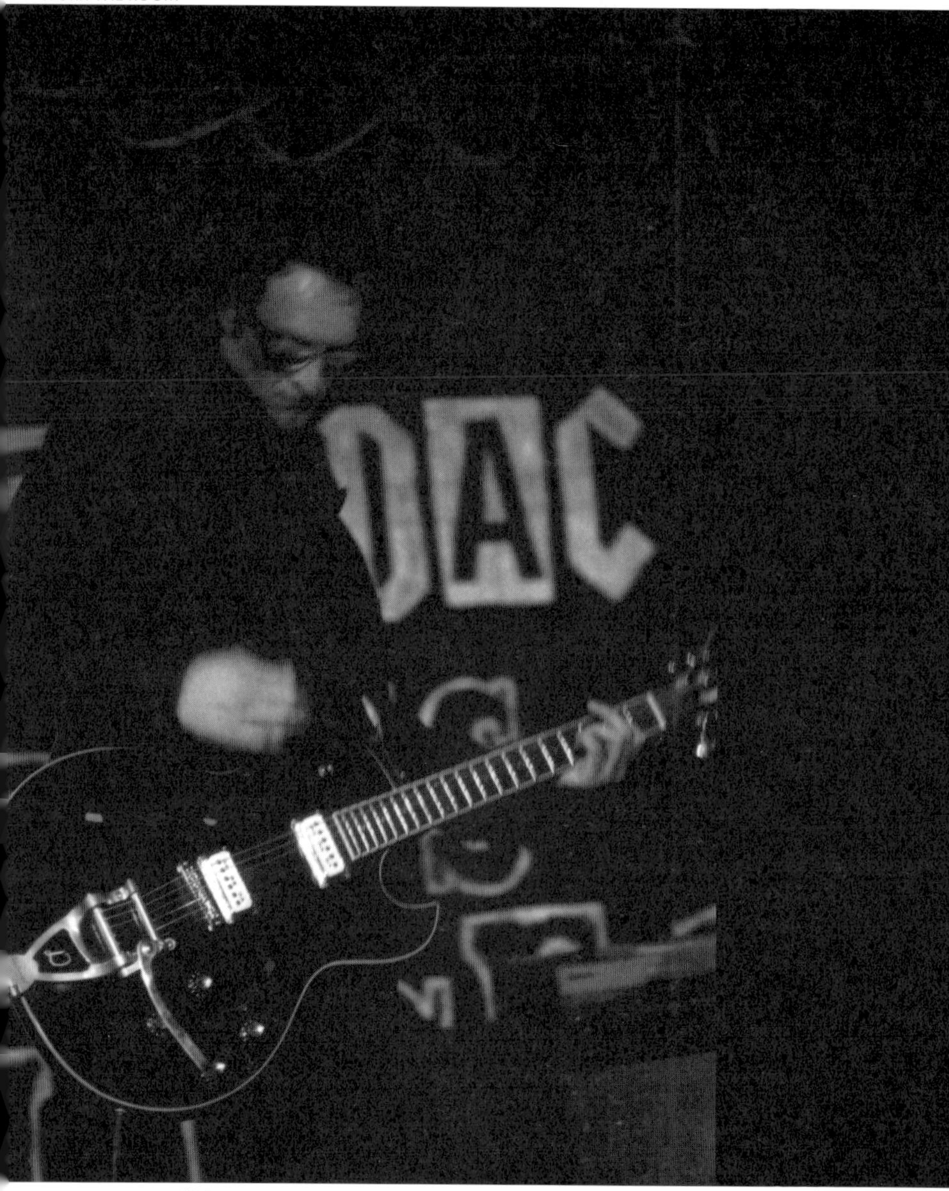

Discoteca Flaming Star

answers questions by Britta Scholze

...

Wolfgang Mayer:

I love the aspect of emotional staging and the relationship with the audience generated by it. I like to share a fictitious memory space with the audience, a space generated through the performance, a space that is strange and confusing without being intimidating.

I like to make myself up, to carry an image of myself on my face. And I really like to sing, to feel the meaning of songs that are crucial for the formation of my identity.

I indulge in celebrations of non-perfection, of failure and vulnerability.

Klaus Kinski is my father, Bonnie Tyler my mother.

Cristina Gómez Barrio:

Discoteca Flaming Star is a dream come true: the dream of sharing a space of artistic encounter without the need for a physical space. Without this kind of performative collaboration, it would be very hard for me to pursue my individual art practice and make it public. I don't believe in the image of the lonely artist working by himself. To be together means to be able to see things not only through your own eyes.

I find a lot of energy in the directness of the performances, because there is space to deal with failure and fragility. I very much enjoy the process of developing the framing of the songs. I feel, work, and see myself more and more as a performer, even when I use different artistic means.

I love to work with songs because it involves working with text and with memories, while also thinking about voice and intonation.

...

DFS:

The smallest unit of our performance is the song, its meaning, the memories it contains. In our working process often we first consider a song and its spatial aspect, the relationship between the performer and the song. This relationship links up with our desires and our strategies as artists.

By intervening in the intentions or in the body of the song we try to shift its memories, or to add something. This can happen in a conceptual or musical way; Robbie Williams's "Supreme," for example, is a fairly optimistic pop song. By way of musical intervention it turns into a torch song that rather reminds one of a middle-aged woman broken by life. For "Aladlona" non-musical aspects play a far bigger role. The cultural misunderstanding that links us to Arab belly dancing interprets the song as much as the guitar or the literal and cultural meaning of the lyrics. Generally, in addition to the fact that we love and respect all of these songs, moments of absurdity and the humor of "displacing" are always very important to us.

All participants in Discoteca Flaming Start are involved in the formation of the space that describes the relationship to the songs. Everybody has an impact on the outcome, through their specific way of thinking, interpreting, dancing, singing, playing, etc.

...

DFS:

The banners are pieces of fabric glued together and subsequently painted with texts. We use them as backdrops for many of our performances, as spatial transformations that capture chaos in words. The texts are references, cryptic thoughts that we've been pregnant with for many months. Thoughts about art practice: for example, "innocence & mystery" relates to Buñuel's filters for his films. The banners are also conceptual; they reflect the relationship of our art to various levels of the everyday experience of artists and viewers. They are fabrics for thought.

Right now we're working on a new banner: "and doubts and exaggeration and amnesia."

...

Sanja Ivekovic, Wiener Gruppe, Alvaro, Anita Berber, El Arroyo los Cagaos, Mahalchick, Mary Shelley, PFFR, Jack Smith, Patti Smith, Cheap Club, Kenneth Anger, Joey Arias, La Pachanga, Félix González-Torres, Karl Valentin, and Lisl Karlstadt ...

...

Ten years from now DFS will be a theater on the outskirts of Marrakesh, where Spaghetti Westerns are performed as three-day-long Greek dramas.

...

DFS at *Public Affairs*. A great freedom of art probably lies in its exemplary functioning as a model. Art as a model, how we propose it, is politically relevant for us. Our proposal is mainly for failure, vulnerability and betrayal. The betrayal of language, genes, provenance, and all given necessities.

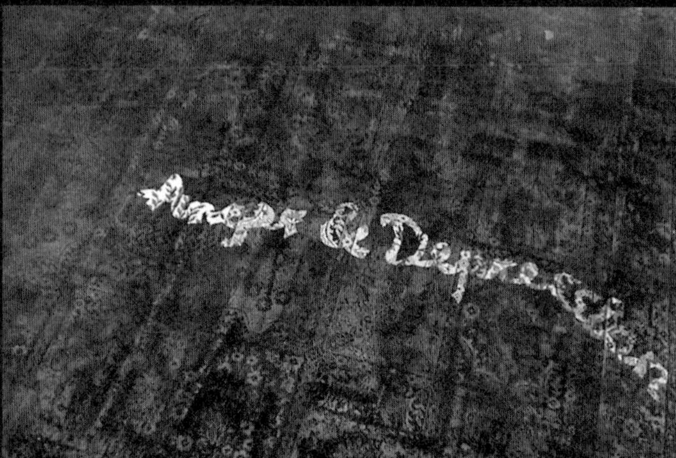

...

Current art as political intervention. We often doubt whether art can intervene in a political way, but our doubts shrink whenever we encounter art that we suspect to have this ability. The works of Félix González-Torres (artist, 1957-1996) are informed by politics and poetry. His works just want to be there; they don't need to be pushy and they don't impose themselves. Ines Schaber (artist, b. 1969) works consistently on aesthetical visual essays that contain politics without excluding poetry and ghosts from the production of new meaning. Alex Arteaga (artist, b. 1969) likes to talk about how aesthetic work is the only relevant basis for real and radical sustainability. There are many artists and collectives who strongly interweave their work with public concerns.

...

Tatsumi Hijikata (dancer, 1928-1986) says that the performer is connected to the audience through provocation, and that the performer does not have to connect with the audience at all. We try to establish a relationship with the audience through openness and pleasure. Fiction seems increasingly provocative.

...

That is what *Public Affairs* was about... for three days we thought about how performance can be a special place for the articulation of socially relevant statements by artists. Over these three days different encounters took place, and that perhaps is the force of performance in this sense: to come together in order to make an artwork possible for a limited time, to choreograph the desire of its production together in order to see something through the eyes of the others along the way. Poetry, emotions, bridges to fiction, to humor... But of course performance is not an exclusive space for social protest.

To stand on a subway platform all day long, singing against the noise of arriving and departing trains, even though nobody came to listen to you: this can be an excellent protest for somebody—considering that he or she is like this, and not different, and not supposed to be different, and uses the means of performance. That is very subversive.

...

We wish to bring people to a space they haven't been to before (maybe we succeeded once so far). We wish to shift the memories of people, to confuse them, to supply them with spirits and lovers.

DFS is meant to be a mental space open to all kinds of artists for experimentation and pleasure. We ask and are asked to collaborate, to make soundtracks, to fight with glamorous intelligence and to go through anger and melancholia. We work with monsters and we want to perform miracles. DFS is a space to challenge the world armed with the weapons of innocence and mystery. We play to heal amnesia, indulging in appropriated songs, hoping to plant roses and to enter your paradise...

At, in, and with this space DFS have been so far:
Guiomar Arjona López (Munich), Edith Mirwald (Munich), Philipp Imdahl (Cologne), David Galbraith (New York), Asana (Berlin), Bene Abel (Berlin), Marita Barnett (Berlin), Ines Gerdes (Berlin), Cristina Gómez Barrio (Berlin), Wolfgang Mayer (Berlin), Imadi (Berlin), Birgit Kramer (Berlin), El Arroyo los Cagaos (Cáceres), Marianne Kirch (Munich), Tom Früchtl (Munich), Stephan Schessl (Munich), Ignaz Schick (Berlin), Rita McBride (New York), Michael Mahalchick (New York), Jim Galbraith (New York), Michael Schultze (Berlin), Dorothy Vallens (Berlin), Circo Interior Bruto (Madrid), Bernd Sevens (Berlin), Helge Slaatto (Copenhagen), Franz Reinecke (Munich), Ursula Rogg (Berlin), Kerstin Rautenberg (Berlin), Laurie Young (Berlin), François Boué (New York), Susan Oetgen (New York), Xenia Riemann (Düsseldorf), Elyce Semenec (New York)

Translated by Ulrike Müller

Discoteca Flaming Star

antwortet auf Fragen von Britta Scholze

...

Wolfgang Mayer:

Ich liebe den Moment der emotionalen Inszenierung und die dadurch entstehende Beziehung zu den Zuschauern. Ich mag es, gemeinsam mit den Zuschauern durch die Performance in einem erfundenen Raum der Erinnerung zu sein, welcher befremdlich und verwirrend, dabei aber nicht bedrohlich ist.

Ich schminke mich gerne, um ein Bild meiner selbst auf meinem Gesicht zu tragen. Ich singe sehr gerne, um die Bedeutung der Lieder zu spüren, die so sehr meine Identität prägten.
Ich genieße die Zelebrierung der Nichtperfektion, die von Fehlern und von Verletzbarkeit.

Mein Vater ist Klaus Kinski, meine Mutter Bonnie Tyler.

Cristina Gómez Barrio:

Discoteca Flaming Star ist die Verwirklichung eines Traumes: des Traumes, einen künstlerischen Begegnungsraum zu teilen, ohne einen physischen Raum haben zu müssen. Ohne die performative Zusammenarbeit in diesem Rahmen würde es mir sehr schwer fallen, meine individuelle künstlerische Tätigkeit weiterführen zu können und in die Öffentlichkeit zu bringen. Ich glaube nicht an das Bild des einsamen, einzeln wirkenden Künstlers. Man ist zusammen, man sieht die Dinge nicht nur durch die eigenen Augen.

Aus der Unmittelbarkeit der Performances beziehe ich viel Kraft, weil es dort Raum für den Umgang mit Fehlern und Zerbrechlichkeit gibt. Ich genieße sehr den Prozess, den Rahmen für die Lieder zu entwerfen. Ich fühle, arbeite und sehe mich mehr und mehr wie eine Performerin, auch wenn ich andere Mittel und Werkzeuge der Kunst benütze.

Ich liebe es, mit Liedern zu arbeiten, weil es bedeutet, mit Text und mit Gedächtnis zu arbeiten, und es zugleich eine Überlegung über die Stimme und die Betonung gibt.

...

DFS

Die kleinste Einheit der Performance ist das Lied, seine Bedeutung, seine Erinnerung. Der erste Schritt im Arbeitsprozess ist meist, einem Lied gerecht zu werden – und auch dem Raum, der Beziehung zwischen dem Performer und dem Lied. Diese Beziehung wird Teil des künstlerischen Begehrens und des künstlerischen Werkzeuges.

Durch Eingriffe in die Intention oder den Körper des Liedes versuchen wir, die Erinnerung des Liedes zu verrücken, ihr etwas hinzuzufügen. Das kann auf konzeptuelle oder musikalische Art und Weise geschehen; z. B. wird auf rein musikalische Weise aus Robbie Williams' „Supreme", welches ein eher optimistisches Popstück ist, ein Torch-Song, der mehr an eine vom Leben gebrochene Frau mittleren Alters erinnert. Bei „Aladlona" spielen nichtmusikalische Momente eine wesentlich größere Rolle. Das kulturelle Missverständnis, das uns mit arabischem Bauchtanz verbindet, interpretiert das Lied genauso stark wie z. B. das Spiel der Gitarre oder die inhaltliche oder kulturelle Bedeutung der darübergesungenen Liedtexte. Allgemein sind neben der

Tatsache, dass wir all diese Lieder lieben und respektieren, Momente von Absurdität und Humor im „Verrücken" immer sehr wichtig.

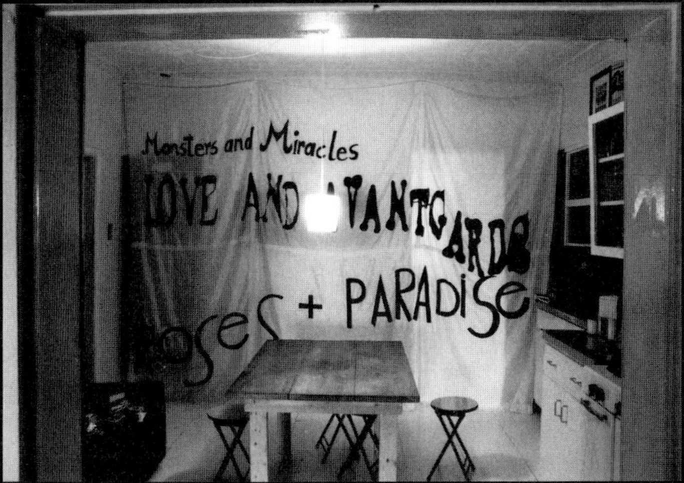

Alle Teilnehmer von Discoteca Flaming Star wirken mit bei der Entstehung des Raumes, der das Verhältnis zu den Liedern beschreibt. Alle daran Beteiligten verändern durch ihre spezifische Art, zu denken, zu interpretieren, zu tanzen, zu singen, zu spielen, etc., das Resultat.

...

DFS

Die Banner sind zusammengeklebte Stoffbahnen, die nachträglich mit Text bemalt werden. Sie dienen als Hintergrundvorhang für viele der Performances, als räumliche Transformation, innerhalb welcher Unordnungen in Worte gefasst werden können. Die Texte sind Referenzen, kryptische Gedanken, mit denen wir über Monate schwanger gehen. Gedanken über die künstlerische Tätigkeit, wie zum Beispiel „innocence &

mystery" sich auf Buñuels Filter für seine Filme bezieht. Sie stellen aber auch Konzepte dar, die das Verhältnis unserer Kunst zu den verschiedenen Ebenen der Alltagserfahrung von Künstlerinnen und Betrachterinnen reflektieren. Es sind Denkstoffe.

Gerade arbeiten wir an einem neuen Banner: „and doubts and exaggeration and amnesia".

…

Sanja Ivekovic, Wiener Gruppe, Alvaro, Anita Berber, El Arroyo los Cagaos, Mahalchick, Mary Shelley, PFFR, Jack Smith, Patti Smith, Cheap Club, Kenneth Anger, Joey Arias, La Pachanga, Félix González-Torres, Karl Valentin und Lisl Karlstadt …

…

In zehn Jahren wird DFS ein Theater am Stadtrand von Marrakesch sein, in welchem Spaghetti-Western als drei Tage dauernde griechische Dramen aufgeführt werden.

…

DFS bei *Public Affairs*. Eine große Freiheit der Kunst liegt wahrscheinlich in ihrer Modellhaftigkeit. Diese Modellhaftigkeit, die wir vorschlagen, hat für uns politische Relevanz. Unser Entwurfsvorschlag steht vor allem für den Fehler, die Verletzlichkeit und den Verrat. Verrat der Sprache, der Gene, des Herkunftsortes und der gegebenen Notwendigkeiten.

…

aktuelle politisch eingreifende Kunst. Oft haben wir Zweifel, ob Kunst wirklich politisch eingreift, aber unsere Zweifel werden immer dann kleiner, wenn wir auf Kunst treffen, bei der wir eben diese Eigenschaft vermuten. Die Arbeiten von Félix González-

Torres (Künstler, *1957, †1996) sind durchdrungen von Politik und Poesie. Seine Arbeiten wollen einfach da sein, sich nicht aufdrängen, sich nicht aufzwingen. Ines Schaber (Künstlerin, *1969) arbeitet rigoros an ästhetisch bildnerischen Essays, die Politik einschließen, aber Poesie und Geister nicht ausschließen und dabei versuchen, neue Bedeutungen zu kreieren. Alex Arteaga (Künstler, *1969) spricht immer davon, dass ästhetische Arbeit die einzig relevante Grundlage bildet, auf der wirkliche und radikale Nachhaltigkeit erzeugt werden kann. Es gibt viele Künstler und Kollektive, die ihre Tätigkeit sehr stark auf einer kommunalen Ebene verweben.

...

Tatsumi Hijikata (Tänzer, *1928, †1986) spricht davon, dass der Performer sich mit dem Publikum über Provokation verbindet, dass aber der Performer sich gar nicht mit dem Publikum verbinden muss. Wir versuchen, uns über Offenheit und Genuss mit dem Publikum in ein Verhältnis zu setzen. Fiktion scheint zunehmend provokativ.

...

Darum ging es in *Public Affairs*...über drei Tage wurde nachgedacht, inwiefern Performance ein besonderer Ort für die Artikulation von gesellschaftlich relevanten Aussagen von Künstlern sein kann. Über diese drei Tage kamen verschiedene Begegnungen zustande, und das ist vielleicht die Kraft der Performance im genannten Sinne: sich zu treffen, um über eine begrenzte Zeit ein Kunstwerk zu ermöglichen und zusammen die Wünsche der Entstehung zu choreografieren, um im Prozess etwas durch die Augen von anderen sehen zu können. Poesie, Emotionen, Brücke zur Fiktion, zum Humor... aber Performance ist natürlich kein exklusiver Ort des sozialen Protests.

Auf einem Bahnsteig mit aller Zartheit den ganzen Tag gegen den Lärm der ein- und ausfahrenden U-Bahnen anzusingen, obwohl niemand gekommen ist, um dich zu hören, kann ein herausragender Protest sein – dafür, dass jemand so und nicht anders ist und auch nicht sein soll, ausgeführt mit den Mitteln der Performance. Das ist sehr subversiv.

…

Wir wünschen uns, die Leute an einen Ort gebracht zu haben, an dem sie so noch nicht waren (haben wir bis jetzt vielleicht einmal geschafft). Wir wünschen uns, die Erinnerung der Leute zu bewegen, sie zu verwirren, ihnen Geister und LiebhaberInnen zu geben.

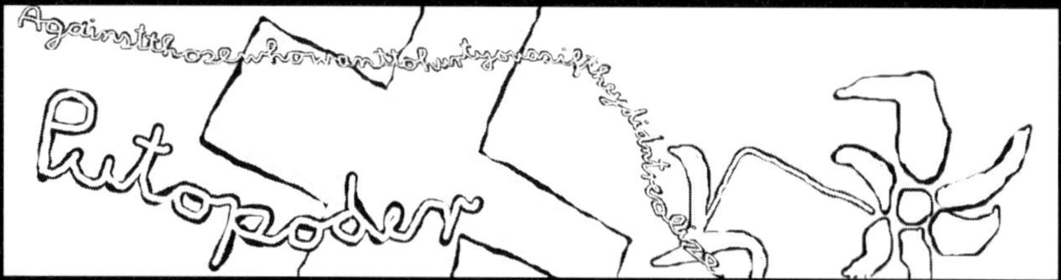

DFS soll ein mentaler Ort sein, den alle möglichen Künstler betreten können, um zu experimentieren und zu genießen. Wir fragen und werden gefragt, zusammenzuarbeiten, Soundtracks zu machen, mit glamouröser Intelligenz zu kämpfen und durch Zorn und Melancholie hindurchzugehen.

Wir arbeiten mit Monstern und möchten Wunder vollbringen. DFS ist ein Ort, die Welt herauszufordern mit Unschuld und Geheimnissen als Waffen. Wir spielen, um die Amnesie zu heilen, in gelernten Liedern badend, mit der Hoffnung, Rosen zu pflanzen, um dein Paradies zu betreten …

An, in und mit diesem Ort DFS hielten sich bis jetzt auf:

Guiomar Arjona López (München), Edith Mirwald (München), Philipp Imdahl (Köln), David Galbraith (New York), Asana (Berlin), Bene Abel (Berlin), Marita Barnett (Berlin), Ines Gerdes (Berlin), Cristina Gómez Barrio (Berlin), Wolfgang Mayer (Berlin), Imadi (Berlin), Birgit Kramer (Berlin), El Arroyo los Cagaos (Cáceres), Marianne Kirch (München),Tom Früchtl (München), Stephan Schessl (München), Ignaz Schick (Berlin), Rita McBride (New York), Michael Mahalchick (New York), Jim Galbraith (New York), Michael Schultze (Berlin), Dorothy Vallens (Berlin), Circo Interior Bruto (Madrid), Bernd Sevens (Berlin), Helge Slaatto (Kopenhagen), Frank Reinecke (München), Ursula Rogg (Berlin), Kerstin Rautenberg (Berlin), Laurie Young (Berlin), François Boué (New York), Susan Oetgen (New York), Xenia Riemann (Düsseldorf), Elyce Semenec (New York)

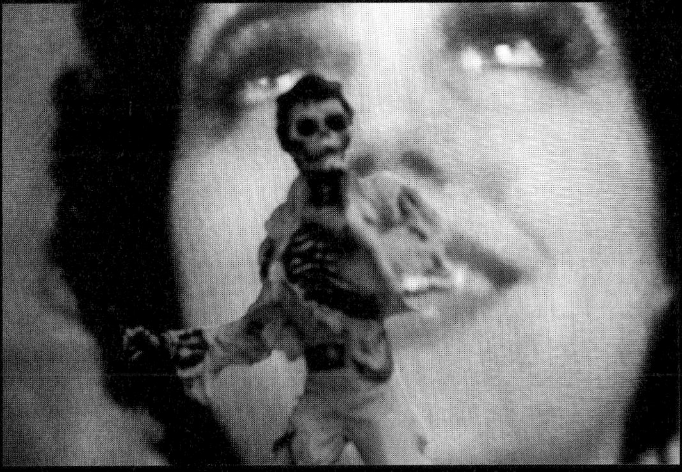

The Discoteca Flaming Star Experience (This is the Remix)

by Matthew Lyons

In his book *Rock My Religion*, Dan Graham described the popular music group Devo as having deftly mixed the seemingly opposed genres of punk and disco in order "to place both attitudes in tension." In a similar way, Discoteca Flaming Star (DFS) combines disparate sound sources, cultural and historical references, and performance modes to subvert the expected trajectory and hierarchies of a staged event. At times a loose performance collective and at times a garage band, DFS calls its activities "hardcore karaoke," implying that the group is some mutant form of a cover band. But Discoteca Flaming Star is more broadly a platform, an approach that can take many shapes.

In its varied formations over the years, Discoteca Flaming Star has included professionals, amateurs, metal rockers, an accordionist, belly dancers, folk musicians, contemporary dancers, and those performing "just this once," among others. Their renditions of the pop rock of Shakira or Prince, the melancholic ballads of Jacques Brel, and the disco of Donna Summer, to name just a few, are extended, spliced together, or transplanted on top of one another, all the while using the classic avant-garde strategy of holding skill and polish at bay. (One DFS classic is ABBA's "Thank You for the Music" superimposed on top of AC/DC's "Big Balls.") Often these songs have been brought together for the political, social, or emotional situations they obliquely reference or evoke. Yet beyond the songs used as sonic material, other clues establish a complementary lineage of artistic heroes, a matrix of inspiration that extends from the cabaret culture of interwar-era Berlin to Jack Smith and his cohorts in New York during the 1960s and beyond. Improvising and faking its way through these unique tributes, DFS employs more than one mode of performance and address at a time. The end result is often what they describe as a "noiserockpiece with pop lyrics." DFS performances react to and interrupt the traditional relation between site, performers, and audience wherever these performances take place, whether in a dive bar in midtown Manhattan, at an outdoor evening performance in a village square in the remote Spanish region of Extremadura, or in the context of an arts space, museum, or gallery. The combination of skilled and unskilled music-making, under-rehearsed moments, ad hoc arrangements, and happy mistakes produces an experience that is both jarring and liberating for the audience.

DFS's emancipatory potential arises from core members Cristina Gomez Barrio and Wolfgang Mayer's dedication to combining wildly diverse elements and continually shifting gears. Furthermore, a lack of "cool" detachment as well as the spirit of generosity towards and trust in their numerous collaborators comes across clearly to the audience. Wolfgang Mayer's stage persona is neither a nostalgic rehearsal of glam rock nor a full-on delivery of camp. He refers to this aspect of his performance as "make-up," and his matter-of-fact execution of it meanders around within the glam-drag spectrum. Overall, in DFS's carefully considered performance practice, potential antagonisms between popular music genres, historical eras, and the conventions of "performance art" versus "rock concert" become neutralized or rather coexist on the inclusive platform created by Discoteca Flaming Star.

The banners, photo-works, and videos which come out of their performances also utilize this kind of combinatory interruption, or interruption through combination. One banner shuffles that odd pairing of the disco group ABBA and the rock band AC/DC into the interruptive sequence AACB/BDAC. Another banner uses the opposite and therefore related approach of continuity with the statement "Ihopeeverythingyoulovediesinyourarms" written in one unbroken line of spray-painted, cursive script. In the photo-works, many snapshots from performances are spliced together to make one compound work—both singular and multiple, comprehensive yet incomplete, and further interrupted by text stenciled over the collaged images. Likewise, in video pieces, adhesive letters are applied directly onto the screen of the monitor, thereby disrupting the seductive nature of the video image.

In all the works, this simultaneously combinatory and interruptive approach serves to prevent a kind of passive absorption on the part of the viewer/audience. By extending to the viewer/audience a DIY energy and liberatory agency, DFS underlines the basic platform fostered throughout its practice for positive and active engagement. Resisting the temptation to hypnotize the viewer/audience, Discoteca Flaming Star's participants bravely accept their vulnerability as sincere, trustful performers and acknowledge their position as hardcore fans themselves. Being so earnest and affirmative without the protection afforded by layers of irony may prove to be one of their most hardcore aspects.

Die Discoteca Flaming Star Experience (der Remix)

von Matthew Lyons

In seinem Buch *Rock My Religion* schreibt Dan Graham, die bekannte Popgruppe Devo habe geschickt die scheinbar gegensätzlichen Genres Punk und Disco vermischt, um „beide Haltungen in ein Spannungsverhältnis zu setzen". Auf ähnliche Weise kombinieren Discoteca Flaming Star (DFS) unterschiedliche Soundquellen, kulturelle und historische Referenzen sowie Aufführungsformen, um die erwartete Ausrichtung und die üblichen Hierarchien eines Bühnenauftritts zu unterlaufen. DFS – manchmal ein loses Performancekollektiv, zuweilen eine Garagenband – verwenden für ihre Aktivitäten den Begriff „Hardcore-Karaoke" und implizieren damit ein Selbstverständnis als eine spezielle Art von Coverband. Im weiteren Sinne sind DFS aber eine Plattform – ein Ansatz, der viele Formen annehmen kann.

Profis, AmateurInnen, Metal-RockerInnen, ein Akkordeonist, BauchtänzerInnen, FolkloremusikerInnen, moderne TänzerInnen und solche, die „nur dieses eine Mal" aufgetreten sind, wirkten bei Discoteca Flaming Star im Lauf der Jahre in wechselnden Formationen mit. Die Interpretationen des Pop/Rock von Shakira oder Prince, der melancholischen Balladen Jacques Brels und der Discomusik von Donna Summer – um nur einige zu nennen – sind erweiterte, kombinierte oder übereinander gesetzte Versionen, stets der klassischen Avantgardestrategie folgend, technisches Können sowie Glanz und Glätte hintanzustellen. (Ein DFS-Klassiker sind die übereinander gelegten Stücke „Thank You for the Music" von ABBA und „Big Balls" von AC/DC.) Kombiniert wurden diese Nummern oft aufgrund der politischen, sozialen oder emotionalen Situationen, die sie indirekt ansprechen oder hervorrufen. Über die Songs als klangliches Material hinausgehend, etablieren jedoch andere Verweise einen komplementären künstlerischen Stammbaum, eine Matrix der Inspiration, die von der Berliner Cabaret-Kultur der Zwischenkriegszeit bis zu Jack Smith und seiner Gefolgschaft im New York der Sechzigerjahre und weiter reicht. Die unverwechselbaren Reverenzerweisungen von DFS sind Improvisationen und Fakes, wobei das Publikum in den vielschichtigen Auftritten stets auf mehrere Arten gleichzeitig angesprochen wird. Am Ende steht oft ein Ergebnis, das DFS als „Noise-Rock-Stück mit Poptexten" bezeichnen. In jedem Kontext reagieren DFS auf das traditionelle Verhältnis zwischen Ort, Auftretenden und Publikum und durchbrechen dieses – egal, ob in einer Kellerbar in Midtown-Manhattan, bei einer Freiluftperformance abends auf einem Dorfplatz in der entlegenen spanischen Region Extremadura oder im Kontext eines Kunstraums, eines Museums oder einer Galerie. Die Kombination aus versiertem und dilettantischem Musizieren, zu wenig geprobten Momenten, Ad-hoc-Arrangements und glücklichen Fehlern ergibt für das Publikum eine Erfahrung, die zugleich verunsichernd und befreiend ist.

Das emanzipatorische Potenzial von DFS beruht auf der Hingabe, mit der die Kernmitglieder Cristina Gomez Barrio und Wolfgang Mayer äußerst verschiedenartige Elemente ins Spiel bringen und ständig die Gangart wechseln. Das Fehlen „cooler" Distanz wird ebenso wie der Geist der Großzügigkeit und des Vertrauens gegenüber ihren Mitwirkenden eindrücklich auf ihr Publikum übertragen. Die Person, die Wolfgang Mayer auf der Bühne verkörpert, stellt weder eine nostalgische Übung in Glam-Rock dar, noch transportiert sie ausschließlich eine Camp-Attitüde. Mayer bezeichnet diesen Aspekt seiner Performance als „Make-up", wobei sich seine durchaus sachliche Umsetzung im Glam-Drag-Spektrum bewegt. Potenzielle Antagonismen zwischen populären Musikgenres, historischen Phasen und den Konventionen von „Performancekunst" versus „Rockkonzert" heben sich in der sorgfältig durchdachten Performancepraxis von Discoteca Flaming Star auf – oder, besser gesagt: Diese

Antagonismen bleiben auf der integrativen, von DFS geschaffenen Plattform nebeneinander bestehen.

Die Auftritte von Discoteca Flaming Star bilden die Grundlage für Banner, Fotoarbeiten und Videos, die ebenfalls diese Art von kombinatorischer Brechung oder Brechung durch Kombination anwenden. So resultiert auf einem der Banner die seltsame Zusammenführung der Discogruppe ABBA mit der Rockband AC/DC in der gebrochenen Sequenz AACB/BDAC. Auf einem anderen Banner findet sich die in Schreibschrift gesprayte Zeile „Ihopeeverythingyoulovediesinyourarms" („Ichhoffealleswasduliebststirbtindeinenarmen") und damit der gegensätzliche – also verwandte – Zugang der Kombination. Die Fotoarbeiten verbinden Schnappschüsse der Liveauftritte zu einem Werk, das gleichzeitig singulär und mannigfaltig, umfassend und doch unvollständig ist und darüber hinaus von über die Bildcollage gelegtem Text gebrochen wird. Bei den Videoarbeiten werden dementsprechend Buchstaben direkt auf den Monitor geklebt, was die Verführungskraft des Videobildes untergräbt.

Dieser Zugang des Kombinierens und der Brechung in den Arbeiten von DFS dient dem Zweck, passives Konsumieren durch die BetrachterInnen/das Publikum zu verhindern. DFS übertragen Do-it-yourself-Energie und die Vorstellung befreienden Handelns auf die BetrachterInnen/das Publikum; dadurch betonen und festigen sie den Plattformgedanken, den Gedanken der positiven und aktiven Teilnahme, der in ihrem gesamten Schaffen von zentraler Bedeutung ist. Discoteca Flaming Star widerstehen der Versuchung, die BetrachterInnen/das Publikum zu hypnotisieren, akzeptieren damit tapfer ihre Verwundbarkeit als aufrichtige, vertrauensvolle PerformerInnen und bekennen sich zu ihrer Position, überzeugte und durch nichts abzubringende Fans zu sein. So ehrlich und bejahend zu agieren, ohne Zuflucht hinter Schichten von Ironie zu suchen, mag sich als einer ihrer zentralsten Aspekte erweisen.

Übersetzt von Martin Gastl und Markus Schmitt

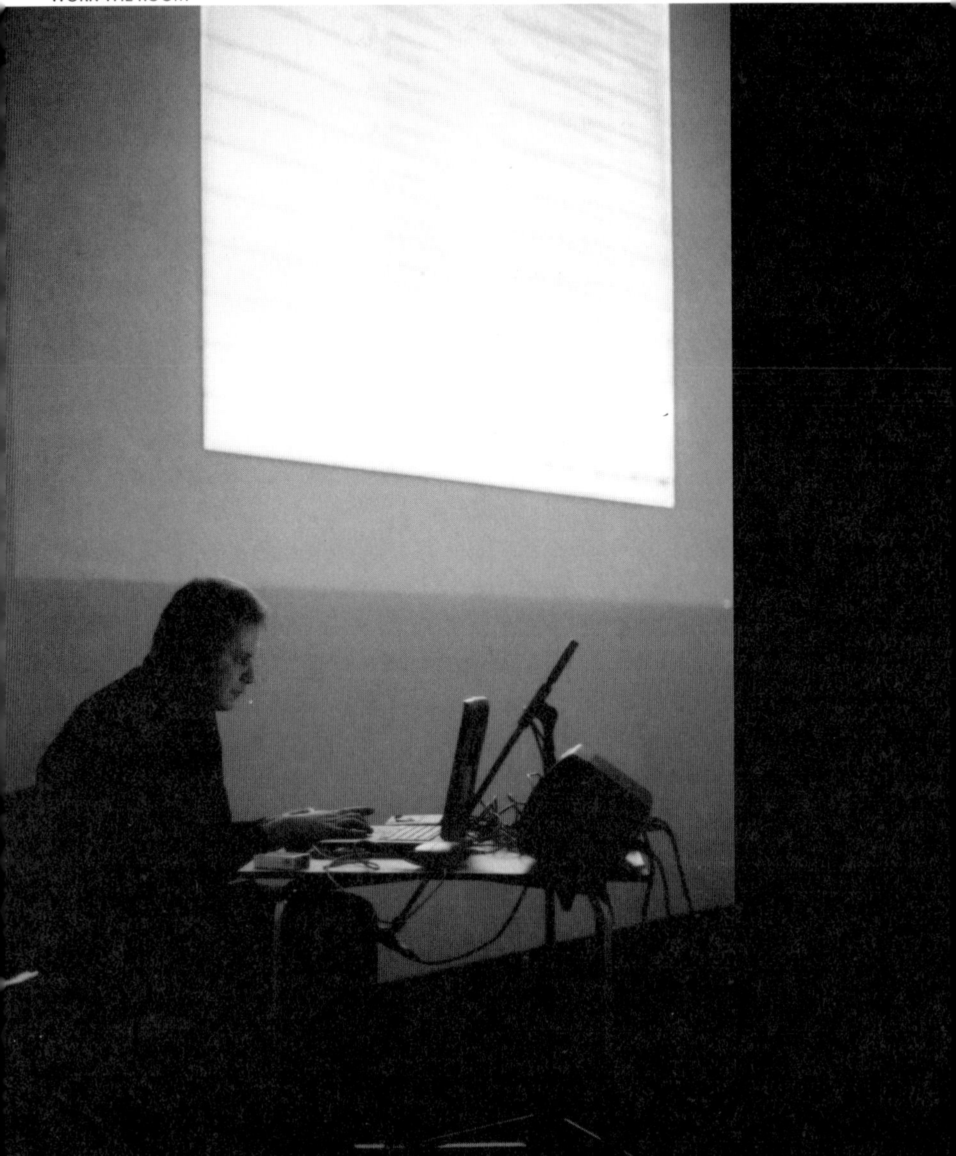

The Air Between

by Christof Kurzmann

When the organizers of the Donaufestival in Krems, Austria invited me to contribute a piece of work on this year's theme, The Deep Tone, my first thought was to return to creating music that followed parameters such as melody or rhythm, things that, except for a few contributions to various compilations, I had paid little attention to on my releases over the past several years.

I had set about building songlike miniatures and sketches, pieces based on low-pitched sounds interspersed with short melodic signatures, when suddenly the flow of my life was interrupted by something that was to change everything: war!

From the moment the U.S. Army and its dubious allies initiated their acts of aggression against Iraq, the first thing I did every morning was to read the news. "Tuned in" as I was, I would then sit down in front of my computer to try to keep working on my music. Before long, I noticed that the ease and lightness so overwhelmingly present at first, this relaxed feeling I needed in order to work in a pop form, had vanished. The sounds flowing from my computer were still deep and low-pitched, but their quality and their relation to the world around them had changed.

For a few days I thought things would come right again, that the aggressors might even see political reason, either by recognizing the injustice on their own or somehow being inspired by the mounting wave of world-wide protest against this war, and that this would eventually lead to a production that would rise up out of the tragic events in a triumphant hymn of human will and intention. However, not only did Iraq's war-torn population end up surrendering, but I too had to give up my faith in justice.

Thus, this album has become an account that documents the surrender of my musical and creative self to my social self, a document of mourning and sadness. Rather than being the result of my wishes, *The Air Between* is a reflection of my mood of resignation. It's a picture of the first days of war, when the air raids were still rare yet nonetheless vehement and disastrous. It's a portrayal of the air between—between the attacks, between hope and despair, between waiting and surrender.

The album *The Air Between* was released on charhizma (cha021, 2003).

Translated from the German by Friederike Kulcsar

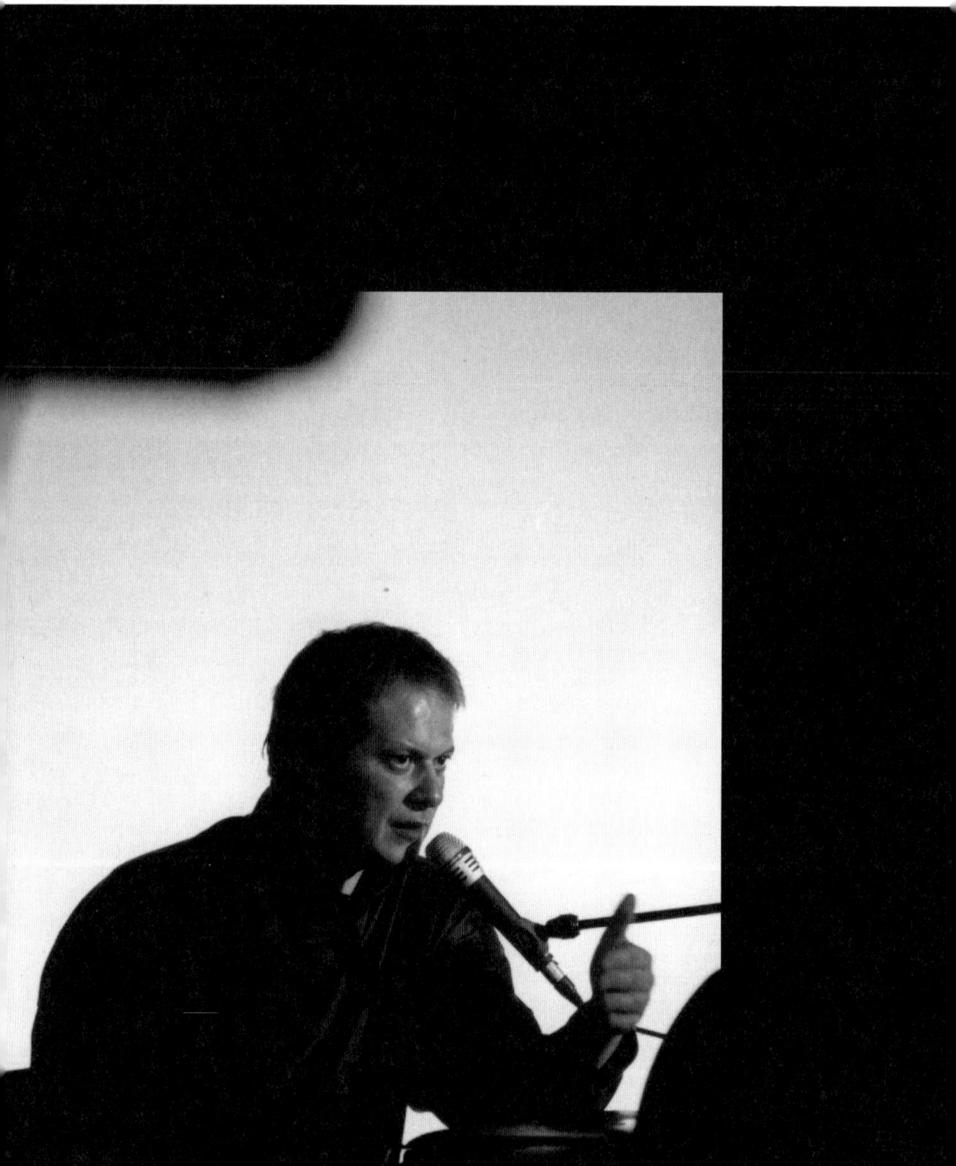

The Air Between

von Christof Kurzmann

Als ich vom Donaufestival Krems 2003 gebeten wurde, mit einem Beitrag zum Thema „der tiefe Ton" teilzunehmen, stand mir der Sinn zunächst einmal danach, wieder etwas zu kreieren, das auf den von mir in den letzten Jahren veröffentlichten CDs – abgesehen von wenigen Beiträgen für diverse Kompilationen – eher ein wenig untergegangen war: eine Musik, die sich mehr entlang von Parametern wie Melodie und Rhythmus bewegt.

Nachdem ich die Arbeit aufgenommen und einige kleine, sehr liedhafte Stücke geschaffen hatte, die, auf tiefen Bässen aufgebaut, mit kurzen, melodischen Signaturen versehen waren, trat ein Ereignis in mein Leben, das alles verändern sollte: Krieg!

Von dem Moment an, da die Aggression der US-Armee und ihrer zweifelhaften Verbündeten gegen den Irak begonnen hatte, stand ich jeden Tag in der Früh auf und las als Allererstes die Nachrichten. So „gestimmt", ging ich an meinen Arbeitsplatz vor dem Computer und versuchte, an meiner Musik weiterzuarbeiten. Schon bald musste ich feststellen, dass die Leichtigkeit, die (m)ich zunächst beherrscht hatte und die für mich nötig ist, um im „Popformat" zu arbeiten, dahin war. Was nun an Klängen aus meinem Computer strebte, waren zwar nach wie vor die tiefen Klänge, aber ihre Qualität und ihr Verhältnis zu ihrer Umgebung hatten sich verändert. Noch einige Tage lang war ich der Ansicht, dies könne sich wieder geben, werde eventuell auch noch durch politische Einsicht in das Unrecht und die massiven weltweiten Proteste gegen den Krieg beeinflusst werden und letztlich zu einer Produktion führen, die aus der Tragik des Geschehens in eine triumphale Hymne des menschlichen Willens emporsteigen würde. Doch dann mussten nicht nur die Menschen im Irak zermürbt aufgeben, sondern auch mein Glaube an die Gerechtigkeit.

So ist das Album *The Air Between* zu einem Dokument der Niederlage meines musikschaffenden Ichs gegenüber dem sozialen Ich geworden, ein Dokument der Trauer und der Tristesse. *The Air Between* ist weiterhin nicht mehr das Ergebnis meines Willens, denn vielmehr ein Stimmungsbild meiner Resignation. Es ist ein Stimmungsbild der ersten Kriegstage, in denen die Angriffe der Flugzeuge zwar noch selten, aber nichtsdestotrotz vehement und verheerend waren. Es ist die Beschreibung der Luft dazwischen. Zwischen den Angriffen, zwischen Hoffen und Verzweifeln, zwischen dem Abwarten und dem Sich-Ergeben.

Das Album *The Air Between* wurde bei charhizma veröffentlicht (cha021, 2003).

Going Fragile

by Mattin

Of course it is not easy to get out of your own material, and it can be painful; there is an insecurity aspect to it. This actually is probably the most experimental level. When do you think real innovation and experimentation are happening? Probably when people are insecure, probably when people are in a situation very new to them and when they are a bit uncertain and afraid. That is where people have to push themselves. People are innovative when they are outside of their warm shit, outside of the familiar and comfortable... I don't know exactly what I want, but I do know exactly what I do not want.

—Conversation with Radu Malfatti

Improvised music forces situations into play where musicians push each other into bringing different perspectives to their playing. Improvised music is not progressive in itself, but it invites constant experimentation. When players feel too secure about their approaches, the experimentation risks turning into Mannerism. What I would like to explore here are the moments in which players leave behind a safe zone and expose themselves in the face of the internalized structures of judgment that govern our appreciation of music. These I would call fragile moments.

During the summer of 2003 I had the opportunity to spend time in Vienna researching the political connotations of improvised music. Not that I found a direct relationship, but through conversations, going to concerts, and playing with other musicians, I became aware of some of the potential and limitations that improvisation has in terms of political agency within the space of music production. For this text, I draw from the conversations I had with the trombonist Radu Malfatti as part of my research. While Malfatti's roots are in the chaotic-sounding improvised free jazz of the 1970s, he is currently more focused on ultra quiet and sparse playing. His approach to performance runs against the stagnation that might occur in sustained improvisation. In his quest to avoid stagnation, Malfatti looks for those insecure situations that I mention above—situations that can call into question the dominant structures of music appreciation.

How could you anticipate what you might achieve if you do not know what you will find on the way? To be open, receptive, and exposed to the dangers of making improvised music, means exposing yourself to unwanted situations that could break the foundations of your own security. As a player you will bring yourself into situations that ask for total commitment. No vision of what could happen is able to bring light to that precise moment. Once you are out, there is no way back; you cannot regret what you have done. You must engage in questioning your security, see it as a constriction. You are aware and scared, as if you were in a dark corridor. Now you are starting to realize that what you thought of as walls existed only in your imagination.

While your senses alert you to danger, you are also going to use them to deal with it. Keep going forward toward what you do not know, to what is questioning your knowledge and your use of it. Keep pushing yourself, knowing that the other players will be pushing you, replacing traces of comfort. This is an unreliable moment, to which no stable definition can be applied. It is subject to all the particularities brought to this moment. The more sensitive you are to them, the more you can work with (or against) them. You are breaking away from previous restrictions that you have become attached to, creating a unique social space, a space that cannot be transported elsewhere. Now you are building different forms of collaboration, scrapping previous modes of generating relations.

Something is happening here, but what is it? It is hard to say, but certainly there is intensity to it. These moments are almost impossible to articulate; they refuse pigeonholing and evade easy representation.

We are forced to question the material and social conditions that constitute the improvised moment—structures that usually validate improvisation as an established musical genre. Otherwise we risk fetishizing "the moment" and avoid its implications.

When we talk about stagnation and progression there is just one instrument to help us explain what we mean, and this is time, history.

—Conversation with Radu Malfatti

When Radu Malfatti talks about the breaks that some musicians have made from musical orthodoxy, he looks at the ways that they have dealt with these breaks. Some seek to consolidate or re-metabolize the fragile moments they have encountered; others simply return to the safety of their previous practices. Only very few manage to keep searching for fragility; it requires musicians to make multiple breaks from their own traditions. It's easier to develop coherence within one's practice: There is a fine line between being persistent in pursuing a particular line of research, and getting comfortable within one's methods.

When something new happens, people do not like it. It's as simple as that... There is nothing I can do about it.

—Conversation with Radu Malfatti

When something different and hard to place appears within the dichotomy of the new and the old of mainstream values, attention cannot easily be drawn to it.

While nobody might recognize the importance of what you have done, you need to keep your confidence. It is difficult to be alone in working toward something and yet not know where it will take you; something which threatens to destroy your artistic trajectory, which you have worked so hard to build up. Of course, when one uses music not as a tool for achieving something else (recognition, status...) but in a more aggressively creative way, it is going to produce alienation. But what do you want to do as an improvised musician? Work toward the lowest common denominator, making music which more people can relate to?

Improvised music has the potential to disrupt previous modes of musical production, but it is up to the players to tear them apart in order to find a way in. Opening new fields of permissibility means to go fragile until we destroy the fears that hold us back.

We are not talking here about changing the labor conditions of a majority of people; but, being aware that culture, creativity, and communication are becoming the tools of the "factory without walls," we need to be suspicious of ways in which cultural practices can be exploited by capital. Because of this we must constantly question our motives, our modus operandi, and its relation to the conditions that we are embedded in, to avoid recuperation by a system that is going to produce ideological walls for us. To be antagonistic to these conditions means danger and insecurity. To go through them will mean commitment and some of what Benjamin described as the "Destructive Character":

The destructive character has the consciousness of historical man, whose deepest emotion is an insuperable mistrust of the course of things and a readiness at all times to recognize that everything can go wrong. Therefore the destructive character is reliability itself. The destructive character sees nothing permanent. But for this very reason he sees ways everywhere. Where others encounter walls or mountains, there, too, he sees a way. But because he sees a way everywhere, he has to clear things from it everywhere. Not always by brute force; sometimes by the most refined. No moment can know what the next will bring.

—Walter Benjamin, "The Destructive Character" (1931)

Zerbrechlich werden

von Mattin

Natürlich ist es nicht einfach, sich vom eigenen Material frei zu machen, und es kann schmerzhaft sein; ein Aspekt dabei ist die Unsicherheit. Eigentlich scheint das die experimentellste Ebene zu sein. Wann finden wohl tatsächliche Innovation und wirkliches Experimentieren statt? Wahrscheinlich dann, wenn Leute unsicher sind, wenn sie sich in einer für sie neuen Situation befinden, wenn sie sich nicht ganz sicher sind und ein wenig Angst haben. Dann müssen sie sich einen Ruck geben, sich anstrengen. Menschen sind innovativ, wenn sie sich außerhalb ihrer warmen Scheiße befinden, außerhalb des Gewohnten und Bequemen ... Ich weiß nicht genau, was ich will, aber ich weiß genau, was ich nicht will.

– Gespräch mit Radu Malfatti

Improvisierte Musik schafft Situationen, in denen sich MusikerInnen gegenseitig ansporonen, andere Perspektiven in ihr Spiel zu bringen. Improvisierte Musik ist nicht per se progressiv, fördert aber permanentes Experimentieren. Wenn MusikerInnen sich ihrer Zugänge zu sicher sind, läuft das Experimentieren Gefahr, manieristisch zu werden. Was ich hier untersuchen möchte, sind die Momente, in denen MusikerInnen sicheres Terrain verlassen und sich den verinnerlichten Beurteilungsstrukturen aussetzen, die unsere Wertschätzung von Musik bestimmen. Diese Momente würde ich zerbrechlich nennen.

Im Sommer 2003 hatte ich die Gelegenheit, in Wien zu sein und die politischen Konnotationen improvisierter Musik zu untersuchen. Zwar konnte ich keine direkte Beziehung finden, aber in Gesprächen, bei Konzertbesuchen und beim Spielen mit anderen MusikerInnen wurde mir einiges bewusst, was das Potenzial und die Limitierungen von improvisierter Musik hinsichtlich einer politischen Wirksamkeit innerhalb der Musikproduktion betrifft. In diesen Text eingeflossen sind Gespräche, die ich im Zuge meiner Untersuchungen mit dem Posaunisten Radu Malfatti führte. Malfattis Wurzeln liegen im chaotisch klingenden improvisierten Free Jazz der Siebzigerjahre; gegenwärtig gilt sein Interesse jedoch hauptsächlich dem ultraleisen und reduzierten Spiel. Sein musikalischer Zugang wendet sich gegen die Stagnation, welche ständige Improvisation mit sich bringen kann. In seinem Bemühen, Stillstand zu vermeiden, sucht Malfatti nach jenen Situationen der Unsicherheit, von denen ich oben gesprochen habe – Situationen, die die vorherrschenden Strukturen der Einschätzung von Musik infrage stellen können.

Wie kann man erahnen, was zu erreichen wäre, wenn man nicht weiß, was unterwegs zu finden ist? Den Gefahren des freien Improvisierens offen und empfänglich gegenüberzutreten heißt, sich ungewollten Situationen auszusetzen, welche die Fundamente der eigenen Sicherheit zertrümmern könnten. Als MusikerIn begibst du dich in Situationen, die dich völlig in Anspruch nehmen. Keine Vision dessen, was passieren könnte, vermag genau diesen Moment zu erhellen. Einmal draußen, gibt es kein Zurück, kein Bedauern. Du musst deine Sicherheiten hinterfragen, als Beschränkungen sehen. Du bist wachsam und verängstigt, als ob du dich in einem dunklen Korridor befändest. Nun beginnst du zu erkennen, dass das, was du für Mauern gehalten hast, nur in deiner Vorstellung existiert hat.

Deine Sinne warnen dich vor Gefahr, und sie helfen dir auch, mit ihr umzugehen. Bewege dich vorwärts in Richtung des Unbekannten, hin zu dem, was dein Wissen und deine Art, es einzusetzen, infrage stellt. Fordere dich selbst, treib dich an, im Bewusstsein, dass die anderen MusikerInnen dich antreiben – dabei werden die letzten Überreste von Bequemlichkeit getilgt. Das ist ein Moment der Ungewissheit, der sich einer fixen Definition entzieht; abhängig von all den spezifischen Umständen, die diesen Moment ausmachen. Je aufmerksamer du diese Umstände wahrnimmst, desto besser kannst du mit ihnen (oder gegen sie) arbeiten. Du machst dich von früheren, gewohnten Beschränkungen frei, du schaffst einen einzigartigen sozialen Raum, der nirgendwo anders existieren könnte. Jetzt entwickelst du andere Formen der Zusammenarbeit, wirfst frühere Arten des Herstellens von Beziehungen über Bord.

Etwas passiert hier – aber was? Das ist schwer zu sagen, aber jedenfalls hat es mit Intensität zu tun. Diese Momente sind praktisch nicht in Worte zu fassen; sie lassen sich nicht einordnen und entziehen sich einer einfachen Darstellung.

Wir sind gezwungen, das Material und die sozialen Bedingungen infrage zu stellen, die den improvisierten Moment bestimmen – Strukturen, die für gewöhnlich Improvisation als etabliertes musikalisches Genre bestätigen. Sonst laufen wir Gefahr, „den Moment" zu fetischisieren, und stellen uns nicht dem, was er impliziert.

Wenn wir über Stillstand und Fortschritt sprechen, gibt es nur ein Instrument, das uns zu erklären hilft, was wir meinen, und das ist Zeit, Geschichte.

– Gespräch mit Radu Malfatti

Wenn Radu Malfatti darüber spricht, wie einige MusikerInnen mit musikalischer Orthodoxie gebrochen haben, sieht er sich dabei an, wie sie mit diesen Brüchen umgegangen sind. Manche versuchen, die zerbrechlichen Momente, die sie erlebt haben, zu festigen oder zu wiederholen; andere kehren einfach zur Sicherheit ihrer früheren Praxis zurück. Nur sehr wenige schaffen es, permanent nach Zerbrechlichkeit zu suchen; dies verlangt von MusikerInnen, häufig Brüche mit ihren eigenen Traditionen zu vollziehen. Einfacher ist es hingegen, innerhalb der eigenen Praxis Kohärenz zu entwickeln: Zwischen dem beharrlichen Verfolgen einer bestimmten Untersuchungsrichtung und dem gemütlichen Einrichten in den eigenen Methoden liegt nur ein kleiner Schritt.

Wenn etwas Neues passiert, gefällt das den Leuten nicht. So einfach ist das ... Ich kann's nicht ändern.

– Gespräch mit Radu Malfatti

Taucht innerhalb der Dichotomie des Neuen und des Alten im Mainstreamwertesystem etwas anderes, etwas schwer Einzuordnendes auf, ist es nicht leicht, die Aufmerksamkeit darauf zu lenken.

Mag auch niemand die Wichtigkeit deines Tuns anerkennen, du musst dein Selbstvertrauen bewahren. Es ist schwierig, allein auf etwas hinzuarbeiten, ohne zu wissen, wohin das führt – auf etwas hinzuarbeiten, das deine künstlerische Ausrichtung zerstören könnte, deine künstlerische Position, die du dir so hart erarbeitet hast. Wenn Musik auf eine aggressivere kreative Weise verwendet wird und nicht als Werkzeug zur Erlangung von etwas anderem (Anerkennung, Status et cetera), führt sie natürlich zu Entfremdung. Aber was willst du als ImprovisationsmusikerIn tun? Auf den kleinsten gemeinsamen Nenner hinarbeiten, Musik machen, mit der mehr Leute etwas anfangen können?

Improvisierte Musik besitzt das Potenzial, die Kontinuität einer früheren Musikproduktion zu unterbrechen; aber es liegt an den MusikerInnen, sich einen eigenen Weg zu bahnen, einen eigenen Zugang zu erschließen. Neues Terrain des Zulässigen zu erschließen heißt, zerbrechlich zu werden, bis wir die uns einschränkenden Ängste überwunden haben.

Wir sprechen hier nicht davon, die Arbeitsbedingungen einer Mehrheit zu verändern; aber angesichts der Tatsache, dass Kultur, Kreativität und Kommunikation zunehmend Werkzeuge der „Fabrik ohne Mauern" werden, müssen wir der Art und Weise misstrauisch gegenüberstehen, wie das Kapital kulturelle Praxen ausbeuten kann. Deshalb müssen wir ständig unsere Motive, unseren Modus Operandi und seine Beziehung zu den uns umgebenden Verhältnissen hinterfragen, um die Vereinnahmung durch ein System zu vermeiden, das ideologische Mauern um uns errichtet. Diesen Verhältnissen ablehnend gegenüberzustehen bringt Gefahr und Unsicherheit mit sich. Dieser Gefahr und Unsicherheit zu begegnen bedeutet Hingabe und Überzeugung und etwas von dem, was Benjamin als „destruktiven Charakter" bezeichnet hat:

Der destruktive Charakter hat das Bewußtsein des historischen Menschen, dessen Grundaffekt ein unbezwingliches Mißtrauen in den Gang der Dinge und die Bereitwilligkeit ist, mit der er jederzeit davon Notiz nimmt, daß alles schief gehen kann. Daher ist der destruktive Charakter die Zuverlässigkeit selbst.

Der destruktive Charakter sieht nichts Dauerndes. Aber eben darum sieht er überall Wege. Wo andere auf Mauern oder Gebirge stoßen, auch da sieht er einen Weg. Weil er aber überall einen Weg sieht, hat er auch überall aus dem Weg zu räumen. Nicht immer mit roher Gewalt, bisweilen mit veredelter. [...] Kein Augenblick kann wissen, was der nächste bringt.

– Walter Benjamin, „Der destruktive Charakter", 1931

Übersetzt von Martin Gastl und Markus Schmitt

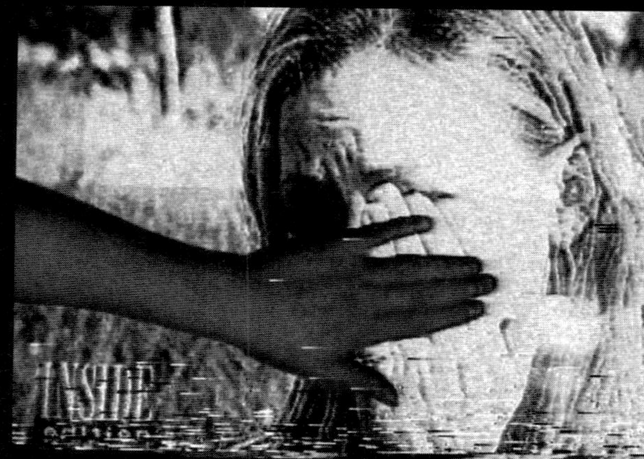

we went from destruction into imitation...

Women as economic factor
gain subjectivity

Men overreact
throw themselves into the river
tear their shirts apart
show (me) bare skin

das business hat längst begonnen:

wir gingen von der destruktion in die imitation. frauen als ökonomischer faktor gewinnen subjektivität. männer reagieren über. werfen sich in den fluss. zerreißen ihre hemden. zeigen (mir) nackte haut. business has begun a long time ago:

Wenn du etwas verkaufen willst, dann

stell dich
auf die
Straße!

If you have something to sell, put yourself on the street!

Who is WE? and who are YOU?

we gather around a microphone

like having something in common

wer ist WIR? und wer bist DU? wir versammeln uns um ein mikrofon. wie etwas gemeinsam haben.

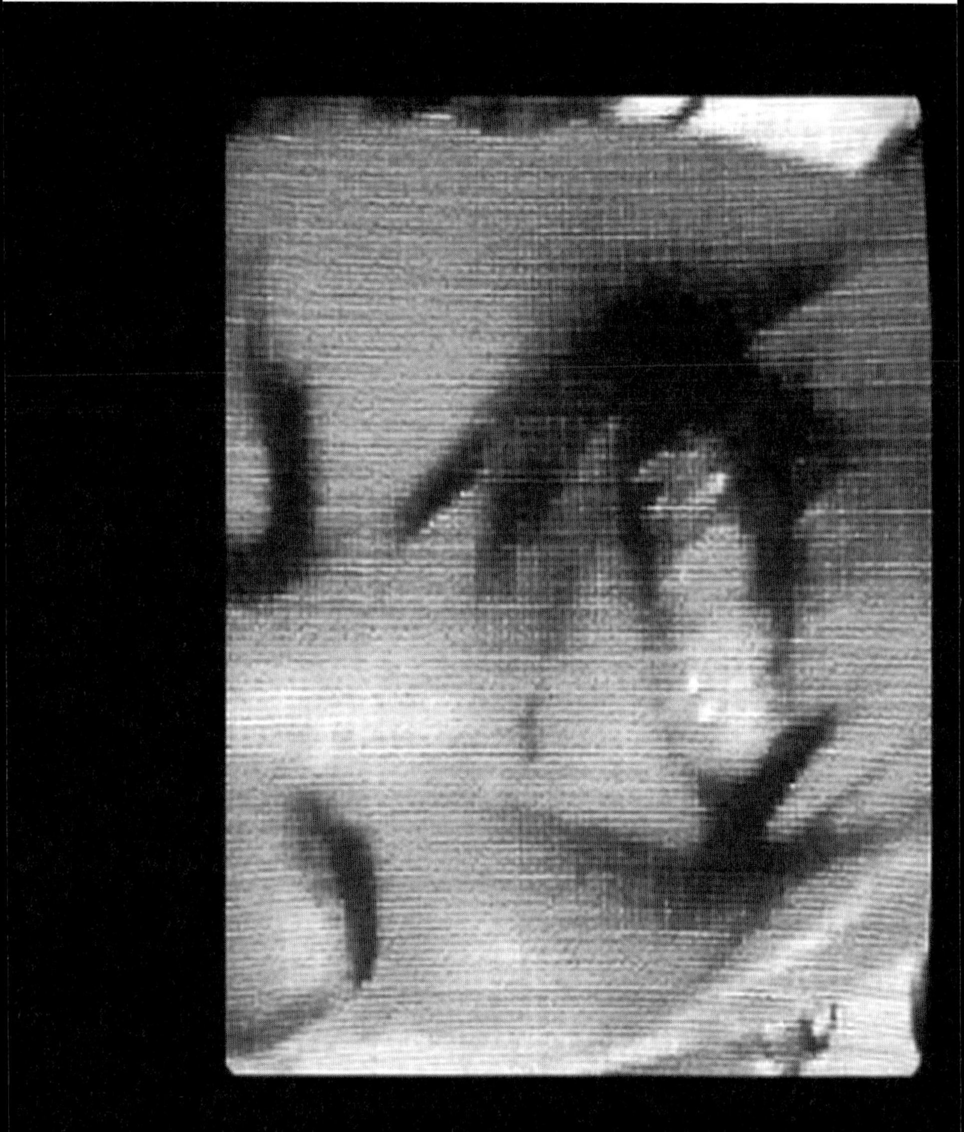

Ich werde euch ein Lied singen, so inbrünstig,
dass das Herzblut rinnt.
Richtige Schmachtfetzen werde ich euch um
die Ohren hauen!

I am going to sing you a song, fervently enough to make your heart blood rush. I am going to slap real tearjerkers into your faces.

by the way:

die Landschaft ist aus

zu Ende

fertig

geht nicht weiteeeeeeerr

ist **flach**

flach wie ein Papiiiiiiiiier!

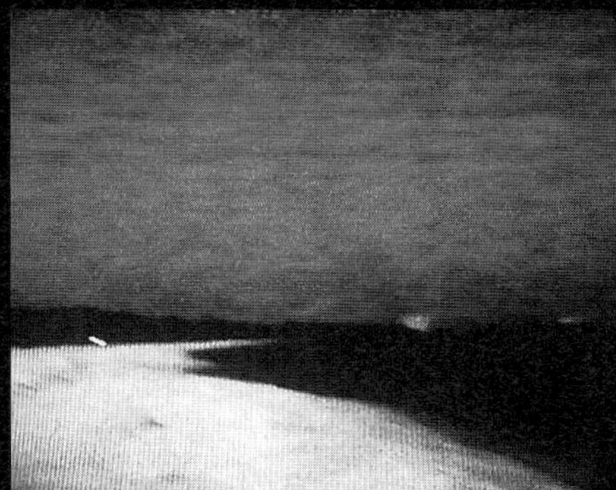

übrigens: the landscape is over. finished. done. doesn’t go ooooooon. is flat. flat like papeeeeeeeeeer!

“Step behind the ropes please! no.2”

On Sabine Marte’s Video-Performance

by Christa Benzer

The television image of a crying woman flickers across the screen. The artist, who stands in front of the projected image, appears to be visibly moved and strokes her hand consolingly. Sabine Marte’s video-performance begins with this simple gesture that perceives the televisual realm as a real sphere of action. Confronted with the dominant media culture, her piece presents us with alternative options for engagement.

A clip from a U.S.-American “true crime” TV series with the telling title *Inside* serves as a narrative model; it revolves around the case of a woman who allegedly set her own house on fire. A radiant heater initiates a tragic story, which the artist retells. She is, however, operating from a completely different set of premises.

Her performative deconstruction of the story uses fragmentation and desynchronization of the plot as techniques to structurally dismantle TV’s function as hegemonic apparatus of image- and meaning-production.

In a first move, Sabine Marte analyzes the conventions of mass-media representation and their perceptual structures. In sync with the rhythm of the visual representation on the screen, she loudly names the individuals, objects, and places illustrated: a woman, a man, a child, a house, a garden, a space heater, etc. By naming what she sees, the artist points to the gap between representation and reality which media perception normally levels out. The vocal affirmation of what can be seen also demonstrates the exchangeability and arbitrariness of representations periodically repeated, however slightly altered, in the televisual realm. Sabine Marte refers to these formations only in order to disassemble them immediately into their individual components.

The emancipatory potential released by such a linguistic and visual dissolution of the representational unit—woman, man, child, and house—is prevalent in the next scene. On the screen appears the face of the woman, who now seeks direct contact with the artist. In contrast to conventional assumptions, she presents herself in dialogue with the performer as an active, obstinately revolutionary subject who acts altogether strategically.

The artist detaches "the woman" from her traditional status as image and lends her her own voice, with which she then eloquently undermines traditional gender-specific attributes. At this point Sabine Marte pays careful attention to the synchronization of image and sound: The woman's lip-movements correspond exactly to the words that the performer puts in her mouth. In the final scene, the cards are again laid out in a new way: "The woman is the house, the man is the child, the child is the garden, the woman stays in bed, the man stays at home, the garden can wait." By using images that are continually in motion, Sabine Marte disturbs potential fantasies projected by the viewers, who can no longer get a grasp on the scene. The desynchronization of image and sound leads to a *tabula rasa* of realistic media representations, while simultaneously effacing the fixed meanings originally generated by the TV images.

Going beyond the mere analysis of hegemonic processes to construct meaning, the artist proposes an alternative model of meaning production—one within which language, medium, gesture, and the body continually and mutually comment, interrogate, and re-evaluate each other. At the same time, she uses the selected TV clip for an exemplary demonstration of the contingent character of media processes of signification and identification.

Translated by Julia Bernard

„Step behind the ropes please! nr. 2"

Zur Videoperformance von Sabine Marte

von Christa Benzer

Das (Fernseh-)Bild einer weinenden Frau flimmert über die Leinwand.

Die Künstlerin, die sich vor der Leinwand positioniert, zeigt sich sichtlich ergriffen und streichelt ihr tröstend über die Hand. Mit dieser einfachen Geste, die den televisuellen Raum als einen realen Handlungsspielraum begreift, beginnt die Videoperformance von Sabine Marte, die in Bezug auf die dominante Medienkultur alternative Handlungsoptionen entwirft.

Als narrative Vorlage dient eine amerikanische „True crime"-Fernsehsendung mit dem bezeichnenden Titel *Inside*. Diese verhandelt den Fall einer Frau, die vermutlich ihr Haus angezündet hat. Ein Heizstrahler setzt dort eine tragische Geschichte in Gang, die die Künstlerin unter vollkommen geänderten Vorzeichen wiedererzählt.

In ihrer performativen Dekonstruktion der Geschichte sind Fragmentierung und Desynchronisation die Verfahren, mit denen sie die Funktion des Fernsehens als hegemoniale Apparatur der Bild- und Bedeutungsproduktion strukturalistisch zerlegt.

In einem ersten Schritt werden die massenmedialen Darstellungskonventionen und Wahrnehmungsstrukturen analysiert: Synchron mit dem Rhythmus der visuellen Repräsentationen auf der Leinwand werden die abgebildeten Personen, Gegenstände und Orte lautstark benannt: eine Frau, ein Mann, ein Kind, ein Haus, ein Garten, ein Heizstrahler et cetera. Indem die Künstlerin das, was sie sieht, auch sprachlich benennt, verweist sie auf die Kluft zwischen Abbild und Realität, deren Nivellierung die mediale Wahrnehmung üblicherweise bestimmt. In der sprachlichen

Affirmation des Sichtbaren zeigt sich aber auch die Austauschbarkeit und Beliebigkeit dieser Repräsentationen, die sich im televisuellen Raum in leicht abgewandelten Formationen stets wiederholen. Sabine Marte zitiert diese Formationen allerdings nur herbei, um sie sofort wieder in ihre einzelnen Bestandteile zu zerlegen.

Das emanzipatorische Potenzial, das die sprachliche und visuelle Auflösung dieser repräsentativen Einheit – Frau, Mann, Kind und Haus – freisetzt, kommt auch in der nächsten Einstellung zum Tragen. Auf der Leinwand erscheint das Gesicht der Frau, die nun den direkten Kontakt mit der Künstlerin sucht. Den üblichen Projektionen entgegengesetzt, präsentiert sie sich im Dialog mit der Performerin als aktives, renitent-revolutionäres Subjekt, das durchwegs strategisch agiert.

Die Künstlerin löst „die Frau" aus ihrem traditionellen Bildstatus und verleiht ihr eine eigene Stimme, mit der sie die üblichen geschlechtsspezifischen Zuschreibungen dann auch eloquent untergräbt. Während Sabine Marte hier penibel auf die Synchronizität von Bild und Ton achtet (die Lippenbewegungen der Frau korrespondieren mit den Worten, die ihr die Performerin in den Mund legt), teilt sie die Karten in der letzten Szene wieder neu aus: „Die Frau ist das Haus, der Mann ist das Kind, das Kind ist der Garten, die Frau schläft sich aus, der Mann bleibt zuhaus, der Garten kann warten." Durch die sich ständig in Bewegung befindlichen Bilder stört Sabine Marte die potenziellen Projektionsfantasien der BetrachterInnen, die hier keinen Halt mehr finden. Die Desynchronisation von Bild und Ton gleicht darüber hinaus einer Tabula rasa medialer Wirklichkeitsbeschreibungen und verwischt gleichzeitig die fixierten Bedeutungen, die die Fernsehbilder ursprünglich generiert haben.

Über die Analyse hegemonialer Bedeutungskonstruktionen hinausgehend, entwirft die Künstlerin so ein alternatives Modell der Bedeutungsproduktion, in dem sich Sprache, Medium, Geste und Körper stets wechselseitig kommentieren, befragen und umwerten.

Gleichzeitig wird der kontingente Charakter medialer Signifikations- und Identifikationsprozesse erfahrbar, der hier anhand des ausgewählten TV-Materials beispielhaft vorgeführt wird.

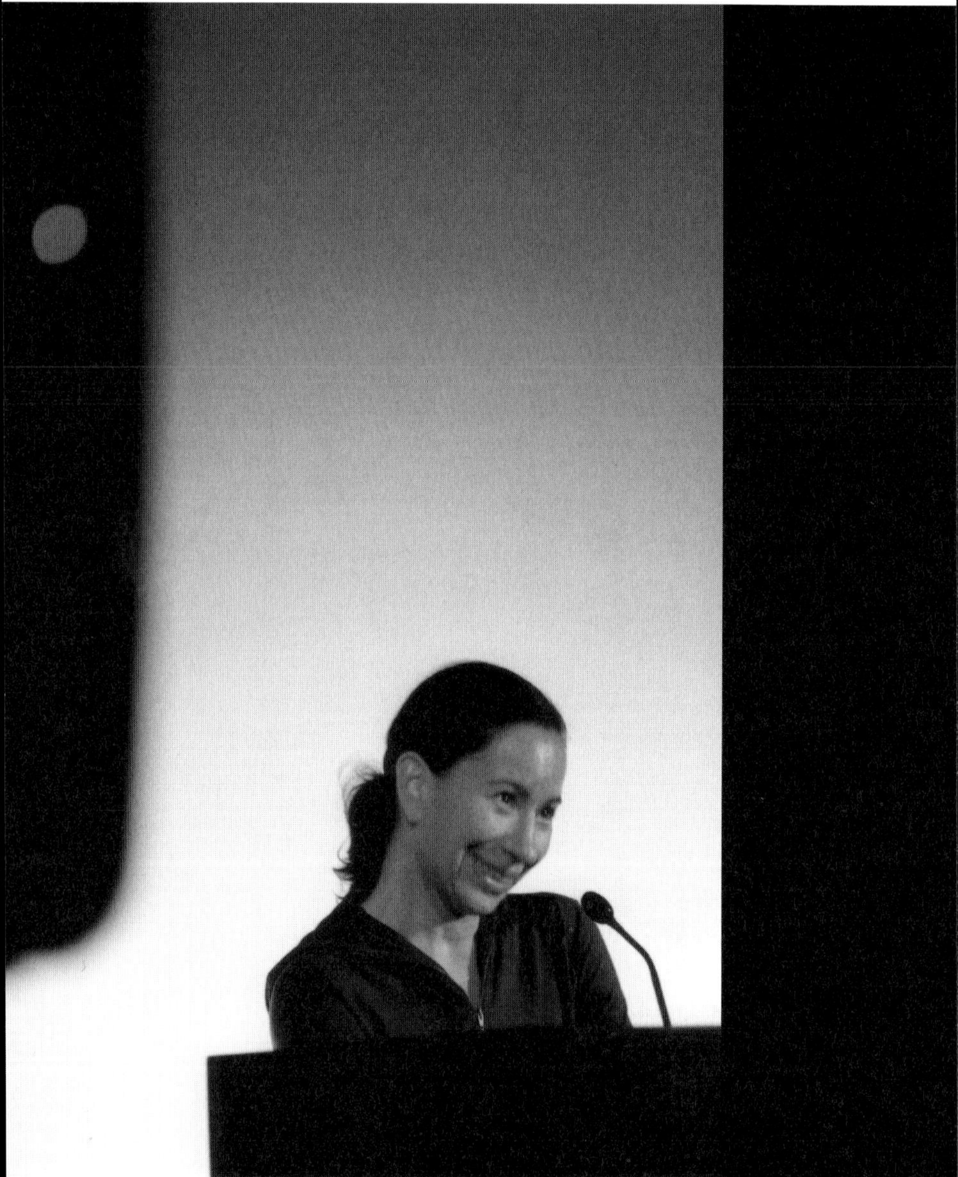

Andrea Fraser
Starting where she's standing

MUMOK, 09/27/04

Introduction

Andrea Fraser approaches the podium and begins to address the audience in a strange sort of German. After about five minutes, she interrupts herself and continues in English.

That, by way of an introduction, was the first part of a performance I developed in 2001 called *Kunst muss hängen*. It's based on a transcript of a speech given by Martin Kippenberger—a kind of drunken *Tischrede* he delivered at a place called Club an der Grenze in Burgenland here in Austria, in 1995. It was a speech he gave on the occasion of the opening of the first art exhibition of one of his best friends, Michael Würthle, who is better known as the owner of the Paris Bar in Berlin.

Kunst muss hängen was the performance in which I began to turn my attention to the position of the artist. I started performing in the mid-1980s. At that time I was already rather identified with institutional critique and neo-conceptualism, but I was also very influenced by feminist performance and feminist psychoanalytic film theory. Combining these two traditions and critical frameworks became my project and the basis for an attempt to develop a practice that would employ performance practice that would critically engage specific sites. Under the influence of feminism and psychoanalysis, however, my conception of site included not only physical, architectural, and geographical spaces and places, but also the often very localized discourses and rituals that frame social and interpersonal relations. Sites in this sense also include situations—situations which are often forms of social and public performance in their own right, like the situation of the conference or lecture, of the exhibition opening, of the tour, of the table speech. I began to conceive of these sites and situations not only as frames of relations, but as sites of the production and reproduction of those relations, of the subject positions they demand, of the subjectivities those subject positions demand, and finally even of the bodies in which those subjectivities are internalized.

Practically speaking, my approach to performance also developed very much out of the strategies of appropriation art that were so prevalent in the 1980s. My interest in appropriation, however, had less to do with problematic of authorship and originality than with the potential for site-specific intervention that more performative forms of appropriation seemed to offer. With my very early work as an "institutional critique," I moved from the appropriation of art historical images and texts to the appropriation of institutional forms and formats—the exhibition brochure, the museum poster. Another turning point came when I wrote about Louise Lawler's work in the mid-'80s. Lawler's early work often involved what I came to see as an appropriation of positions and functions within the field of art: as a publicist, sending out invitations, producing matchbooks; as a curator, presenting installations of other artists' work, etc. Under the influence of Lawler's work, I began to sort of move from the appropriation of institutional forms and formats to the appropriation of positions and functions within museums and galleries. This led to live performances in the form of museum tours, gallery sales presentations, academic panel discussions (with the group The V-Girls), and opening speeches, as well as projects and installations in which I would perform the functions of a curator, a consultant, an educator, etc. After about fifteen years of that, I had managed to take up or otherwise engage the positions of collectors, dealers, docents, museum educators, trustees and board members, curators, art journalists—the list could go on.

In the late '90s, however, I began to turn my attention to the position of the artist, and *Kunst muss hängen* was my first work in that direction. What I'd like to show today is a videotape of the performance that I gave at the opening of a retrospective of 20 years of my work that just opened at the Kunstverein in Hamburg. The performance, called *Official Welcome*, was originally commissioned by two New York collectors, Barbara and Howard Morse, and first performed in their living room in 2001. *Official Welcome* is the only performance I've ever performed in more than one site and I was thinking of just performing it here today. But to perform it here would ultimately function as no more than a demonstration, like the little bit of *Kunst muss hängen* with which I began this introduction. Even though *Official Welcome* does not require a specific physical site, it does require a specific kind of situation: a situation in which an artist is being honored, as I certainly was at the opening of my retrospective at the Kunstverein in Hamburg. So I decided that showing the video of its performance in that site would actually convey more of its meaning than re-performing it here today.

Thank you.

The script of *Official Welcome* has been published in:

Alexander Alberro (ed.), *Museum Highlights: The Collected Writings of Andrea Fraser*. Cambridge, Massachusetts 2005.

Kunsthaus Dresden (exhibition catalog), *Madonna*. Dresden 2005. (German translation by Nikolaus G. Schneider)

Andrea Fraser, "Official Welcome," in: Documents, No. 24, Winter 2004.

Belkin Art Gallery (exhibition catalog), *Exhibition: New Video Work by Andrea Fraser*. Vancouver2004.

Kunstverein in Hamburg (exhibition catalog), *Andrea Fraser, Works 1983 to 2003*. Cologne 2003.

Andrea Fraser, "Official Welcome," in: The MICA Foundation Newsletter, Vol. 1, No. 2, 2001.

Discussion

Andrea Fraser [on the verge of tears]: I don't know whether I'll be able to say much about my emotional state... [Begins to weep; recovers. Laughingly, to the audience:] So maybe I'll just open the floor for questions... I need to find a tissue, I'll be right back. [Returns; blows her nose. With humor:] You all should have been here last night when Gregg Bordowitz was talking about affects.

Ulrike Müller: *Thank you, Andrea.* [To the audience:] *Gibt es jemanden, der die erste Frage stellen möchte?*

Question from the audience: *Wer waren die Künstler [unverständlich]? translated by U.M.: Who were the artists you were using during your research?*

A. F.: The script of *Official Welcome* is published with a list of sources. Not all of the voices are specific people; many of them are hybrids. I am not attempting to impersonate the people I quote, as I was, for example, in my performance as Martin Kippenberger. Basically, I worked with text. Of all the people I quote, there's only one I have actually heard speak, and that's Benjamin Buchloh, on whom the first voice is based. So it begins with Benjamin Buchloh on Thomas Hirschhorn as well as a little bit on Gabriel Orozco and Richard Serra. And then it's Thomas Hirschhorn, with a little bit of Gabriel Orozco mixed in [joins in laughter from the audience], and then it's Daniel Birnbaum on Thomas Hirschhorn. And then it's a number of other critics on Gabriel Orozco and then on Matthew Barney and then Shirin Neshat. And then, when I'm having difficulties speaking, what I'm saying there (I don't actually say all that much) uses the words of Shirin Neshat, Ross Bleckner and Cy Twombly. It's a strange combination. My delivery is very much of an invention. I was thinking of some abstract expressionist who probably really did suffer and struggle but then bought into the whole truckload of humanist ideology. And then it's Kirk Varnedoe. "Arma virumque cano" is Kirk Varnedoe quoting the first line of the *Aeneid* from a speech at the opening of Cy Twombly's retrospective at MOMA. And then it's Varnedoe on Jasper Johns. And then there are a number of different people talking about Julian Schnabel, Francisco Clemente, and Ross Bleckner. And then it's mostly Ross Bleckner, the artist with the "social strategy," who wants to be remembered. And then it's Dave Hickey, mostly on Francisco Clemente, whose Guggenheim retrospective he describes as "the most elegant beauty salon in the universe." And then it's Katy Siegel on Matthew Barney—who *is* better than us. I changed the gender there so that description becomes a lead-in to Vanessa Beecroft—"it's about emptiness." And then it's mostly Larry Gagosian on Damien Hirst. And then it's Damien Hirst. And then there are a number of different collectors and critics on different artists, although it finishes up with a combination of somebody on Nan Goldin and Bill Arning on Tracy Emin. And then it's Tracy Emin—[laughs]—now you're getting the whole list, but I hope this is entertaining. Then it's Tracy Emin with a couple of other people mixed in. And then it's C. Carr on Karen Finley, Lucy Lippard on Andres Serrano, Michael Kimmelman on Paul McCarthy, and Maurice Berger on Kara Walker. And then it's Kara Walker, and then it's Bill Clinton. [Laughs with laughter from the audience.] And then it's me [smiles], I'm the one who cries. And then it's Bill Clinton again [laughs], saying good night. So, those are the sources.

Official Welcome was commissioned by the collectors Barbara and Howard Morse and I first performed it in their living room in New York in November 2001. I began that first performance by thanking them, of course. But I also asked them to write a page about me, what they might say if they were actually introducing me. So after thanking them for their support, I then spoke about myself as them. That was the original introduction. I performed *Official Welcome* a couple of other times since then, and I always ask whoever invites me to write something for me about me, so I can incorporate it into a new introduction to keep the piece somewhat site-specific. But in Hamburg, as I said in my introduction, I didn't have time to do that. [With emotion, speaking with difficulty.] So I was actually quite serious.

[Question from the audience, not recorded.]

A. F.: What are you surprised about? That I mix?

Woman from the audience: *Yes—yes, that you bring yourself in, in fact.*

A. F.: In fact, I would be happy to bring myself in more. What I say about this piece is [on the verge of tears] that it's not "there go I, but for the grace of God." It's "there *go* I." I mean, there I go. I consider myself a Bourdieuan, and I like to quote Bourdieu (actually quoting Bachelard) to the effect that who we are, positions we occupy, may be quite specific and individual, even unique, but they are nevertheless always only "particular instances of the possible"—of the positions that are possible in our given fields at a given point in time. So my position as an artist in the field of art is a particular instance of the possible positions that one can occupy, as an artist, in the field of art, as are all the other positions that I perform in *Official Welcome*. For me, this is central. Because most of my work has involved quotation for a long time, and also humor, particularly my performance work, what I always have to struggle against is letting it sink into a facile kind of irony or ironic distancing, where I might give the impression that I think that I'm outside or beyond... [fighting back tears, clears her throat] ...the structures that I'm engaging and trying to articulate and perform and critique.

That's not what I believe. So in fact, while it's central to *Official Welcome* that I couldn't possibly be many of the people that I perform—who are, for example, men—it's equally central that there are moments of ambiguity, when I could be describing myself, or speaking as myself, or at least as "Andrea Fraser," as I might want to be perceived.

For me, one of the most complicated parts of *Official Welcome* is when I quote Benjamin Buchloh. [Very moved, recovers, blows her nose.] He is one of the very few people I have ever really wanted to write about my work [with a smile], but he never did. So to quote him, as if about myself, in words that could serve to describe what I intend to do in the performance, when in fact he is speaking about another artist, is a deeply ambivalent piece of wish fulfillment. *Official Welcome* is a deeply, painfully ambivalent performance that involves many things I might want to pretend that I don't intend, such as competition and envy and jealousy and aggressive incorporation. But these dynamics are as central to the structure of the field as those of legitimation and other, shall we say, more sublimated forms of symbolic struggle. I don't believe it's possible to pursue institutional critique without taking such problematically subjective and intimate forms of ambivalence into account. They are precisely what need to be critically engaged and situated in relationship to institutional structures of "possible" positions. *Official Welcome* is particularly concerned with the extent to which those positions remain gender-defined. When I quote Buchloh, the moment when the listener must realize that I am not talking about myself is when I introduce the masculine pronoun. The artist being celebrated there is male.

Judith Hopf*: May I ask a question about the term affirmation you bring in? You describe yourself at the beginning as a person using this strategy as a critique form, and in this piece I find it very impressive how the power system is visible, because you give it so much with your impressive acting, and you are playing* *with it. And I was asking myself, while I was looking at it, whether there is a border you really can't go over, because of this affirmation. Giving power to it, but deconstructing it at the same time, and it shifts. Do you think there is a limit to affirmation?*

A. F.: I don't really understand your question.

***J. H.**: Maybe you can describe your own term of affirmation, in the way you did in this performance? My impression is now—also, it's hard for me to talk in English—it's that you accept this power at the same level as you fight against it. There is, as you said, the competition thing in between, but then there's also a limit to it, because, you know, I feel that reality is really as gendered, in this power system. You don't give another possibility or body to it, you fulfill it somehow, you are acting within the power system. You know what I mean? I don't mean it as a critique, I mean it as question.*

A. F.: I'm still not entirely clear on what the question is. But I think it has to do with a kind of ambivalence between affirmation and critique?

***J. H.**: And also stabilizing the belief in the power system, that it's not changeable, not by five millimeters, by not bringing in another concept.*

A. F.: Oh, I think I understand the question. You could say that *Official Welcome* is based on a kind of realism and argue that realism is not a very effective critical strategy when it implies simply re-performing certain structures of power that have to do with gender, that have to do with forms of institutional incorporation [fighting back tears], as they exist. And it sounds like you are also saying that my acting skill undercuts the critique, or it might.

***J. H.**: I am not saying that your ability is disturbing your critique, I think that the impressive thing about your performance is that you really see the power, it really builds up the power system somehow by playing it—it's also a power for you, it hurts also. I ask myself whether this could be an interesting point to think about. I was very impressed by that, and I feel a little bit lost also about it.*

A. F. [speaking with difficulty]: I do feel that acting is necessary to the performance, to maintain the ambiguity of me/not me; to be "convincing" in some way, at least for a few moments; to produce a layering of conflicting positions that I think of as a kind of grotesque. For example, when I strip down as a woman but then, still in lingerie, start performing as a man, the effect does depend on how convincingly I can perform as a man, or at least perform my body differently.

I am not sure if this is your question, but what I'm hearing in your question is one of the perennial questions about institutional critique as a site-specific critique that locates itself solidly and self-consciously within the field and structures that it takes as its objects. For me that practice is partly rooted in a kind of pessimism about the possibility of there being any other way. It's not that I think there is no outside of the art world or its institutions; there is an outside. But my definition of art is that art is art if and when it exists for discourses and practices that can recognize and appropriate it as art—this is Bourdieu. So if it exists as art, it exists within these structures of power of the artistic field, and if it doesn't exist as art, then it doesn't have any impact on those structures of power. [Fighting back tears.] I mean, this could be a very long discussion. So what a lot of my work ends up being about are the underlying homologies that exist within the field of art between apparently opposed positions, and the relations of complicity those homologies support. I'm not interested so much in the cynicism of complicity, as if it's an attitude or choice or a moral failing or something of that sort. I see our participation in these relations of power as structural. But I also believe that this participation is facilitated by the interests and desires we invest in those relations.

J. H.: *That was really my question, your relation to the power system.*

Question from the audience: *I'm not sure that this is really a question, but somehow it came up in relation with this question. What's interesting to me about watching the video tonight is—I've seen other documentation of your work, I've never seen your performance work live, and what's interesting is your decision not to perform it live, it points out this certain thing about the way in which your work is site-specific, and maybe this is very dominant and I should have seen this a long time ago—but there's something that I appreciate and that I also find implicated in your question, which is that the site-specificity to me seems specifically about positions and a relational site-specificity. That it's not the site-specificity of a building, of an architecture, of a land, a location, a geography, but actually one of relation. And as much as it has existed in your work, I have not seen it in quite this way, and it makes a lot of sense to me.*

A. F. [nods]: I'm glad that that distinction between what I've called relational site-specificity and a more spatial or geographical site-specificity comes through. To some extent *Official Welcome* could be reduced to the list of names I ran off at the start of this discussion. But, for me, *Official Welcome* is less about performing those individual positions than about performing the relations between those positions and the homologies and contradictions and hierarchies that structure those relations. In non-performance projects I've tried to accomplish the same thing through a kind of mapping of positions. Sometimes this has been a mapping in physical space, like my audio installation for the Austrian pavilion in the Venice Biennale in 1993, or my installations of collections at the

Kunstverein in Munich or the Generali Foundation here in Vienna. Sometimes it is a mapping on a page, as with my Generali *Report*, which is composed of fragments of quotations from interviews with a range of people in different positions in the corporation and the foundation. My hope is that such mapping doesn't only produce a representation of those relations that one can reflect on, but also produces a dynamic reading or dynamic listening that impacts and implicates the position of the reader/listener as well.

Response from the audience: *...There's something very specific then about your choice, which I very much appreciate, of repetition within performance. A decision about whether to repeat a performance is linked to this mapping that you are suggesting. That is something that is very interesting to me in how terms of how performance exists particularly in an art context.*

U. M.: *I'm still working on my question, I'm not sure where to begin... But taking up what Judith said, I do see this five millimeter shift and maybe even more in the act of undressing and what that is to me, and also in the crying, I think.*

A. F. [blows her nose]: Wait, what was the first part?

U. M.: *The description of the power structure that is described as a stable one, that is not shifting—and then for me the act of undressing opens up something that adds up a completely different layer where I can link to the thing emotionally. And maybe it's not more than a kind of sadness that art presents itself in this stability—does this make sense or should I go on working on my question?*

A. F. [laughing]: I can work on the answer while you work on the question.

***U. M.** [also laughing]: Yes, let's do that.*

A. F.: The question of the stability of the structures that I am performing is a really good one. It's a question I have not thought enough about. I guess I intend a destabilizing to happen not in the performance itself so much as in the context—you know, maybe that's my answer—in the audience, or in the relationship between my position as a performer and the context.

***Question from the audience**: I'm interested in whether, by stripping, do you criticize the patterns of expectations people have towards women, that they should strip, symbolizing expectation patterns, or is it rather a criticism of exhibitionism in art, being used as a form in art?*

A. F.: There's an obvious dimension of quotation to the act of stripping and to the nudity in *Official Welcome*, first with reference to Vanessa Beecroft and then, more generally, to what I like to call the grand old tradition of nudie performance art. I used to joke that I'm not really nude because I'm in quotation marks. Of course, it's a tradition that's most associated with the work of women, or with women performing in works by male artists, that is, with female nudity, and most of the people I quote while I'm nude, particularly the artists I quote, are women. But in fact, taking all my clothes off has much more to do with, again, trying to [speaking with difficulty] escape an ironic reading of the performance. It's one of the points in the performance where the tension between the me/not me is hopefully most acute. Because, even if you're quoting, when you're standing naked in front of a bunch of people [laughing], *you're standing naked in front of a bunch of people*. It's not the body of any of the people I might be quoting standing there, it's my body standing there. I hoped that it would further complicate an assumption of my distance from the positions I am performing. I hoped crying would function that way as well. When I cry in *Official Welcome* I'm not quoting but speaking as myself. And while it is, of course, scripted and has been repeated and therefore cannot be considered spontaneous, I never feel that I'm "acting." Rather, I cry because what I'm saying, what I scripted myself to say, makes me cry. Acting would be stopping myself from crying at the moment. It's also an opportunity for a release of the accumulated tension of doing the performance. And it's probably also a way of absolving myself of some of the bitter aggressivity of the performance—one of the function of tears, according to some psychoanalysts. And as you can see from what happened here today, I actually have a history of crying when I speak in public [laughter mixing with tears], although usually unintentionally if not uncontrollably. The first time I performed *Official Welcome*, I did feel it to be a cathartic kind of experience and I think that may have had less to do with the nudity than with allowing myself to cry in public intentionally, rather than unintentionally.

U. M.: *Thank you, Andrea.*

A. F.: Thank you.

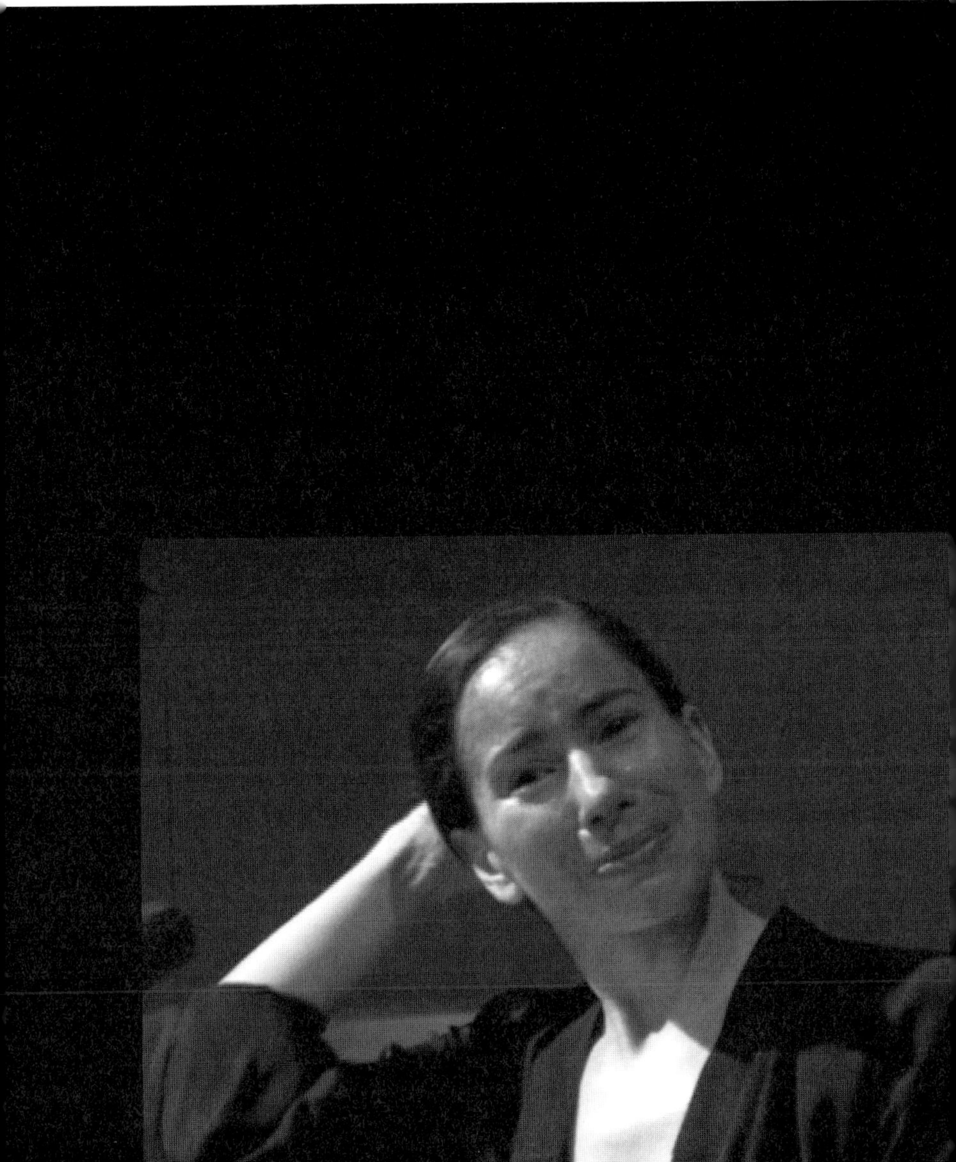

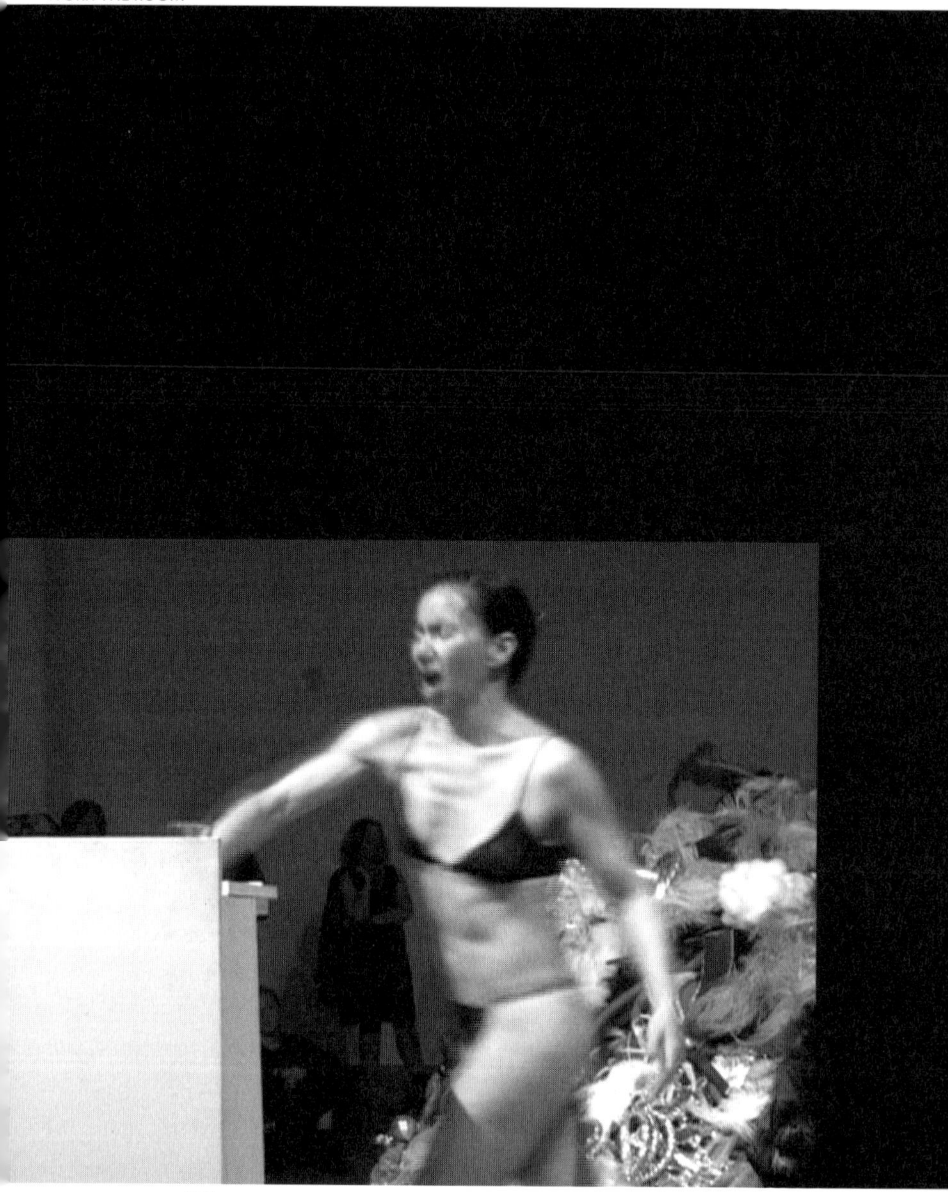

Andrea Fraser
Starting where she's standing

MUMOK, 27.09.2004

Einführung

Andrea Fraser geht zum Rednerpult und beginnt, das Publikum in einem seltsamen Quasideutsch anzusprechen. Nach etwa fünf Minuten unterbricht sie sich und spricht englisch.

Die Einleitung war der erste Teil meiner Performance *Kunst muss hängen* aus dem Jahr 2001. Sie basiert auf dem Transkript einer Rede von Martin Kippenberger – einer Art betrunkener Tischrede, die er 1995 in einem Ort namens „Club an der Grenze" im Burgenland hier in Österreich gehalten hat. Er hielt die Rede anlässlich der Eröffnung der ersten Ausstellung eines seiner besten Freunde, des Künstlers Michael Würthle, der vor allem als Besitzer der Paris Bar in Berlin bekannt ist.

Kunst muss hängen war die Performance, mit der ich begann, mich mit der Position der Künstlerin und des Künstlers auseinander zu setzen. Als ich Mitte der Achtzigerjahre mit Performance zu arbeiten begann, wurde ich bereits stark mit Institutionskritik und Neokonzeptualismus identifiziert, war aber auch sehr von feministischer Performance und feministischer psychoanalytischer Filmtheorie beeinflusst. Ich machte es zu meinem Projekt, diese beiden Traditionen und kritischen Modelle zu kombinieren und als Grundlage für den Versuch zu verwenden, eine Performancepraxis zu entwickeln, die sich kritisch mit verschiedenen Orten befasst. Beeinflusst von Feminismus und Psychoanalyse, beinhaltete mein Ortsbegriff jedoch nicht nur physische, architektonische oder geografische Plätze und Räume, sondern auch die oft ebenso an Orte gebundenen Diskurse und Rituale, die soziale und zwischenmenschliche Beziehungen rahmen. Orte sind in diesem Sinne auch Situationen – Situationen, die oft selbst Formen sozialer und öffentlicher Auftritte bedingen, wie etwa die Situation der Konferenz oder des Vortrags, der Ausstellungseröffnung, der Museumsführung oder der Tischrede. Ich begann, diese Orte und Situationen nicht nur als Rahmenbedingungen von Beziehungen zu denken, sondern als Orte der Produktion und Reproduktion dieser Beziehungen sowie der Produktion entsprechender Subjektpositionen – welche wiederum Formen von Subjektivität fordern – und schließlich der Körper, die diese Formen von Subjektivität verinnerlicht haben.

Was die Praxis betrifft, entwickelte sich mein Zugang zu Performance stark aus den in den 1980ern weit verbreiteten Strategien der Appropriationskunst. Mein Interesse an Appropriation hatte allerdings weniger mit der Problematik von Autorschaft und Originalität zu tun als vielmehr mit dem Potenzial für ortsspezifische Interventionen, das performative Formen von Appropriation zu bieten versprachen. Mit meiner sehr frühen Arbeit als „Institutionskritikerin" bewegte ich mich weg von der Appropriation kunsthistorischer Bilder und Texte hin zur Appropriation institutioneller Formen und Formate – der Ausstellungsbroschüre, des Museumsposters. Ein anderer Wendepunkt war, als ich Mitte der Achtzigerjahre über Louise Lawlers Arbeit schrieb. Lawlers frühe Arbeiten bezogen oft etwas ein, das ich als die Appropriation von Positionen und Funktionen im Feld der Kunst zu betrachten lernte: als Öffentlichkeitsarbeiterin, die Einladungen ausschickt und Streichholzbriefchen produziert, als Kuratorin, die in Installationen die Arbeit anderer Künstlerinnen und Künstler präsentiert, et cetera. Beeinflusst von Lawlers Arbeit, begann ich, mich sozusagen von der Appropriation institutioneller Formen und Formate zur Appropriation von Positionen und Funktionen in Museen und Galerien zu bewegen. Dies führte zu Liveperformances in Form von Museumsführungen, Verkaufspräsentationen in einer Galerie, akademischen Paneldiskussionen (mit der Gruppe The V-Girls) und Eröffnungsreden, aber auch zu

Projekten und Installationen, in denen ich die Funktionen einer Kuratorin, Beraterin, Vermittlerin et cetera aufführte. Nach etwa 15 Jahren der Arbeit damit hatte ich es geschafft, mir die Positionen von Sammlerinnen und Sammlern, Händlerinnen und Händlern, Dozentinnen und Dozenten, Museumsvermittlerinnen und -vermittlern, Kuratoriums- und Vorstandsmitgliedern, Kuratorinnen und Kuratoren sowie Kunstjournalistinnen und -journalisten – die Liste könnte fortgesetzt werden – anzueignen oder mich auf andere Art damit zu befassen.

In den späten Neunzigern begann ich jedoch, meine Aufmerksamkeit auf die Position der Künstlerin respektive des Künstlers selbst zu richten, und *Kunst muss hängen* war meine erste Arbeit in diese Richtung. Heute würde ich gerne ein Video meiner Performance zeigen, die ich gerade im Hamburger Kunstverein zur Eröffnung einer Retrospektive auf 20 Jahre meiner Arbeit aufgeführt habe. Diese Performance mit dem Titel *Official Welcome* war ursprünglich von den New-Yorker Sammlern Barbara and Howard Morse beauftragt und 2001 erstmals in deren Wohnzimmer aufgeführt worden. *Official Welcome* ist die einzige Performance, die ich an mehr als einem Ort aufgeführt habe, und ich hatte überlegt, sie auch heute hier aufzuführen. Das wäre jedoch letztendlich nicht mehr als eine Vorführung – wie das kleine Stück, der kleine Ausschnitt, Auszug aus *Kunst muss hängen*, mit dem ich diese Einführung begonnen habe. Obwohl *Official Welcome* keines spezifischen physischen Ortes bedarf, muss doch eine spezifische Art von Situation gegeben sein: eine Situation, in der eine Künstlerin oder ein Künstler geehrt wird, so wie ich das gewiss bei der Eröffnung meiner Retrospektive im Kunstverein in Hamburg wurde. Also beschloss ich, dass die Vorführung des Videos der Performance an diesem Ort die Bedeutung besser transportieren würde als die Wiederaufführung der Performance hier und heute.

Vielen Dank.

Das Skript von *Official Welcome* wurde veröffentlicht in:

Alexander Alberro (Hg.), *Museum Highlights: The Collected Writings of Andrea Fraser*. Cambridge, Massachusetts 2005.

Kunsthaus Dresden (Ausstellungskatalog), *Madonna*. Dresden 2005. (ins Deutsche übersetzt von Nikolaus G. Schneider)

Andrea Fraser, "Official Welcome", in: Documents, No. 24, Winter 2004.

Belkin Art Gallery (Ausstellungskatalog), *Exhibition: New Video Work by Andrea Fraser*. Vancouver 2004.

Kunstverein in Hamburg (Ausstellungskatalog), *Andrea Fraser, Works 1983 to 2003*. Köln 2003.

Andrea Fraser, "Official Welcome," in: The MICA Foundation Newsletter, Vol. 1, No. 2, 2001.

Andrea Fraser: [den Tränen nahe] Ich weiß nicht, ob ich viel über meine emotionale Verfassung sagen kann ... [beginnt zu weinen, fängt sich, lachend zum Publikum] Vielleicht öffne ich einfach das Podium für Fragen aus dem Publikum ... Ich brauche ein Taschentuch, ich bin gleich zurück. [kommt zurück, schnäuzt sich, humorvoll] Sie hätten gestern hier sein sollen, als Gregg Bordowitz über Affekte gesprochen hat ...

Ulrike Müller: *Danke, Andrea. [zum Publikum] Gibt es jemanden, der die erste Frage stellen möchte?*

Kaum verständliche Frage aus dem Publikum, die U. M. übersetzt: *Welche Künstler und Künstlerinnen haben Sie für Ihre Recherchen verwendet?*

A. F.: Das Skript zu *Official Welcome* ist mit Quellenangaben veröffentlicht worden. Nicht alle Stimmen sind bestimmte Personen – viele sind Hybride. Ich versuche nicht, die zitierten Personen darzustellen – wie etwa in meiner Performance als Martin Kippenberger. Im Grunde genommen, habe ich mit Text gearbeitet. Von allen zitierten Personen habe ich nur eine tatsächlich sprechen gehört: Benjamin Buchloh, auf dem die erste Stimme basiert. Es beginnt also mit Benjamin Buchloh über Thomas Hirschhorn – und ein bisschen über Gabriel Orozco und Richard Serra. Und dann kommt Thomas Hirschhorn, dem ein wenig Gabriel Orozco beigemengt wurde, [stimmt in das Lachen des Publikums ein] und dann Daniel Birnbaum über Thomas Hirschhorn. Und dann kommt eine Reihe anderer Kritiker über Orozco und dann über Matthew Barney und dann Shirin Neshat. Und dann, wenn es mir schwer fällt zu sprechen, basiert, was ich sage, auf Texten von Shirin Neshat, Ross Bleckner und Cy Twombly – eigentlich sage ich nicht viel. Es ist eine seltsame Mischung. Mein Auftritt ist ziemlich erfunden. Ich dachte dabei an einige abstrakte Expressionisten, die vielleicht tatsächlich litten und zu kämpfen hatten, aber schlussendlich auch die gesamte Ladung humanistischer Weltanschauung kauften. Und dann kommt Kirk Varnedoe.

„Arma virumque cano" ist Kirk Varnedoe, der in seiner Eröffnungsrede zur Cy-Twombly-Retrospektive im MoMA die ersten Zeilen der *Äneis* zitiert. Und dann kommt Varnedoe über Jasper Johns. Und dann eine Reihe anderer Leute, die über Julian Schnabel, Francesco Clemente und Ross Bleckner sprechen. Und dann kommt hauptsächlich Ross Bleckner, der Künstler mit der „sozialen Strategie", der erinnert werden möchte. Dann Dave Hickey über Francesco Clemente, dessen Guggenheim-Retrospektive er als „den elegantesten Schönheitssalon des Universums" beschreibt. Und dann Katy Siegel über Matthew Barney – der tatsächlich besser ist als wir. Ich habe hier das Geschlecht geändert, sodass die Beschreibung zu Vanessa Beecroft überleitet: „Es geht um Leere." Dann kommt größtenteils Larry Gagosian über Damien Hirst. Und dann Damien Hirst. Danach folgt eine Reihe anderer Sammler und Kritiker über verschiedene Künstler, was dann mit einer Kombination von jemandem über Nan Goldin und Bill Arning über Tracey Emin endet. Und dann kommt Tracey Emin – [lacht] nun bekommen Sie also die gesamte Liste. Ich hoffe bloß, es ist unterhaltsam. Dann kommt Tracey Emin, mit ein paar anderen Personen vermischt. Und dann C. Carr über Karen Finley, Lucy Lippard über Andres Serrano, Michael Kimmelman über Paul McCarthy und Maurice Berger über Kara Walker. Dann Kara Walker und dann Bill Clinton. [lacht mit dem Lachen des Publikums] Und dann komme ich, [lächelt] ich bin diejenige, die weint. Und dann kommt noch mal Bill Clinton, [lacht] der Gute Nacht sagt. Das sind also die Quellen.

Official Welcome war von den Sammlern Barbara und Howard Morse beauftragt worden, in deren Wohnzimmer in New York ich es im September 2001 zum ersten Mal aufführte. Ich begann diese erste Performance selbstverständlich damit, ihnen zu danken. Aber ich hatte sie auch darum gebeten, eine Seite über mich zu schreiben, was sie so sagen würden, wenn sie mich tatsächlich vorzustellen hätten. Nachdem ich mich also bei ihnen für ihre Unterstützung bedankt hatte, sprach ich als sie über mich selbst. Das war die ursprüngliche Einführung. Seither habe ich *Official Welcome* noch einige weitere Male aufgeführt und immer die Person, die mich eingeladen hat, gebeten, etwas für mich über mich zu schreiben, um es in eine neue Einführung aufzunehmen und somit die Arbeit etwas ortsspezifisch zu halten. Aber wie ich in meiner Einleitung schon gesagt habe, hatte ich in Hamburg keine Zeit dazu. [ergriffen, mühsam sprechend] Und so war ich tatsächlich ziemlich ernst.

[Frage aus dem Publikum, die nicht aufgezeichnet wurde.]

A. F.: Was überrascht Sie? Dass ich mixe?

Frau aus dem Publikum: *Ja, ja, dass Sie sich eigentlich selbst einbringen.*

A. F.: Eigentlich wäre ich froh, wenn ich mich selbst mehr einbringen könnte. Was ich über das Stück sage, [den Tränen nahe] ist nicht: „Das war knapp, es hätte mich auch erwischen können." Ich sage: „Es ist knapp." Ich meine, es erwischt mich auch. Ich sehe mich selbst als Bourdieuianerin, und ich zitiere gerne Bourdieu, der, eigentlich Bachelard zitierend, sagt, dass – wer wir sind – die Positionen, die wir einnehmen, sehr spezifisch und individuell sein mögen, sogar einzigartig, aber dass sie dennoch immer nur „bestimmte Momente des Möglichen" darstellen – Positionen, die in unserem bestimmten Feld zu einem bestimmten Zeitpunkt möglich sind. Meine Position als Künstlerin im künstlerischen Feld ist demnach also ein bestimmtes Beispiel der möglichen Positionen, die man einnehmen kann – als Künstlerin im künstlerischen Feld eben –, und das gilt auch für alle anderen Positionen, die ich in *Official Welcome* performe. Für mich ist das entscheidend. Weil Zitieren ebenso wie Humor seit langem Teil meiner Arbeit ist – vor allem in meinen Performances –, muss ich immer kämpfen, nicht in eine zu einfache Form von Ironie oder in ironische Distanz abzugleiten, was den Eindruck vermitteln könnte, ich wäre der Ansicht, mich selbst außerhalb oder jenseits [kämpft mit den Tränen, räuspert sich] der von mir verwendeten Strukturen zu befinden und von so einer externen Position aus artikulieren, vorführen und kritisieren zu können. Das glaube ich nicht. Während es also wesentlich für *Official Welcome* ist, dass ich viele der Personen, die ich performe, unmöglich sein könnte – zum Beispiel wenn es Männer sind –, ist es gleichermaßen wichtig, dass es mehrdeutige Momente gibt, in denen ich mich selbst beschreiben oder als ich selbst sprechen könnte – oder zumindest als „Andrea Fraser", so wie ich vielleicht gerne wahrgenommen werden würde.

Eine der schwierigsten Stellen in *Official Welcome* ist für mich, wenn ich Benjamin Buchloh zitiere. [sehr ergriffen, fängt sich, schnäuzt sich] Er ist eine der ganz wenigen Personen, von denen ich mir gewünscht habe, dass sie über meine Arbeit schreiben [lächelnd] – aber er hat es nie getan. Ihn also zu zitieren, als ginge es um mich, mit Worten, die beschreiben könnten, was ich mit meiner Performance beabsichtige, während er eigentlich über einen anderen Künstler spricht, ist ein zutiefst ambivalentes Stück Wunscherfüllung. *Official Welcome* ist eine zutiefst und schmerzhaft ambivalente Performance, die vieles enthält, was ich vielleicht lieber nicht zugeben würde, etwa Konkurrenz und Neid und Eifersucht und aggressive Vereinnahmung. Aber diese Dynamiken sind genauso zentral für die Struktur des Feldes wie die der Legitimation und andere – sagen wir mal: sublimiertere – Formen symbolischen Kampfes. Ich glaube nicht, dass es möglich ist, institutionelle Kritik fortzuführen, ohne diese problematisch subjektiven und intimen Formen der Ambivalenz zu berücksichtigen. Genau diese müssen kritisch einbezogen und in Bezug zu den institutionellen Strukturen „möglicher" Positionen gebracht werden. *Official Welcome* beschäftigt sich insbesondere mit dem Ausmaß, in dem solche Positionen geschlechtsspezifisch bleiben. Wenn ich Buchloh zitiere, müssen die Zuhörerinnen und Zuhörer in dem Moment, wenn ich das männliche Fürwort verwende, erkennen, dass ich nicht über mich selbst spreche. Der Künstler, der an dieser Stelle zelebriert wird, ist männlich.

***Judith Hopf**: Ich würde gerne eine Frage zu dem von Ihnen eingebrachten Begriff der Affirmation stellen. Am Anfang haben Sie sich als jemand beschrieben, die diese Strategie* *als Form der Kritik verwendet, und ich finde es beeindruckend, wie in dieser Arbeit das Machtsystem sichtbar wird, weil Sie es schauspielerisch so gut darstellen und weil Sie damit spielen. Ich habe mich beim Zusehen gefragt, ob es eine Grenze gibt, die aufgrund dieser Strategie der Affirmation unüberschreitbar ist. Sie anerkennen Macht und dekonstruieren sie zugleich – dadurch findet eine Verschiebung statt. Glauben Sie, dass der Affirmation Grenzen gesetzt sind?*

A. F.: Ich verstehe Ihre Frage nicht wirklich.

***J. H.**: Vielleicht können Sie Ihren eigenen Begriff von Affirmation im Bezug auf diese Performance beschreiben? Ich habe jetzt den Eindruck – es fällt mir auch schwer, englisch zu sprechen –, dass Sie diese Macht auf der gleichen Ebene akzeptieren, auf der Sie sie bekämpfen. Es gibt, wie Sie gesagt haben, diese Konkurrenz dazwischen, aber dann gibt es auch eine Grenze, weil ... wissen Sie, meinem Gefühl nach ist die Realität in diesem Machtsystem eigentlich genauso geschlechtsbestimmt. In Ihrer Arbeit gibt es keine andere Möglichkeit und keinen anderen Körper, sondern Sie erfüllen es gewissermaßen, Sie handeln innerhalb des Machtsystems. Verstehen Sie, was ich meine? Das ist nicht kritisch gemeint, sondern als Frage.*

A. F.: Ich bin mir noch immer nicht ganz sicher, was Ihre Frage ist. Aber ich nehme an, dass sie etwas mit einer Form von Ambivalenz zwischen Affirmation und Kritik zu tun hat.

***J. H.**: Und auch damit, den Glauben an das Machtsystem zu stärken, dass es unveränderlich ist – um nicht fünf Millimeter verschiebbar –, da Sie kein anderes Konzept einführen.*

A. F.: Oh, ich glaube, ich verstehe die Frage. Man könnte sagen, dass *Official Welcome* auf einer Art von Realismus basiert, und argumentieren, dass Realismus keine sehr effektive kritische Strategie ist, wenn das bedeutet, bloß bestimmte geschlechtsspezifische Machtstrukturen, die mit existierenden Formen institutioneller Vereinnahmung zu tun haben, in der Performance zu wiederholen. [kämpft gegen Tränen an] Und es klingt, als würden Sie außerdem finden, dass meine schauspielerischen Fähigkeiten die Kritik untergraben – oder sie zumindest untergraben könnten.

***J. H.**: Ich sage nicht, dass Ihr Können die Kritik stört. Ich finde, dass das Eindrucksvolle an Ihrer Performance ist, dass Sie wirklich die Machtstrukturen sichtbar werden lassen; irgendwie wird das Machtsystem durch die Aufführung hergestellt – es bedeutet für Sie Macht, und es ist auch schmerzhaft für Sie. Ich frage mich, ob das ein interessanter Punkt zum Nachdenken sein könnte. Ich war sehr beeindruckt davon und fühle mich zugleich ein wenig verloren.*

A. F.: [mit Mühe sprechend] Ich finde durchaus, dass das Schauspielen notwendig für die Performance ist, um die Ambiguität des Ich/Nichtich zu erhalten; um – zumindest für einige Momente – in gewisser Hinsicht zu „überzeugen"; um eine Überlagerung widersprüchlicher Positionen herzustellen, die ich auf eine Art grotesk finde. Wenn ich zum Beispiel als Frau strippe, aber dann – noch in Dessous – als Mann zu performen beginne, hängt die Wirkung durchaus davon ab, wie überzeugend ich einen Mann darstellen oder zumindest meinen Körper anders performen kann. Ich bin mir nicht sicher, ob das Ihre Frage ist, aber was ich aus der Frage heraushöre, ist eine der ewigen Fragen zur Institutionskritik als ortsspezifischer Kritik, die sich genau und bewusst in dem Feld und den Strukturen verortet, die sie zum Gegenstand hat. Für mich gründet diese Praxis zum Teil auf einer Art Pessimismus, was Alternativen betrifft. Nicht dass ich denken würde, es gäbe kein Außerhalb der Kunstwelt oder ihrer Institutionen – es gibt ein Außerhalb. Aber meine Definition von Kunst ist, dass Kunst Kunst ist, wenn sie für Diskurse und Praktiken existiert, die sie als Kunst erkennen und sich aneignen können – das ist Bourdieu. Was also als Kunst existiert, befindet sich innerhalb dieser

Machtstrukturen des künstlerischen Feldes, und wenn es nicht als Kunst existiert, hat es keinen Einfluss auf diese Machtstrukturen. [kämpft gegen Tränen an] Das könnten wir sehr lange diskutieren. Worum es letztendlich also in vielen meiner Arbeiten geht, sind die grundlegenden Homologien, die im Kunstfeld zwischen scheinbar gegensätzlichen Positionen existieren, und die Komplizenschaft, die von diesen Homologien gefördert wird. Mich interessiert weniger der Zynismus dieser Komplizenschaft, als ob es eine Haltung oder Entscheidung oder moralische Schwäche oder etwas Ähnliches wäre. Ich betrachte unsere Teilnahme an diesen Machtverhältnissen als strukturell. Aber ich glaube auch, dass diese Teilnahme durch die Interessen und das Begehren ermöglicht wird, die wir in diese Verhältnisse investieren.

J. H.: *Das war eigentlich meine Frage: Ihr Verhältnis zum Machtsystem.*

Frage aus dem Publikum: *Ich weiß nicht, ob dies wirklich eine Frage ist, aber irgendwie kam das im Zusammenhang mit dieser Frage auf. Was mich am Anschauen des Videos heute Abend interessiert – ich habe andere Dokumentationen Ihrer Arbeiten gesehen, aber nie eine Ihrer Performances live –, ist Ihre Entscheidung, nicht live zu performen, was zeigt, auf welche bestimmte Art Ihre Arbeiten ortsspezifisch sind. Vielleicht ist das sehr offensichtlich – und ich hätte es vor langer Zeit bemerken sollen –, aber da ist etwas, das ich schätze und das ich auch in Ihrer Frage enthalten finde, nämlich dass es bei der Ortsspezifik besonders um Positionen und um eine relationale Ortsspezifik zu gehen scheint. Dass es nicht um die Ortsspezifik eines Gebäudes geht, einer Architektur, eines Grundstückes, eines Ortes, einer Geografie, sondern vielmehr um eine der Relation. Und so sehr das auch in Ihrer Arbeit vorkam, habe ich es so noch nicht gesehen, und es erscheint mir sehr plausibel.*

A. F.: [nickt] Ich bin froh, dass die Unterscheidung zwischen dem, was ich relationale Ortsspezifik genannt habe, und einer eher räumlichen oder geografischen Ortsspezifik deutlich wird. Zu einem gewissen Grad könnte *Official Welcome* auf die Liste der Namen reduziert werden, die ich am Anfang der Diskussion genannt habe. Aber für mich geht es bei *Official Welcome* weniger um das Vorführen dieser Einzelpositionen als um das Aufführen der Relation zwischen diesen Positionen und um die Homologien und Widersprüche und Hierarchien, die diese Relationen strukturieren. In Projekten, die nicht performativ waren, habe ich versucht, das Gleiche durch eine Form von Mapping von Positionen zu erreichen. Das war manchmal ein Mapping im physischen Raum – wie in meiner Audioinstallation für den Österreichischen Pavillon auf der Biennale in Venedig 1993 oder in meinen Sammlungsinstallationen im Münchner Kunstverein oder in der Generali Foundation hier in Wien. Manchmal handelt es sich um ein Mapping auf einer Buchseite – wie etwa beim *Generali Report*, der aus Zitatfragmenten aus Interviews mit einer Reihe von Leuten in unterschiedlichen Positionen innerhalb des Unternehmens und der Foundation besteht. Meine Hoffnung liegt darin, dass ein solches Mapping nicht nur eine Repräsentation dieser Verhältnisse darstellt, über die man nachdenken kann, sondern dass dadurch zudem ein dynamisches Lesen oder dynamisches Zuhören erzeugt wird, das auch die Position des Lesers/Hörers beeinflusst und einbezieht.

Bandwechsel – kurze Unterbrechung.

Antwort aus dem Publikum: *... dann hat Ihre Entscheidung, in der Performance zu wiederholen, etwas äußerst Spezifisches, was ich sehr schätze. Die Entscheidung, ob eine Performance wiederholt wird, hängt mit diesem Mapping zusammen, das Sie anbieten. Das interessiert mich sehr im Bezug darauf, inwiefern Performance spezifisch im Kunstkontext verortet ist.*

U. M.: *Ich arbeite noch an meiner Frage, ich bin mir nicht sicher, wo ich anfangen soll ... aber um aufzugreifen, was Judith Hopf gesagt hat: Ich glaube, ich sehe diese fünf*

Millimeter oder vielleicht sogar mehr an Verschiebung durchaus im Akt des Entkleidens und darin, was das für mich bedeutet, und ebenso im Weinen.

A. F.: [schnäuzt sich] Einen Moment, bitte – was war der erste Teil?

U. M.: *Die Beschreibung der Machtstruktur, die als stabil beschrieben wird, sich also nicht verschiebt, und dann der Akt des Entkleidens eröffnen etwas, das eine ganz neue Ebene hinzufügt, in der ich mich mit der Sache emotional verbinden kann. Und vielleicht geht es um nicht mehr als eine Form von Traurigkeit darüber, dass Kunst sich selbst in dieser Unverrückbarkeit präsentiert – ergibt das Sinn oder soll ich weiter an meiner Frage arbeiten?*

A. F.: [lachend] Ich kann an der Antwort arbeiten, während Sie an der Frage arbeiten.

U. M.: *[ebenfalls lachend] Ja, das können wir so machen.*

A. F.: Die Frage nach der Beständigkeit der Strukturen, die ich performe, ist sehr gut. Über diese Frage habe ich nicht genug nachgedacht. Ich vermute, dass ich eine Destabilisierung weniger in der Performance selbst zu erreichen beabsichtige als vielmehr im Kontext – wissen Sie, vielleicht ist das meine Antwort –, im Publikum oder im Verhältnis zwischen meiner Position als Performerin und dem Kontext.

Frage aus dem Publikum: *Mich würde interessieren, ob Sie mit dem Entkleiden die Erwartungsmuster kritisieren, die Frauen gegenüber existieren – dass diese sich, Erwartungsmuster symbolisierend, ausziehen sollen –, oder geht es eher um eine Kritik am Exhibitionismus in der Kunst, der als eine Kunstform verwendet wird?*

A. F.: Es gibt eine offensichtliche zitathafte Dimension des Entkleidens und der Nacktheit in *Official Welcome*, zunächst als Referenz auf Vanessa Beecroft und dann – allgemeiner – auf das, was ich gerne als die große alte Tradition der „Nackedei-Performancekunst“ bezeichne. Ich habe auch schon gescherzt, dass ich nicht wirklich nackt bin, da ich in Anführungszeichen stehe. Natürlich ist das eine Tradition, die vor allem mit der Kunst von Frauen in Verbindung gebracht wird oder mit Frauen, die in Werken männlicher Künstler auftreten, also mit weiblicher Nacktheit; und die Mehrzahl der Personen, die ich zitiere, wenn ich nackt bin, vor allem aus dem Kunstbereich, sind Frauen. Aber all meine Kleider auszuziehen hat wiederum tatsächlich viel mehr mit dem Versuch zu tun, [mit Mühe sprechend] einer ironischen Lesart der Performance zu entkommen. Das ist einer der Momente der Performance, wo die Spannung zwischen mir und nicht mir hoffentlich am stärksten ist. Auch wenn man zitiert: Wenn man nackt vor einer Gruppe von Menschen steht, [lachend] steht man nackt vor einer Gruppe von Menschen. Es sind nicht die Körper der Personen, die ich zitiere, die dort stehen, sondern es ist mein Körper. Ich hoffte, dass dadurch die Vermutung einer Distanz zu den aufgeführten Positionen zusätzlich verkompliziert wird. Ich hoffte, dass Weinen die gleiche Wirkung hätte. Wenn ich in *Official Welcome* weine, zitiere ich nicht, sondern äußere mich als ich selbst. Und während der Text natürlich vorher geschrieben worden ist und wiederholt aufgeführt wurde und daher nicht als spontan bezeichnet werden kann, habe ich nie das Gefühl zu schauspielern. Ich weine vielmehr, weil mich das, was ich sage, was ich selbst geschrieben habe, zum Weinen bringt. Zu schauspielern würde mich in diesem Moment vom Weinen abhalten. Es ist eine Gelegenheit, die vom Ausführen der Performance angestaute Spannung zu entladen ... Und vielleicht ist es auch eine Form, etwas von der bitteren Aggressivität der Performance loszuwerden – was einigen Psychoanalytikern zufolge eine der Funktionen von Tränen ist. Und wie Sie an dem, was heute Abend hier geschehen ist, sehen können, ist es tatsächlich Teil meiner Geschichte, beim Sprechen in der Öffentlichkeit zu weinen, [Lachen mischt sich mit Tränen] auch wenn es normalerweise unbeabsichtigt, wenn nicht gar unkontrolliert ist. Als ich *Official Welcome* das erste Mal aufführte, empfand ich es als eine Form kathartischer Erfahrung, und ich glaube, das mag weniger mit der Nacktheit zu tun gehabt haben als damit, dass ich mir vorsätzlich erlaubt habe, in der Öffentlichkeit zu weinen, statt es unbeabsichtigterweise zu tun.

U. M.: *Danke, Andrea.*

A. F.: Ich danke auch.

Übersetzt von Barbara Schröder

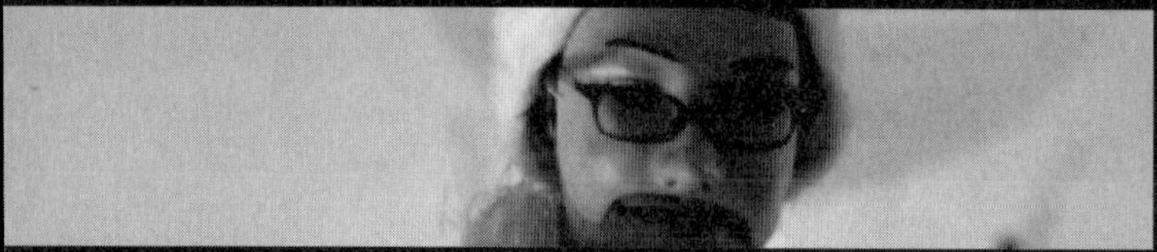

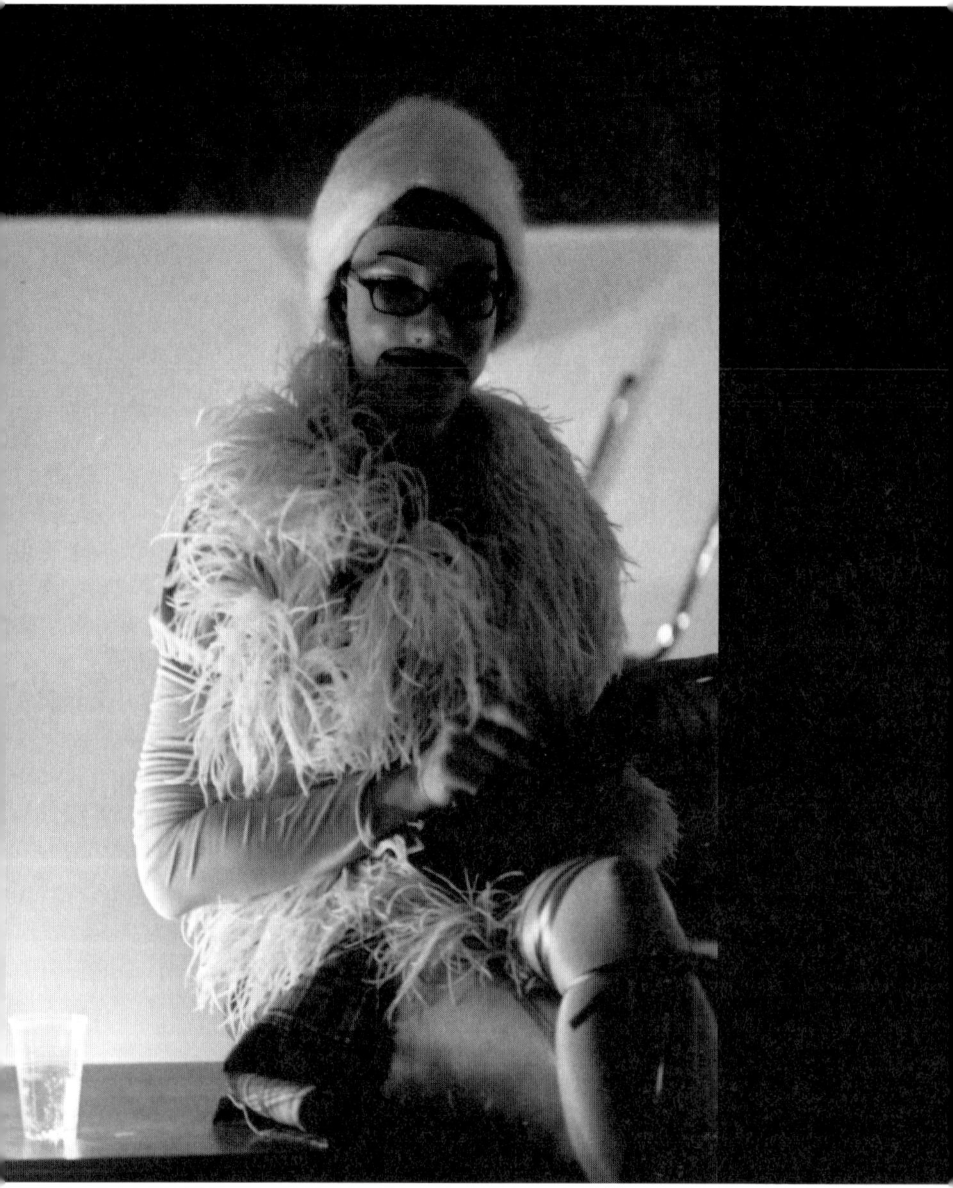

“In Exquisite Attire, the Rococo Stands Amok”

A Conversation Between Stephan Dillemuth and Achim Hochdörfer

Achim Hochdörfer: Your appearance in *Public Affairs* consisted of two parts: First, you gave an overview of your art work in a lecture-like presentation. Then at the symposium's conclusion we saw a very moving and amusing performance of your theatrical work *Improvisations on the Bassoon*,[1] in the royal stables behind the Museum Moderner Kunst (MUMOK) in Vienna's Museum Quarter. The piece was very appropriately set in a late Baroque *mise-en-scène* in which you built an improvised stage-set out of chairs stacked up on top of each other, candles, and other things.[2] Let's speak first about your talk during the symposium.

Stephan Dillemuth: I can hardly remember that first part, but what remains is a feeling that something screwed up there.

A. H.: At the beginning of the presentation you explicitly emphasized that what you were doing was not a performance. Yet nonetheless, during the subsequent course of your presentation, you played with various aspects of the history of happenings and performance art: you quoted John Cage, and you attempted to activate the public, to animate it, to break out of its institutionally determined role.

S. D.: Yes, that was a mistake. I wanted to avoid the possibility that my lecture, within the framework of a symposium on the topic of "Performance as Political Acts," would automatically be perceived as a "performance." Of course, this interpretation offers itself, especially when one stands on the stage as an artist. My announcement that "this is not a performance" intended to make this moment explicit; at the same time, I risked that my lecture would all the more—or precisely just for this reason—be misunderstood as a performance. Therefore I suggested to the public to go ahead and imagine itself in the role of the performer, to see itself as part of a collective sit-and-listen performance. However, through playing with this notion, I confused myself so much that my actual lecture became unconcentrated and stagnant. On top of that, as if to perfect my stupidity, I subsequently suggested to the public to break out of the performance prescribed by me. That was at the point when I was talking about *Corporate Public* and dramatization. I hoped that something like an occupation of the stage could take place.

A. H.: Was your stage appearance really aimed at provoking an occupation of the stage?

S. D.: That was a metaphor, for the occupation of reality.

A. H.: I actually believe that your lecture did not simply go awry, but that the apparent accidentalism and uncouthness of your appearance were altogether programmatic. You switched between a theoretically-elaborated, meta-artistic position—you speak at one point of your "role of professor"—and intentionally inserted theatrical or performative moments. From the beginning your lecture is thereby set up to get entangled in these contradictions: You refer to existing *topoi* of the performance tradition, and simultaneously distance yourself from them.

S. D.: Apart from the fact that in this case I tripped myself up, I indeed have an interest in bringing performance, research, and communication together or having them compete against each other in different roles. I am also tempted to try out things that have actually been checked off.

A. H.: Your art practice seems to me in a basic way conceived as something consciously pieced together. During your lecture alone, you worked with models, diagrams, with personal impressions, with theatrical moments in which the roles are constantly changing. In your artistic production, intellectual movement is continually displayed and brought to the fore; the theoretical assumptions and conceptual movements themselves are exposed, the brittleness and composite nature of your system are revealed. Following Lévi-Strauss, one could speak of a kind of "intellectual bricolage," which you performatively execute.

S. D.: If art has to do with reversing the division between scientific and mythic-artistic means of understanding, and with returning sensuality to a scientific mode of thought, then I would be d'accord with Lévi-Strauss' concept of "bricolage". In contrast to an engineer who, following the parameters of greatest efficiency, attempts to eliminate the traces of his working- and thinking-processes in order to be able to present a resolved end-product, the handicrafting amateur consciously accentuates the imponderable, accidental, and combinatory aspects of his intellectual production. But in the case of Lévi-Strauss, the hobbyist in his handicrafting is unfortunately subjected to the ethnologist's cultivated gaze. This naiveté attributed by the ethnographic stance bothers me.

A. H.: Could your work with performative forms perhaps be characterized as an allegorization, a revision of activist performative practices of the 1960s, in analogy to institutional critique? You distance yourself from the naiveté and unmediatedness of avant-garde escape fantasies, while at the same time you attempt to salvage their sociopolitical objectives.

S. D.: Okay, if you as a critic want to describe it like that. But I cannot go to work with such an intention. In the case at hand, I simply wanted to try out reversing the projections and expectational attitudes, and turn the performative element around, pointing it toward the audience. Also in order to let them feel how we are all prescribed a passive role of consuming, looking, and listening within this "society of the spectacle." However, through this trick, up on the stage there, I experienced a completely unexpected expansion of my power over the audience, and the consequences were uncanny to me. Because I could have—or would have had to—go far beyond affronting the spectators, in order to motivate the audience to violate its passive role. Now I could no longer simply let my lecture roll, but I also could not figure out how to make the provoked situation really productive. With productive here I do not mean occupation of the stage, but rather the transparency of a theatrical model for the purpose of artistic reflection.

A. H.: What would such a productive employment of a theatrical model look like? You spoke about the nineteenth-century workers' theater. Which sort of perspective are you hoping to gain there?

S. D.: I was reporting about my two-part research project in Norway: *The Academy and the Corporate Public*, and *Art Production in a Dramatized Field*. In short, they are driven by questions about the extent to which artistic means can be used as a form of dramatization within the creative field, in order to develop a self-reflective visual-perceptual and organizational model, that would then—possibly interventionally—help rewrite social-corporate stagings. The workers' theater of the 1870s and '80s captured my interest precisely because the workers in their self-organized clubs did not imitate bourgeois theater, but rather developed a kind of theater that involved mutual agitation and education. In addition, it was of course recreational fun and entertainment. Conventional plays were not written in these clubs, nor were already-existing pieces staged. It was more like evenings of music and entertainment, with songs, live spectacles, and improvised staged dialogues, for example about Karl Marx's recently published *Capital*. All of that was not in a strict sense class struggle, but rather self-enlightenment, a means of creating class-consciousness. It did not take place on the basis of a party doctrine dictated from above, but instead playfully from below, from the political base. I am invested in producing such a class-consciousness within the art field that would enable us to reflect on our own situation and our own possibilities—but you know how hopeless that is.[3]

A. H.: Does not the idealized image of an oppressed class resonate in your description of these workers' theaters, a class that on its own takes in hand its emancipation from the shackles of dominant relations—and the idea that this free and originary impulse would finally be brought to a halt by the Party, that is by processes of regimentation and institutionalization? To ask this question in a different way: Does your resorting back to the model of these workers' theaters, to something like a utopia of the past, link up with a concrete social and political perspective for the present?

S. D.: Utopias are actually there to ignite the desire for an improvement of social conditions. By the way, my knowledge about the workers' theater was supplied by a work of Peter von Rüden's[4] that proved to be relevant for me in many respects—historically speaking, because there was indeed a point at which the workers' movement might have been able to create its own notion of culture through sociably organized self-education. That was effectively botched at the time, as the Party found it more appropriate to communicate bourgeois values to the workers— Goethe, Schiller, and all of that.

Considering my interest in the academy and theater, it seems to me worthwhile to point out how collective play became a medium for reflecting upon and appropriating knowledge. It was like fathoming common possibilities—to try out agitational techniques, and attempt to create class-consciousness—before one supposedly unanimously confronts the outside world and takes political action.

I see all of this—then as now—in contrast to the self-appointed enlighteners, most of them of bourgeois origin, who want to make "political art." In any case, such a general addressing of a culturally bourgeois public is even less effective today than it already was then. But in relation to an increasingly fragmented and segmentary public, this early workers' theater provides illustrative material about how self-reflection and self-organization could be achieved with the help of a dramatizing play, and how the next step to be taken in common might look.

Finally—excuse me for being so long-winded here—in retrospect and with astonishment, I found a formal parallel with *Improvisations on the Bassoon*.

A. H.: Namely?

S. D.: Since I have no experience with theater, I had to go for an altogether simple option: As if in a rehearsal, the conversation between father and son is read off from a script by two performers, slips of the tongue are okay.

A. H.: And...?

S. D.: At the time when the first volume of *Capital* appeared, a man by the name of Schweitzer published a kind of summary in the newspaper *Social-Demokrat*. For this, he used the form of a dialogue, a kind of discussion between two people. The workers' clubs made use of this text, which had not been written for the stage at all, and put it on as a "reading drama" piece. For the next ten years, this was for many the only way to familiarize themselves with Marx's theories, as the book sold very poorly in the beginning. Schweitzer then also wrote a stage version especially for this purpose.

A. H.: Good, but I only see similarities in the fact that it is a dialogically constructed piece—and maybe in that it is read out loud... Do you know anything about its staging?

S. D.: No, but I would be very much interested in that.

A. H.: And how did you stage your piece?

S. D.: I have always performed the piece in an art context, and in the corresponding spaces. To demarcate the stage, I generally use what is available in the space. Candlelight is intended to give the scene a grotto-like or festive mood. The son is usually "adopted" on-site, he's often played by a woman, both of us wear face-masks, and as costumes we wear mostly whatever is found in the closet. I have only once used a theater for the performance. It even had a working-class history.[5] There also, the piece was staged for a small art audience. Although the conditions there were seemingly more suitable—a stage, lighting, etc.—it nevertheless did not work as well as in an art context. An effect of alienation results from the displacement of theater into the realm of visual arts—perhaps the allegorization that you mentioned earlier—and a point of view opens up that allows the artistic field's constructedness to appear as if it were a theater.

A. H.: Okay, let us return to MUMOK. The performance of *Improvisations on the Bassoon* seems to me to be an exemplification of your performance theory. In this miniature theater-piece with concertlike intermezzos, you sketch a bleak scenario: In the year 2033, the aging court painter Werner von Delmont and his son Hans-Dieter are looking back and conversing about the insidious and unstoppable decline of bourgeois society. Political developments of the 1980s and '90s—above all the collapse of the Soviet Union and the increasing process of globalization—appear as central markers along the way toward a final liquidation of a critical political general public, ending up with a "global and new absolutism" which you call "Corporate Rococo." *Improvisations on the Bassoon* can be interpreted as if it were a terminal stanza devoted to institutional critique, with all its futile attempts at saving a critical Modernism. How would you evaluate the diagnoses that you handed over with your conception of a "Corporate Rococo" from today's perspective?

S. D.: Then, in 1996, the piece was in a way a sort of taking account of the '90s and the various artistic positions of that time.

A. H.: In what way an account-taking? Which positions were you objecting to?

S. D.: That was putting two and two together from allusions, and it would be tedious and misleading to concretely label that now and here. What is important is that diverse positions from the early 1990s had by that point in time either become academic or were so far infiltrated by the art market that one could without hesitation throw them straight onto the scrap-heap.

But it had also to do with an attempt to embroil these political and aesthetic positions in a new game, to observe them against the horizon of an economy striving toward totalization as if looking backwards, quasi-retrospectively. Yet I would by no means view this scenario as the concluding stanza of institutional critique or a critical general public, but rather as its being saved from limbo. The question is precisely how critique can survive, critique of and within a courtly state set on total appropriation. Should I now also answer your question as to how alarmed I am about how deeply we are already embedded in corporate absolutism? Actually it would interest me more to know what you think about that...

A. H.: I do not view these developments so apocalyptically. Above all I am not able to recognize the totalization or absolutization of our society which you describe, at least not to this degree of inevitability, given how enormously differentiated and highly complex our society is. The simplifying parallelization of capitalism and totalitarianism reminds me too much of the inescapable development in the direction of a "managed world," the "instrumental common sense" which critical theory prophesized in the 1940s.

This parallelization is indeed a prevailing motif of the political left—from Marx, through Lukács's reification theory, continuing up to the (in my view unspeakable) *Empire* of Hardt and Negri. I do not personally believe that one can adequately describe the development of Western society since 1945 using this range of intellectual tools. And if I perceive this correctly, then the whole philosophical effort that Jürgen Habermas pursued was in the service of unraveling the contradictions in which critical theory had entangled itself in the 1930s. In his attempt to save Modernism, he resorted back to the beginnings of the Enlightenment and the terminology of a political public sphere developed at that time, which, following the Revolution of 1848, became more and more diffusely defined. Hence, what consequences for your art work would arise if your political and social theory turned out to be too simple? Would this do any damage to your art practice, or would it not have any effect on them? Does this in the end mean that the autonomous field of art production is—structurally speaking—in fact precisely so socially irrelevant that no emancipatory movement can originate from it? To phrase the question polemically: What actually remains from *Improvisations on the Bassoon* if your political and social analyses are not quite correct?

S. D.: Achim, oh Achim! In fairy tales the beautiful girl is still named Bella, and King Neoliberalism reigns over the empire of global economy. But if you want, we can also start a political discussion—if this is motivated by my piece, then all the better. We must however distinguish between the play and its objectives. For it is not intended to develop any kind of scientific prognoses about the future of capitalism, nor to sell them as facts. Moreover it is also irrelevant whether the theses are correct or not, since what will one day remain of it all is in any case only a pile of rubble.

A. H.: On the basis of the scenery, the amateurish lecturing style, and the entertaining text as well, your piece is prone to a comedic lightness. As a listener, one is actually tempted to grin about the fact that all the political and cultural-theoretical exertions with which we are grappling have in fact proven themselves as pointless. In light of this ironical, consciously paradoxical structure, I ask myself if your cultural pessimism is ultimately an attitude.

S. D.: Which cultural pessimism are you actually speaking about?

A. H.: Well, the one where we are moving toward a hopeless, reified, corporate society in which any form of a critical public sphere will be dissolved.

S. D.: Precisely that is the matter in question—and in order to approach this *status quaestionis*, I use humorous performance as scientific method. I know the term "cultural pessimism" from the 1920s. At that time, it contributed to the rise of National Socialism, and nowadays it is slapped around the ears of everyone dealing with Neoliberalism and Neoconservatism in any kind of critical fashion. While writing the piece, to me a critique that would only bemoan the loss of the welfare state seemed too conservative. I wanted to confront these new givens, and playfully pushed the logic of Neoliberalism further, looking for possibilities in which a critical position could function within the courtly state of "Corporate Rococo."

A. H.: Then I would call this ironic nostalgia. Already in its form, your conception of the "Corporate Rococo" is nostalgic, or let's say, elegiac. One could describe the elegy as a literary form in which the present is always experienced in a past mode. Your salvaging recourse to emancipatory projects such as early Enlightenment bourgeois society or the nineteenth-century workers' theater is in this sense formulated from the perspective of unfulfillable yearning and failure. The decisive moment of workers' theater does exactly not turn up in your conception: It arises from the proletarian class itself, and finds a form. If I speak polemically of a cultural-political attitude, I mean to say that you on the one hand flirt with the radical political implications of such regressions, but on the other ignore the present-tense requirements for their concrete realization. Or, to put it another way: Whenever you refer back to the late nineteenth-century workers' theater in the performative lecture and the formulation of your allegorical performance theory—that is, you refer to a set of instruments of active political emancipation and change—you actually end up eliminating the hope for real political interventions.

S. D.: Veto! It is you who speaks, on the one hand, of allegories while at the same time assigning me a one-to-one relationship with the workers' theater, which leads you to conclude—because this cannot work within your analogy—that it must be entirely unserious, that is to say ironical... But what is the workers' theater for me, in fact? Nothing other than a good historical example for self-organization, auto-reflection, and self-generated agitation, as I would like to see these three elements more strongly shaping our fragment of the art public. Only then can art aim for more change within a broader social context! But first, behind all of that stands the question whether we, as artists—and critics—can take up the new tasks that a transforming public sphere bring along with it:

In exquisite attire, the Rococo stands amok,
Brocades and coquillages to the helm,
Announcing the start of a sparkling epoch
Of the Coin in the global realm.

Well, artists, where are you, are you also fit
And fully prepared its charmes
To assault? Yet, oh! I would feel the pity of it
Were you to perish at last in its armes.

Translated by Julia Bernard

Notes:

1. To be found in Werner von Delmont, *Corporate Rokoko and the End of the Civic Project* (Copenhagen: Pork Salad Press, 2035).
2. See illustration below and page 220.
3. What is interesting is how this workers' theater ended: on the one hand, it was discredited by the Party as a waste of time, because the workers should carry out party-work. On the other hand, the workers' theater was professionalized by the literati of naturalism and taken up into the roundelay of bourgeois theater: Workers' life was set on the stage and their sentiments played by professional actors for a—no longer proletarian—public of upwardly mobile employees. This type of theater did not interest the workers themselves.
4. Peter von Rüden, *Sozialdemokratisches Arbeitertheater (1848-1914)* (Frankfurt/Main: Athenäum, 1973). An English summary can be found online at: *http://www.societyofcontrol.com/coal/workerstheater.htm* [2005-10-05].
5. Hoxton Hall in London.

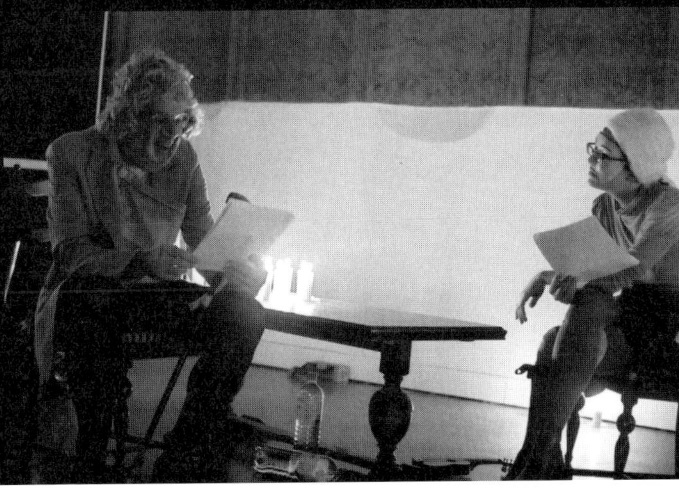

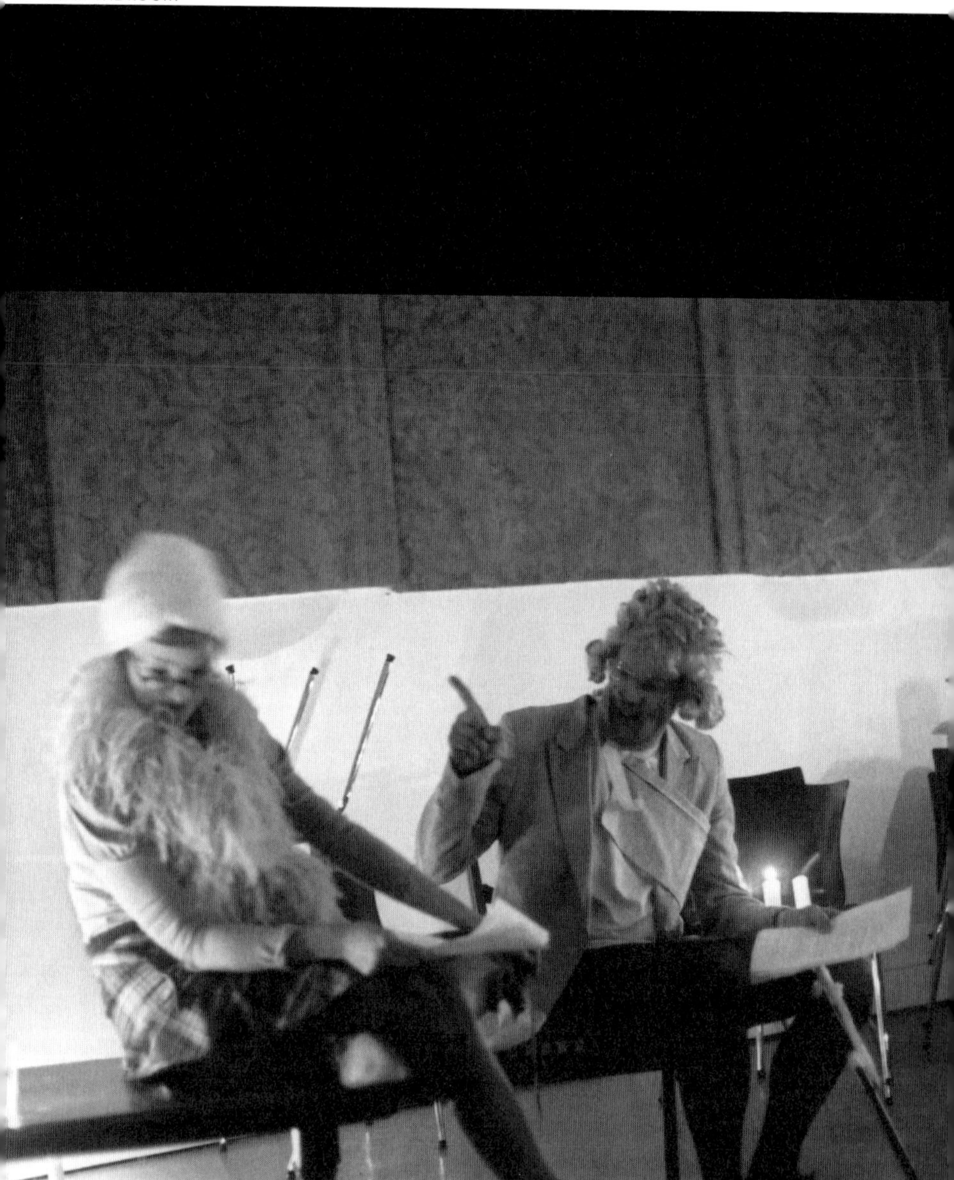

„Der Rokoko steht lachend im köstlichen Kleid"

Ein Gespräch zwischen Stephan Dillemuth und Achim Hochdörfer

Achim Hochdörfer: Dein Auftritt bei *Öffentliche Angelegenheiten* bestand aus zwei Teilen. Zunächst hast du in einer vortragsähnlichen Präsentation einen Überblick deiner künstlerischen Arbeit gegeben. Zum Abschluss des Symposiums kam es dann zu einer sehr stimmungsvollen und lustigen Aufführung deines Theaterstücks *Improvisationen auf dem Fagott*[1] in den Hofstallungen hinter dem Museum Moderner Kunst im MuseumsQuartier – passend zum Stück also in einer spätbarocken Szenerie, in der du ein improvisiertes Bühnenbild aus übereinander gestapelten Stühlen, Kerzen und anderem aufgebaut hast.[2] Lass uns zuerst über deinen Auftritt während des Symposiums sprechen.

Stephan Dillemuth: An den ersten Teil kann ich mich kaum noch erinnern, aber es verblieb das Gefühl, dass da ziemlich was in die Hose gegangen ist.

A. H.: Gleich zu Beginn der Präsentation betonst du ausdrücklich, dass es sich bei dem, was du tust, nicht um eine Performance handelt. Und dennoch spielst du im weiteren Verlauf deiner Präsentation mit verschiedenen Aspekten der Geschichte von Happening und Performance: Du zitierst Cage, versuchst, das Publikum zu aktivieren, animierst es, aus den institutionell verordneten Rollen auszubrechen.

S. D.: Ja, das war ein Fehler. Ich wollte vermeiden, dass man meinen Vortrag im Rahmen eines Symposiums zum Thema „Performance als politisches Handeln" automatisch als

Performance ansieht. Vor allem wenn man als Künstler auf der Bühne steht, bietet sich eine solche Sichtweise an. Meine Ankündigung: „Dies ist keine Performance", wollte dieses Moment begreifbar werden lassen; zugleich riskierte ich, dass mein Vortrag aber umso mehr – oder gerade nun erst recht – als Performance missverstanden wird. Deshalb schlug ich dem Publikum vor, sich doch nun selbst in die Rolle der Performer zu imaginieren – sich als ein Teil einer kollektiven Sitz- und Zuhörperformance zu sehen. Durch das Spiel mit diesen Vorstellungen hatte ich mich selbst aber so weit aus dem Konzept gebracht, dass mein eigentlicher Vortrag unkonzentriert und stockend wurde. Zu allem Überdruss, wie um meine Blödheit perfekt zu machen, schlug ich dem Publikum später vor, aus dieser von mir verordneten Performance auszubrechen. Das war an dem Punkt, als ich über *Corporate Public* und Dramatisierung redete. Ich hoffte, so etwas wie eine Bühnenbesetzung könnte nun stattfinden.

A. H.: War dein Auftritt wirklich auf eine Bühnenbesetzung angelegt?

S. D.: Das war eine Metapher – für die Besetzung der Wirklichkeit.

A. H.: Ich glaube ja, dass dein Vortrag nicht einfach schief gelaufen ist, sondern dass die scheinbare Zufälligkeit und Flapsigkeit deines Auftritts durchaus Programm sind. Du changierst zwischen einer theoretisch erläuternden, metakünstlerischen Position – du spricht einmal von deiner „Rolle des Professors" – und gezielt eingestreuten theatralischen beziehungsweise performativen Momenten. Dein Vortrag ist damit von vornherein so angelegt, dass du dich in diese Widersprüche verstrickst: Du berufst dich auf bestehende Topoi der Performancetradition und distanzierst dich gleichzeitig von ihnen.

S. D.: Abgesehen davon, dass ich mir in diesem Falle selbst ein Bein gestellt hatte, gibt es tatsächlich das Interesse, Performance, Forschung und Vermittlung miteinander zu verbinden beziehungsweise sie in verschiedenen Rollen gegeneinander antreten zu lassen. Es reizt mich auch, Dinge auszuprobieren, die man eigentlich schon abgehakt hat.

A. H.: Deine Kunst scheint mir von Grund auf als etwas bewusst Zusammengestückeltes konzipiert zu sein. Allein während deines Vortrags arbeitest du mit Modellen, Diagrammen, mit persönlichen Eindrücken, mit theatralischen Momenten, in denen Rollenbilder immer wechseln. In deiner künstlerischen Produktion findet ein ständiges Ausstellen und Hervorkehren der intellektuellen Bewegung statt; die theoretischen Annahmen und gedanklichen Bewegungen werden selbst bloßgelegt, die Brüchigkeit und Zusammengesetztheit deines Systems offen gelegt. Mit Lévi-Strauss könnte man von einer Art „intellektueller Bastelei“ sprechen, die du performativ vorträgst.

S. D.: Wenn es in der Kunst darum geht, die Trennung zwischen wissenschaftlicher und mythisch-künstlerischer Erkenntnisweise rückgängig zu machen und der wissenschaftlichen Denkweise ihre Sinnlichkeit zurückzuerstatten, dann bin ich mit Lévi-Strauss' „bricolage“-Begriff d'accord. Im Gegensatz zum Ingenieur, der nach Maßgabe größtmöglicher Effizienz die Spuren seines Arbeits- und Denkprozesses zu eliminieren sucht, um ein schlüssiges Endprodukt vorstellen zu können, hebt der Bastler das Unwägbare, Zufällige und Kombinatorische seiner gedanklichen Produktion bewusst hervor. Aber bei Lévi-Strauss ist der Bastler in seiner Bastelei leider dem kultivierten Blick des Ethnologen unterworfen. Diese zugewiesene Naivität stört mich am ethnografischen Ansatz.

A. H.: Könnte man deine Auseinandersetzung mit Formen der Performance vielleicht als eine Allegorisierung, als eine der Institutionskritik vergleichbare Revision der aktivistischen performativen Praxis der Sechzigerjahre bezeichnen? Du distanzierst dich von der Unschuld und Unmittelbarkeit der avantgardistischen Ausbruchsfantasien, versuchst aber gleichzeitig, ihre gesellschaftspolitischen Zielsetzungen zu retten.

S. D.: Gut, wenn du das als Kritiker so beschreiben willst. Aber ich kann nicht mit so einem Vorhaben an die Arbeit gehen. Im vorliegenden Falle wollte ich es einfach einmal ausprobieren, die Projektionen und Erwartungshaltungen umzudrehen, und das performative Element aufs Publikum wenden. Auch um erfahrbar werden lassen, wie uns allen in dieser „Gesellschaft des Spektakels" eine passive Rolle des Konsumierens, Zuschauens, Zuhörens verordnet ist. Durch diesen Trick erfuhr ich aber dort oben auf der Bühne einen ganz unerwarteten Zuwachs an Macht über das Publikum, und das wurde mir in seiner Konsequenz unheimlich. Denn ich hätte weit über die Zuschauerbeschimpfung hinausgehen können – oder müssen –, um das Publikum zum Durchbrechen seiner verordneten passiven Rolle zu bewegen. Jetzt konnte ich meinen Vortrag nicht einfach nur mehr abrollen lassen, aber die provozierte Situation konnte ich auch nicht richtig produktiv machen. Produktiv meint hier nicht die Bühnenbesetzung, sondern die Anschaulichkeit des Modells Theater für künstlerische Reflexion.

A. H.: Wie könnte ein solch produktiver Gebrauch des Modells Theater aussehen? Du sprachst über das Arbeitertheater des 19. Jahrhunderts. Welche Perspektive versprichst du dir davon?

S. D.: Ich berichtete von meinem zweiteiligen Forschungsprojekt in Norwegen: *The Academy and the Corporate Public* und *Art Production in a Dramatised Field*. Kurz gesagt, geht es mir dabei um die Frage, inwieweit man künstlerische Mittel als eine Form der Dramatisierung im künstlerischen Feld dazu benutzen kann, ein selbstreflexives Anschauungs- und Organisationsmodell zu entwickeln, um dann – eventuell interventionistisch – gesellschaftlich-corporate Dramaturgien umzuschreiben. Das Arbeitertheater in den 1870er- und 1880er-Jahren war für mich deswegen so interessant, weil die Arbeiter in selbst geschaffenen Klubs eben kein bürgerliches Theater nachahmten, sondern ein Theater machten, das gegenseitige Agitation und Ausbildung bedeutete. Zudem war es natürlich auch Freizeitspaß und Unterhaltung. Es wurden da aber keine Stücke im herkömmlichen Stil geschrieben oder bereits bestehende Stücke aufgeführt, eher waren das improvisierte bunte Abende mit Gesang, lebende Bilder und improvisiert aufgeführte Dialoge, zum Beispiel über das eben erschienene *Kapital* von Karl Marx. All das war nicht im eigentlichen Sinne Arbeiterkampf, sondern Selbstaufklärung, ein Mittel, um Klassenbewusstsein zu schaffen. Dies geschieht aber nicht aufgrund einer von oben verordneten Parteidoktrin, sondern spielerisch, von unten, von der Basis. Es wäre mir daran gelegen, so ein Klassenbewusstsein im künstlerischen Feld zu erzeugen, das uns befähigt, die eigene Situation und die eigenen Möglichkeiten zu reflektieren – aber du weißt, wie aussichtslos das ist.[3]

A. H.: Schwingt in deiner Beschreibung des Arbeitertheaters nicht das idealisierte Bild einer unterdrückten Klasse mit, die aus freien Stücken ihre eigene Emanzipation aus den Fesseln der herrschenden Verhältnisse in die Hand nimmt – und die Ansicht, dass dieser freie und ursprüngliche Impuls schließlich nur von der Partei, von Reglementierungs- und Institutionalisierungsprozessen gestoppt wurde? Anders gefragt: Verbindest du mit deinem Rückgriff auf das Modell des Arbeitertheaters, eine quasi rückwärts gewandte Utopie, heute eine konkrete gesellschaftliche und politische Perspektive?

S. D.: Utopien sind ja dazu da, den Wunsch nach einer Verbesserung der gesellschaftlichen Umstände zu befeuern. Im Übrigen habe ich mein Wissen über das Arbeitertheater aus einer Arbeit von Peter von Rüden[4] bezogen, die sich mir in mehrfacher Hinsicht als relevant erwies:

Historisch, weil die Arbeiterbewegung wohl an einem Punkt war, wo sie durch gesellig organisierte Selbsterziehung durchaus einen eigenen Kulturbegriff hätte schaffen können. Das wurde damals nachhaltig vermasselt, denn die Partei hielt es für angemessener, den Arbeitern die bürgerlichen Werte zu vermitteln, Goethe, Schiller, Wagner und all das.

In Hinblick auf mein Interesse an Selbstorganisation von Akademie und Theater schien es mir bemerkenswert, wie das gemeinsame Spiel ein Mittel der Reflexion und Aneignung von Wissen wurde. Das war wie ein Ausloten gemeinsamer Möglichkeiten – ein Erproben agitatorischer Techniken, ein Versuch, ein Klassenbewusstsein zu schaffen –, bevor man geschlossen nach außen tritt und politisch handelt.

All dies sehe ich – damals wie heute – im Unterschied zu den selbst ernannten Aufklärern meist bürgerlicher Herkunft, die politische Kunst machen wollen. Allerdings ist so eine allgemeine Adressierung an eine kulturbürgerliche Öffentlichkeit heute noch ineffektiver, als sie es ohnehin schon war. Im Hinblick auf zunehmend fragmentierte und segmentierte Öffentlichkeiten liefert das frühe Arbeitertheater aber Anschauungsmaterial, wie Selbstreflexion und Selbstorganisation mithilfe eines dramatisierenden Spiels erreicht werden können und wie der nächste gemeinsame Schritt aussehen könnte.

Schließlich – entschuldige, dass ich hier so ausführlich werde – habe ich auch rückblickend und mit Erstaunen eine formale Parallele zu *Improvisationen auf dem Fagott* gefunden.

A. H.: Nämlich?

S. D.: Weil ich gar keine Ahnung vom Theater habe, musste ich mich für eine ganz einfache Möglichkeit entscheiden: Wie bei einer Theaterprobe wird das Gespräch zwischen Vater und Sohn in verteilten Rollen vom Blatt abgelesen, Versprecher sind okay.

A. H.: Und?

S. D.: Beim Erscheinen des ersten Bandes von *Das Kapital* veröffentlichte ein Mann namens Schweitzer eine Art von Zusammenfassung in der Zeitung *Social-Demokrat*. Allerdings benutzte er dazu die Dialogform, also eine Art Diskussion zwischen zwei Leuten. Die Arbeiterklubs bedienten sich dieses Textes, der gar nie für die Bühne geschrieben war, und führten ihn als „Lesedrama" auf. Für die nächsten zehn Jahre war dies für viele der einzige Weg, sich mit den Theorien von Marx vertraut zu machen, denn das Buch verkaufte sich anfangs sehr schlecht. Schweitzer schrieb alsbald auch noch extra eine Bühnenversion dafür.

A. H.: Gut, aber Übereinstimmungen sehe ich nur in dem Fakt, dass es ein dialogisch aufgebautes Stück ist – und vielleicht abgelesen ... Weißt du etwas über dessen Inszenierung?

S. D.: Nein, würde mich aber sehr interessieren.

A. H.: Und wie hast du dein Stück inszeniert?

S. D.: Ich habe das Stück immer nur im Kunstkontext und in dementsprechenden Räumen aufgeführt. Zur Markierung der Bühne wurde meist das Inventar vor Ort verwendet. Kerzenschein sollte der Szene eine grottenartige oder auch feierliche Stimmung verleihen. Der Sohn wurde meist erst vor Ort „adoptiert", oft auch von einer Frau gespielt, beide trugen wir Gesichtsmasken, und als Kostüm hatten wir meist das, was man so im Kleiderschrank fand.

Nur einmal habe ich zur Aufführung ein Theater benutzt, sogar eines mit Arbeitergeschichte,[5] allerdings wieder nur für ein kleines Kunstpublikum. Obwohl ich da mit Bühne, Licht et cetera auf anscheinend günstigere Verhältnisse traf, hat es dennoch nicht so gut funktioniert wie im Kunstkontext. Denn durch die Verschiebung des Theaters in den Bereich bildende Kunst ergibt sich ein Verfremdungseffekt – vielleicht die Allegorisierung, die du erwähnt hast –, und es eröffnet sich ein Blick, der die Konstruiertheit des künstlerischen Feldes wie ein Theater erscheinen lässt.

A. H.: Ja, gehen wir zurück zum MUMOK. Dein zweiter Auftritt dort, die Aufführung von *Improvisationen auf dem Fagott*, scheint mir eine Exemplifikation deiner Performancetheorie zu sein. In diesem Miniaturtheaterstück mit konzertanten Einlagen entwirfst du ein düsteres Szenario: Im Jahr 2033 unterhalten sich der alternde Hofmaler Werner von Delmont und sein Sohn Hans-Dieter rückblickend über den schleichenden und unaufhaltsamen Niedergang der bürgerlichen Gesellschaft. Die politischen Entwicklungen der 1980er- und 1990er-Jahre – allen voran der Zusammenbruch der Sowjetunion und der zunehmende Globalisierungsprozess – erscheinen als zentrale Wegmarken einer endgültigen Liquidierung einer kritischen politischen Öffentlichkeit, hin zu einem „globalen und neuen Absolutismus", den du „Corporate Rokoko" nennst. *Improvisationen auf dem Fagott* liest sich wie ein Abgesang auf die Institutionskritik mit all ihren vergeblichen Versuchen einer Rettung einer kritischen Moderne. Wie würdest du aus heutiger Sicht die Diagnosen beurteilen, die du mit deiner Konzeption eines „Corporate Rokoko" abgibst?

S. D.: Damals, 1996, war das Stück einerseits eine Art Abrechnung mit den Neunzigerjahren und den verschiedenen künstlerischen Positionen dieser Zeit.

A. H.: Inwiefern eine Abrechnung? Gegen welche Positionen wendest du dich?

S. D.: Das war aus Andeutungen zusammengereimt, und es wäre öde und irreführend, das jetzt hier konkret zu benennen. Wichtig ist, dass die unterschiedlichen Ansätze der frühen 1990er zu diesem Zeitpunkt entweder akademisch geworden waren oder vom

Kunstmarkt so weit durchgenudelt, dass man sie getrost zum alten Eisen werfen konnte.

Aber es ging eben auch um einen Versuch, die politischen und ästhetischen Ansätze in ein neues Spiel zu verwickeln, sie nämlich vor dem Horizont einer zur Totalisierung strebenden Ökonomie quasi rückwärts blickend zu betrachten. Dieses Szenario würde ich aber keinesfalls als Abgesang auf Institutionskritik oder kritische Öffentlichkeit sehen, sondern als deren Errettung aus dem Fegefeuer. Die Frage ist doch, wie die Kritik an und in einem auf totale Appropriation gestellten Hofstaat überleben kann. Und soll ich nun auch noch auf deine Frage antworten, wie erschreckt ich darüber bin, wie tief wir schon im corporaten Absolutismus drinstecken? Es würde mich eigentlich mehr interessieren, was du darüber denkst ...

A. H.: Ich sehe die Entwicklung nicht so apokalyptisch. Vor allem kann ich die von dir beschriebene Totalisierung beziehungsweise Verabsolutierung unserer Gesellschaft, die ja eine enorm ausdifferenzierte und hochkomplexe ist, zumindest nicht in dieser Zwangsläufigkeit erkennen. Mich erinnert deine vereinfachende Parallelisierung zwischen Kapitalismus und Totalitarismus zu sehr an die ausweglose Entwicklung hin zu einer „verwalteten Welt", der „instrumentellen Vernunft", die die Kritische Theorie in den Vierzigerjahren prophezeit hat. Diese Parallelisierung ist ja ein durchgängiges Motiv der politischen Linken – von Marx über Lukács' Verdinglichungstheorie bis hin zu dem in meinen Augen unsäglichen *Empire* von Hardt/Negri. Ich persönlich glaube nicht, dass man mit diesem Instrumentarium die Entwicklung der westlichen Gesellschaften seit 1945 angemessen beschreiben kann. Und wenn ich richtig sehe, dann dient der ganze philosophische Aufwand, den Jürgen Habermas betreibt, dazu, die Widersprüche aufzulösen, in die sich die Kritische Theorie in den Dreißigerjahren verstrickt hat. In seinem Rettungsversuch der Moderne greift er auf die Anfänge der Aufklärungsbewegung und den damals entwickelten Begriff einer politischen Öffentlichkeit zurück, der dann nach der Revolution von 1848 mehr und mehr aufgeweicht wurde.

Also, welche Konsequenzen auf deine künstlerische Arbeit würden sich ergeben, falls sich deine politisch-gesellschaftliche Theorie zu simpel erweist? Schadet es deiner künstlerischen Praxis oder hat es keine Auswirkungen auf sie? Bedeutet das letztlich nur, dass das autonome Feld der künstlerischen Produktion – strukturell – eben doch gesellschaftlich so irrelevant ist, dass davon keine Emanzipationsbewegung ausgehen kann? Polemisch gefragt: Was bleibt eigentlich von *Improvisationen auf dem Fagott* übrig, wenn deine politisch-gesellschaftlichen Analysen so nicht stimmen?

S. D.: Achim, ach, Achim! Im Märchen heißt das schöne Mädchen eben Bella, und es regiert der König Neoliberalismus im Reich der globalen Münze. Aber wenn du willst, können wir hier auch eine politische Diskussion beginnen – wenn sie von dem Stück motiviert wird, dann umso besser. Wir müssen aber zwischen dem Spiel und seinen Absichten unterscheiden. Denn die Absicht ist es nicht, irgendwelche wissenschaftlichen Prognosen über die Zukunft des Kapitalismus zu entwickeln oder sie als Tatsachen zu verkaufen. Das ist zudem auch egal, ob die Thesen stimmen oder nicht, denn was eines Tages davon übrig bleiben wird, ist ohnehin nur ein Haufen Schrott.

A. H.: Aufgrund des Bühnenbildes, des amateurhaften Vortragsstils und auch des unterhaltsamen Textes eignet deinem Stück eine komödiantische Leichtigkeit. Als Zuhörer muss man eigentlich eher darüber schmunzeln, dass all die politischen und kulturtheoretischen Anstrengungen, mit denen wir uns herumschlagen, sich doch als sinnlos herausgestellt haben. Angesichts dieser ironischen, bewusst paradoxen Struktur frage ich mich, ob dein Kulturpessimismus letztlich eine Attitüde ist.

S. D.: Von welchem Kulturpessimismus sprichst du eigentlich?

A. H.: Na, von dem, dass wir uns auf eine ausweglose, verdinglichte, corporate Gesellschaft zubewegen, in der jede Form einer kritischen Öffentlichkeit liquidiert wird.

S. D.: Genau das ist doch der zu befragende Gegenstand – und um mich diesem Status Quaestionis zu nähern, benutze ich als wissenschaftliche Methode das heitere Spiel.

Den Begriff „Kulturpessimismus“ kenne ich aus den 1920ern. Damals hat er zum Aufstieg des Nationalsozialismus beigetragen, heute wird er all jenen um die Ohren geschlagen, die sich mit Neoliberalismus und Neokonservatismus in irgendeiner Form kritisch auseinander setzen. Als ich das Stück schrieb, erschien mir eine Kritik als konservativ, die nur dem Verlust des Sozialstaates nachweint. Ich wollte mich den neuen Gegebenheiten insofern stellen, als ich die Logik des Neoliberalismus spielerisch weitertrieb und eine Möglichkeit suchte, wie eine kritische Position im Hofstaat des „Corporate Rokoko“ funktionieren könnte.

A. H.: Dann nenne ich das eben ironische Nostalgie. Schon von der Form her ist deine Konzeption des „Corporate Rokoko“ doch nostalgisch oder, sagen wir, zumindest elegisch.

Man könnte die Elegie als eine Sprachform beschreiben, in der die Gegenwart immer schon im Modus der Vergangenheit erlebt wird. Deine rettenden Rückgriffe auf emanzipatorische Projekte wie die frühaufklärerische bürgerliche Gesellschaft oder das Arbeitertheater des 19. Jahrhunderts sind insofern aus der Perspektive der unerfüllbaren Sehnsucht und des Scheiterns formuliert. Das entscheidende Moment des Arbeitertheaters taucht nämlich gerade nicht in deiner Konzeption auf: Es entsteht aus der Mitte der proletarischen Klasse und findet eine Form. Wenn ich polemisch von kulturpolitischer Attitüde spreche, dann meine ich damit, dass du einerseits durchaus mit den radikalpolitischen Implikationen von solchen Rückgriffen kokettierst, andererseits aber die heutigen Bedingungen einer konkreten Umsetzung ausblendest. Oder anders ausgedrückt: Wenn du dich mit deiner allegorischen Performancetheorie in der Gestaltung beziehungsweise im performativen Vortrag auf das Arbeitertheater des späten 19. Jahrhunderts berufst – also auf ein Instrumentarium der aktiven politischen Emanzipierung und Veränderung –, annullierst du doch letztlich die Hoffnung auf realpolitische Intervention.

S. D.: Veto! Denn du bist es, der einerseits von Allegorien spricht und mir gleichzeitig immer ein Eins-zu-eins-Verhältnis zum Arbeitertheater unterstellt und dann daraus schließt – weil es in der Analogie nicht funktionieren kann –, dann müsse es wohl unernst, das heißt ironisch gemeint sein ... Aber was ist das Arbeitertheater für mich eigentlich? Nichts anderes als ein gutes historisches Beispiel für Selbstorganisation, Selbstreflexion und Selbstagitation, denn diese drei Elemente möchte ich in unserem Kunstöffentlichkeitsfragment stärker ausgeprägt sehen. Erst dann kann Kunst in einem breiteren gesellschaftlichen Kontext auf mehr Veränderung abzielen! Aber erst einmal steht hinter allem die Frage, ob wir uns als Künstler – und Kritiker – den neuen Aufgaben stellen können, die ein sich wandelnder Öffentlichkeitsbegriff mit sich bringt:

Der Rokoko steht lachend im köstlichen Kleid,
Brokat samt Muscheln zur Seite,
Und kündet den Beginn einer glänzenden Zeit
Der Münze in globaler Weite.

Nun, Künstler, wo steht ihr, seid ihr auch bereit
Und gefeit, seinen Charme
Zu bekämpfen? Doch, ach, gar leid ihr mir seid,
Stürbet ihr in seinem Arme.

Anmerkungen:

1. Zu finden in: Werner von Delmont [d. i. Stephan Dillemuth], *Corporate Rokoko und das Ende des bürgerlichen Projektes*, Köln 2035 [tatsächlich 1998].
2. Siehe Abbildung S. 219 und 220.
3. Interessant ist das Ende dieser Art von Arbeitertheater: Einerseits wurde es von der Partei als Zeitverschwendung diskreditiert, denn lieber sollten die Arbeiter Parteiarbeit leisten. Andererseits wurde das Arbeitertheater durch die Literaten des naturalistischen Theaters professionalisiert und aufgenommen in den Reigen des bürgerlichen Theaters: Arbeiterleben wurden auf die Bühne gestellt und Sentiments von professionellen Schauspielern für ein – nicht mehr proletarisches – aufstrebendes Angestelltenpublikum gespielt. Die Arbeiter selbst interessierte diese Form von Theater nicht.
4. Peter von Rüden, *Sozialdemokratisches Arbeitertheater (1848–1914)*, Frankfurt/M. 1973. (Eine englische Zusammenfassung findet sich unter http://www.societyofcontrol.com/coal/workerstheatre.htm [2005-10-05].)
5. Hoxton Hall, London.

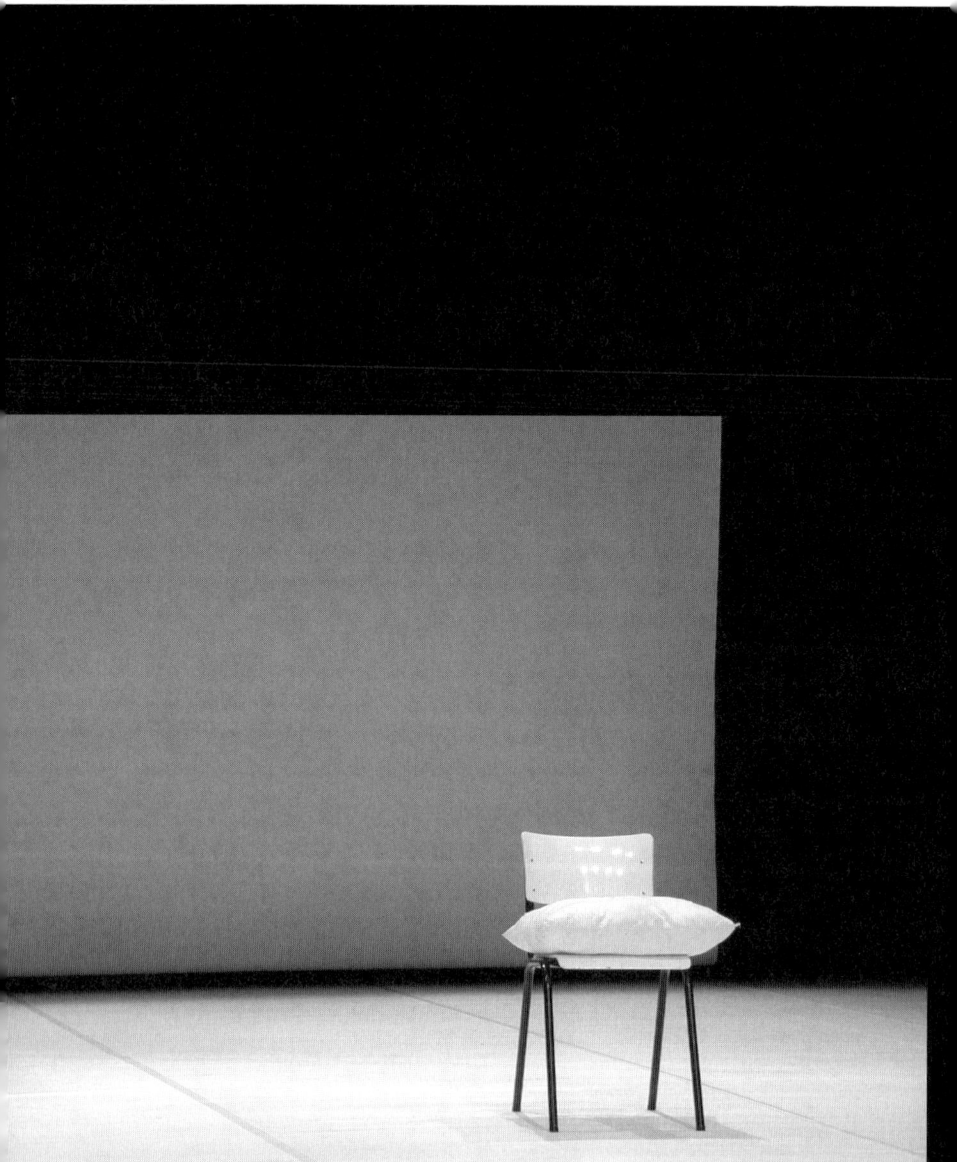

Product of Circumstances

(1999)

by Xavier Le Roy

This performance was originally presented in a theater (Podewil Berlin) and can be presented in any situation allowing an audience in front of a stage and a screen for slide projection (theaters, conference rooms, and so on). The light should be, to the degree possible, the same on stage and in the audience space. The intensity should go down for slide projection but never be black. The light is there at the beginning and at the end of the performance and never goes off. Depending on the space, you might use a microphone, a conference desk, a slide projector, a chair, a pillow, or any other props you want to transform the performance. The text is written in English correspondent to my ability in this language; it is part of the presentation and should be read as clearly as possible. The performance should, as much as possible, present each element as a matter of fact, trying not to emphasize any of the aspects. Try to perform without irony, sarcasm, romanticism, or any affect that could transform the facts. The performance of each element should stay as close as possible to fact. Every text that is not italicized should be said or read. The texts in italic are instructions.

Good evening, ladies and gentlemen. I will do this performance in English; if you have questions afterwards I will be glad to answer them.

The title of this performance is "Product of Circumstances."

In 1987 I started work on my thesis for my PhD in molecular and cellular biology, and at the same time I began to take two dance classes a week.

I finished my master's degree and received a scholarship from the French government to write my thesis. The same year, I was admitted to work in a laboratory specializing in research on breast cancer and hormones. Also, I started to see a lot of dance performances during the summer festivals in the south of France where I lived. The same year was the painful ending of a three years long love relationship.

I was still playing a lot of basketball and my body was trying to get some stretch.

1. I leave paper and microphone, go three steps to the side. I do a stretching exercise, bending my torso over and trying to reach the floor with my hands in 20 light bounces. My hands don't get closer than 20 cm from the floor, like it was in 1987. Then I go back to the microphone.

Can you please turn on the slide projector and change the lights. Thank you.

The title of the thesis I presented in October 1990 was:

SLIDE # 1 is the title of the thesis: STUDY OF ONCOGENES EXPRESSION AND HORMONAL REGULATION IN BREAST CANCER USING QUANTITATIVE IN SITU HYBRIDIZATION (HIS)

When I was in the laboratory, my task was to study in vivo the expression of oncogenes in breast cancer. Oncogenes are genes that, after alteration at a structural or expressive level, have the ability of transformation and are then part of some cancer mechanisms. Oncogenes can be altered by the punctual mutation, genetic re-arrangement, amplification, or over-expression of the oncogenes.

The usual techniques used to study the RNA or protein expression are not well-adapted to detect gene expression in human biopsies, so we chose to develop the technique of in situ hybridization (HIS), because with this technique it is possible to detect very low quantities of RNA expression and to localize it in the studied tissue.

HIS reveals the presence of messenger RNA (mRNA) on tissue sections by using a probe of the tested gene marked with radioactivity. After hybridization we observe the tissue section under a microscope and the presence of mRNA is visible as black dots or grains on the tissue sections.

SLIDE # 2 is a photograph of tissue section under the microscope after in situ hybridization with the oncogene c-myc. *On this slide you can see a section from a biopsy of ductal breast carcinoma, and the black grains reveal the expression of the oncogene* c-myc *in cancer cells.*

SLIDE # 3 is a photograph of tissue section under the microscope after in situ hybridization with the oncogene c-erbB-2. *On this slide you can see the expression of the oncogene* c-erbB-2 *at the RNA level in an invasive ductal breast carcinoma. The different genes always appear in black; there are no color differences.*

It's easy to see a difference in the number of grains in the two previous examples and also in the next one.

SLIDE # 4 is a photograph of tissue section under the microscope after in situ hybridization with the oncogene c-myc. *In this example, it is also clear to see that the grains are visible in some zones but not in others. It shows how this technique allows the localization of the expression of the tested gene. You can see here the expression in the epithelial tissue but not in the stromal tissue.*

Can you please turn off the slide projector and change the lights. Thank you.

As you can see, the technique allows the localization of the expression of the tested gene, and the different examples show a clear difference in the quantity of grains.

But to get usable results from these experiments, we had to be able to translate them into numbers for making comparative and quantitative studies of the RNA expression for statistic studies.

Of course it was possible to count the grains visually one by one, but it takes about two hours to count the grains in each chosen field under the microscope. So my first task was to develop, in collaboration with computer scientists from the corporation IMSTAR, a method for mechanically counting the level of RNA detected by HIS on tissue sections.

2. I go to a chair which is almost in the middle of the stage. Staying at one third on the left side, I take the pillow off the chair, put it down on the side of the stage, and stand up on top of the chair to perform the first five minutes from a piece I did in 1994 called Things I Hate To Admit. *The dance is made up of movements in which my arms are stuck (without artifice, only physically and mentally) against my torso from the armpit to the elbows, which I imagine to be my shoulders.*

Then I go back to the microphone.

To count the black dots mechanically, we use a microscope connected to a camera and a computer with software developed specifically for this task.

First, we select a field from the studied tissue section under the microscope. Then we take a picture from this field with the video camera that is on top of the microscope. This picture then goes into a computer, where it is digitized, and the digitized pictures appear on a video monitor where the processing of the counting can be followed.

Using this technique it takes us ten minutes with the help of the computer to count one field observed under the microscope. This is already much better than the two hours needed for a visual counting.

These results were published, and it was the first time that I participated in a scientific publication.

At that time, I was taking two or three dance classes a week and trying to learn how to do the following kind of exercises.

3. I leave my papers and the microphone, do several steps to the side and do the exercise in 6 (or another) from Merce Cunningham. After that, I do a diagonal with a combination of triplets with port de bras and curves from the torsos, which have to be changed according to the space where I perform. Then I go back to the microphone.

During this period I spent a lot of time looking at sections of human tissue under the microscope, trying to learn how to recognize the histological differences between normal and cancer cells and also between the different types of cancer. I remember that, even for the very experienced researcher, it was difficult to make a clear and objective decision to put the observed tissue in one of the numerous existing categories. But the decisions had to be as objective as possible. Looking into the microscope I very often had the feeling that I was both observing and transforming what I was observing.

I had the feeling that my decisions were made under influence. I thought every decision challenged my "objectivity" and that I could not be objective.

I asked myself at this time, how objective do I have to be to be able to continue to practice science, or more specifically, biomedical research?

But I quickly forgot these thoughts, so as to be able to continue my work of research in the laboratory.

After we developed this mechanical method of quantification, we first studied the expression of oncogenes from the group of the fibroblast growth factor-like genes.

We tested six different genes and oncogenes in twenty breast cancer biopsies.

The level of expression of these oncogenes was very low and at the limit of detection.

This work became the first subject of discord with Henry Rochefort, my laboratory director.

We argued a lot, and I quickly found out that his experience and social position was much more important than any scientific argument. The discussions were rarely about scientific problems or questions; it was all about career, power, and hierarchy.

He wanted to publish these results and I thought that they were not relevant enough to be published.

I was learning the importance of publication and that publishing articles is the scientist's best way to create and protect his position in society. Like researcher use to say, "publish or perish." I was learning that research has to follow and use the methods of capitalism.

I was asked to produce science, and not to search.

At that time I took at least one dance class a day. I did some yoga and I began to visit an osteopath regularly. These corporeal experiences laid the foundation for the necessity of a new corporeality or new theories about the human body.

4. I leave my papers and microphone and walk to the center of the stage. I lie down on my back with the soles of my feet on the floor and my knees toward the ceiling. I stay there for one minute. Then I go back to the microphone.

The next step of my work in the laboratory was to study the regulation in vivo of oncogenes with Tamoxifen.

Tamoxifen is a chemical used for breast cancer therapy because it has the ability to inhibit the effect of steroid hormones, which probably play a role in the development of breast cancer.

We studied the effect of Tamoxifen on the RNA levels of four different oncogenes—*c-myc*, *c-erbB-2*, *hst*, and *int-2*—in nineteen breast cancer biopsies from patients treated by tamoxifen three weeks prior surgery. We then compared the results with twenty-two control patients who were not treated with Tamoxifen prior to surgery. The RNA levels were measured by in situ hybridization and with computer-aided quantification, as described before.

We found that all four oncogenes were expressed in breast epithelial cells and that the expression in the stromal tissue was negligible. I will show some examples of this.

Can you please turn on the slide projector and change the lights. Thank you.

SLIDE # 5 is an example of c-myc *(can be the same as slide #3).*
You can see here an example of a clear difference of the gene *c-myc* expression in stromal and epithelial cells in an invasive ductal breast carcinoma.

SLIDE # 6: an example of c-erbB-2 *(can be the same as slide #4).*
This is the same area from the same cancer tested with the gene *c-erbB-2*, which is clearly more expressed than *c-myc*.

SLIDE # 7: a graphic with differences of expression in c-myc *and* c-erbB-2 *in two populations.*
In this figure are represented the expression of *c-myc* and *c-erbB-2* in the two

different populations (one treated with Tamoxifen and the control group). For both genes, expression is high in the control population (with a mean value of 23.4 for *c-myc* and 29.1 grains/cell for the gene *c-erbB*-2), and significantly decreased in the Tamoxifen-treated population (mean value 14.6 and 7.4 grains/cell).

The results for the genes *hst* and *int*-2 were much less spectacular.

SLIDE # 8 is a photograph of tissue section under the microscope after in situ hybridization with the oncogenes int-2 *and* hst.

SLIDE # 9: As you can see in this example, int-2 *and* hst *RNA show very low levels of expression, with an average of 2 to 3 grains/cell.*
This is a graphic with difference of expression of *int*-2 and *hst* between two populations. The *int*-2 and *hst* RNA levels were not found to be significantly altered by the treatment with Tamoxifen.

All these results were used for statistical analysis, to look for possible correlation.

SLIDE #10 is a table of correlation between oncogene, RNA expression, and their DNA amplification in control and treated populations of ductal breast carcinomas.
The statistical analysis showed a correlation between gene amplification and expression for *c-erbB*-2 (with a p-value of 0.0005) and for *hst* (with a p-value of 0.02) in the control population. No correlation was detected for the oncogenes *int*-2 and *c-myc* in either population.

SLIDE # 11, table 3, is a statistical analysis, correlation with estrogen receptor status.

The effect of Tamoxifen on the RNA expression in ductal breast carcinoma with or without estrogen receptor showed that Tamoxifen significantly decreased *c-myc* gene expression in the estrogen-receptor-positive population (p=0.04), while, surprisingly, the elevated *c-erbB*-2 RNA expression was more significantly diminished in the estrogen-receptor-negative population (p=0.02).

Can you please turn off the slide projector and change the lights. Thank you.

So as I conclude at the end of my thesis for my doctorate: The results suggest that Tamoxifen in vivo decreases *c-myc* and *c-erbB*-2 RNA levels in breast cancer cells and has no effect on the expression of *hst* and *int*-2. And it seems that the mechanisms of regulation of these two oncogenes by anti-estrogens are different.

Tamoxifen seems to be able to interfere at both the DNA and the RNA levels, with or without an interaction with the estrogen's receptors.

To study these different mechanisms, the approach would be to develop an experimental protocol using, for example, different lineages of breast cancer cells with different estrogen receptor status.

I had from these three years of work some other conclusions and questions, such as, why do we try to give a homogenous picture of the results when they look so heterogeneous? Can we trust statistics? What is the meaning of statistical results?

In regard to statistics, I would like to quote some material about the risks of breast cancer pointed out by Yvonne Rainer in her film *MURDER and murder*. She says that lesbians have a two to three time higher risk of developing breast cancer than heterosexual women. Which means, between other conclusions that you can make about these statistics, that when a woman comes out as a lesbian, she is more exposed to breast cancer from one day to the other by changing her relationship towards women.

During my practice of science, I also asked myself, what is the aim in getting more and more specific? Is it a way to understand the human body?

It seems very strange to study it by isolating micro-systems out of their context for an analysis in a laboratory environment.

This experimental system, like any other technical-scientific disposition, is responsible for its results. It imposes the answers to problems, which are no longer about the original questions but about their transformation.

I thought that trying to understand the cell as a microcosm of our body could be a very interesting model if it were not described and studied only by using mechanistic systems that make a myth out of it.

The human body is not organized only in the way that biology tries to organize it. All these remarks may sound pretty naïve, but I had the feeling that science was about understanding problems made up to give us the impression and satisfaction of total control of questions on, for example, the human body. I had another idealistic idea of science, and slowly I lost my belief in it. I lost this very distinguished belief specific to science, which is presented as the right of access to truth and to a different world.

5. I leave the microphone, go to the chair, sit almost in the center of the stage with my back to the audience, and perform a part (the beginning) of Burke*, a piece created in 1997. This part plays with movement that gives the illusion, when I fold my lower arms behind the rest of my arms, that my arms are cut off at the elbow. I perform this simultaneously thinking and imagining that my arms stop at the elbow. When I am finished I go back to the microphone.*

These three years of work in the laboratory taught me that doing research is, for fifty percent of the time, making reports, writing articles for publications,

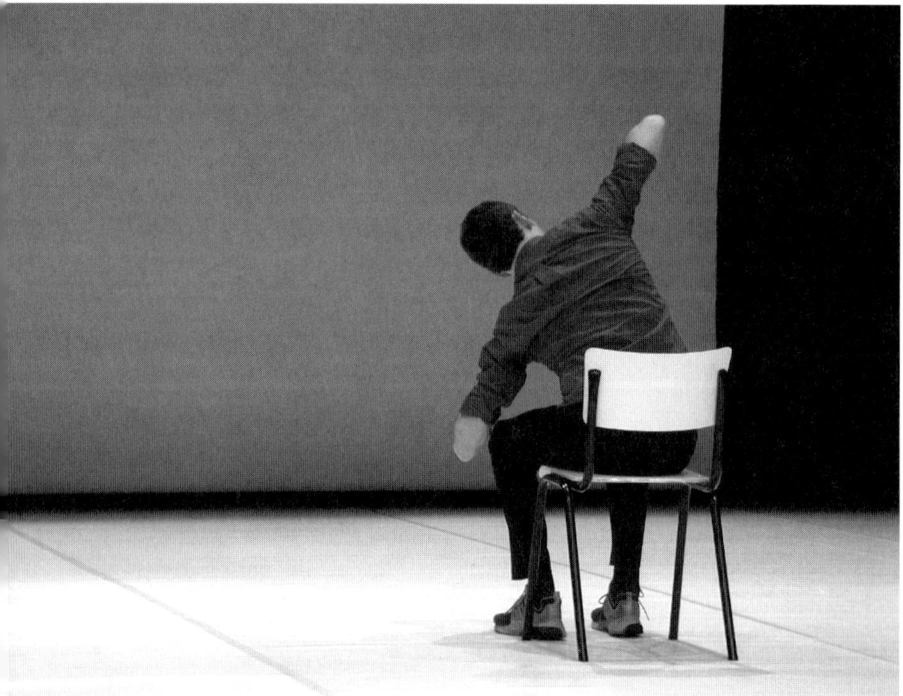

or proving that you're actually working on a productive subject. Thirty percent of the time is used to think about how you could be productive. The rest of the time is for experiments, observations, and analysis.

I realized that research in biology was a lot about power and "politics" and rarely about an understanding of the human body, which was actually my interest.

As Guy Debord wrote in *Commentaire sur la société du spectacle* (*Comments on the Society of Spectacle*), published in 1988, "We notice very quickly that today's medicine is not allowed to defend the population's health against the pathogen environment because it would mean being opposed to the state or to the chemical industry. We don't ask anymore that science understands or improves the world. We ask it to instantly justify everything that is done. In order to obey this final request it's better not to know how to think and to have a very good practice in the discourse of the spectacle."

Maybe my experience is very specific to biomedical research?

Maybe it would have been different if I had done fundamental research in physics, for example?

In 1990, after I presented my thesis, I quit my career as a molecular biologist. I escaped. I decided to do more dance.

Thinking became a corporeal experience.

My body became simultaneously active and productive, object and subject, analyzer and analyzed, product and producer.

I went to Paris, where I took more dance classes. And I did some of these.

6. I leave the microphone and repeat the second part of 3 (the triplets). Then I go back to the microphone and say:

During this year in Paris I went to auditions. I remember that one time I was refused because I was too skinny, but most of the time I was not accepted because of my lack of technique. So I tried to practice more of this.

7. I leave the microphone, step aside, and do some exercises like Cunningham's développés, *front, side, back on each leg; then I go back to the microphone and continue.*

It didn't really help. My enthusiasm for dance was mixed with disappointment and a feeling of exclusion. Somehow my body was resisting the norms of dance. Maybe I was too old?

Maybe there was something wrong with my body?

Maybe it was this?

8. I leave the microphone, go to a wall or screen backstage and I extend my arms against it from the floor to the highest point I can reach. I keep this point with my finger, stand against the wall under the point, still marked by my finger, marking with my hands the distance between the top of my head and the highest point. Then I show this distance to the audience and go back to the microphone.

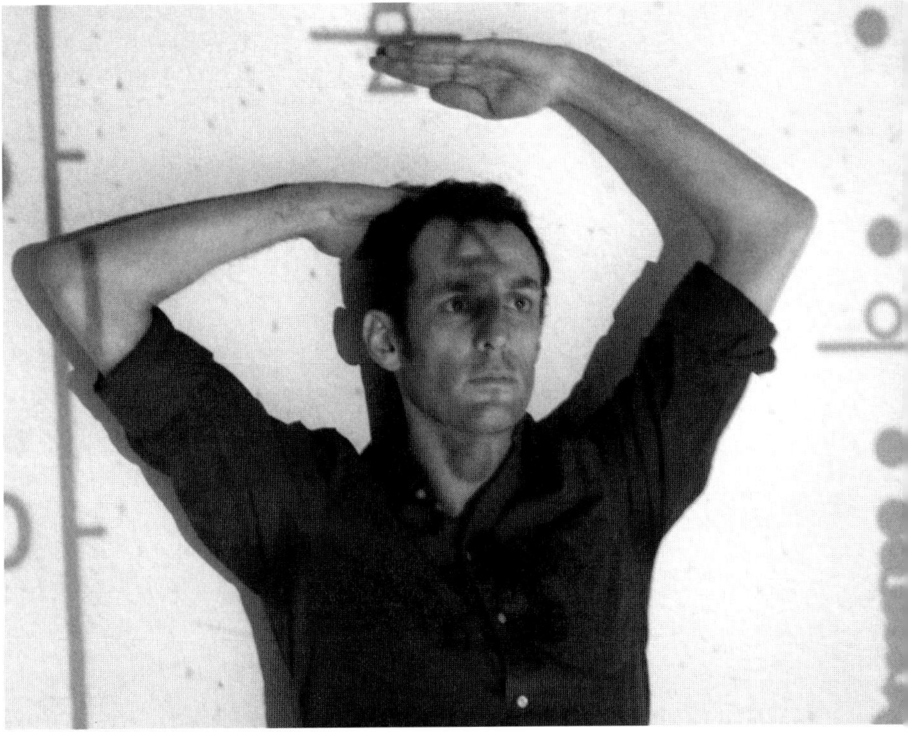

After a year of dance classes and auditions, I got a job as a dancer in a company called La compagnie de l'Alambic. I was fitting in. I remember we were working on or using the body to produce metaphors. We were improvising under the direction of Christian Bourigault, the choreographer, to produce movements. We were trying to express something by creating movement sequences supposed to answer to his questions and desires. I also had to learn movements composed by the choreographer or other dancers in order to be part of the group's dances. Most of the time this was very difficult for me and I will now show you an excerpt of one of these dances.

9. I leave the microphone, go to front stage left, and dance a part of a dance called La caresse *from a piece titled* Matériau-Désir *created by Christian Bourigault in 1993. Then I go back to the microphone.*

In 1992, I moved to Berlin for reasons of love.

Except for one or two groups, I found the dance scene not very exciting, but I began to practice a little bit of contact improvisation and I also took some Alexander Technique classes. These experiences changed a lot of my perceptions about the human body.

After a year in Berlin, I began to work with a group called Detektor. This multi-disciplinary group was using video, theater, and dance, and mixing them all for performances. Working with them I began to ask myself questions about the definition of dance. At the same time I was more and more disappointed by most of the performances that I saw. Watching a lot of them from a lot of different groups from all over, I could less and less imagine working with one of these groups, companies, and choreographers.

So in 1993, I began to work alone. My body became the practice of a critical necessity.

I began to use my body for questions about body images, identity, differences.

I worked on creating functions and dis-functions of the body with a quite analytical method, if not to say a scientific one.

The first choreographies were constructed by creating links between fragments of bodies voluntarily taken apart, as a biologist might do to analyze them. Performing these movements was about inscribing something that could be described as a go-between for mind and body, as a moving entity.

It was a way to redefine the mind/body opposition and to work on the idea that, just as the mind organizes the rest of the body's tissues into a life process, sensations and perceptions, to a large degree, organize the mind. Sensations and perceptions do not simply give the mind material to organize; they are themselves a major organizing principle.

But this doesn't mean that dance should only be about sensations and perceptions. I don't think that choreography is reduced to handle these questions. On the opposite I think that choreography has a much wider field of action.

Since 1995 these reflections have been enriched by collaboration with Laurent Goldring who questions the status of body pictures or human figures within the history of photography and produces video works as well as texts.

This collaboration helped me to continue my research which at that time was centered on deconstructing and reconstructing my body to produce movement sequences.

I have already showed two different examples of this, extracts from a triptych called *Narcisse Flip*. I will now show another one from Burke, the third part of the triptych.

10. Parts from Burke: I go from side to side, arms leading around and changing the direction three times. Then I move my body parts in all directions until my arms accelerate, all performed as if my arms were not mine. This brings me back to the chair where I sit down before a last movement sequence where my body tries to get rid of my arms as if they were not mine. Then I go back to the microphone.

The first choreographies I worked on were presented during private events called *Pressure Presents*. The first one was at the end of 1993.

It was the proposition of Alexander Birntraum, a musician and musicologist friend, who suggested that we could offer each other music or dance, to force ourselves to find a form to present them.

It was a way to take the works out of an exclusively personal experience and find a direct exchange without engaging all the dynamics of theater's organization of presentation.

The decision on the presentation of a piece of dance, music, or anything else, could be quick, and the exchange was rich.

After that, we have been invited to present some works which emerged out of these *Pressure Presents*, in a couple of venues.

In 1996 I got some support from institutions from the city of Berlin, I was invited to be artist in residence at the Podewil, and I started to be invited to present different works in different places in Europe.

But this small success, recognition, and attention were slightly changing my way of thinking.

I lost a certain kind of independence.
I slowly noticed that the systems for dance production had created a format that influenced and, sometimes to a large degree, determined how a dance piece should be. I think that to a large extend dance producers and programmers essentially follow the rules of the global economy.

I had integrated the economical dynamics of dance production because I wanted to be able to make a living with what I had decided to do.

But even though I was very careful not to bow to that particular logic, and tried to resist, I was not always completely convinced by my decisions.

It reminded me of some earlier experiences and made me think about the utopic and idealistic reasons that made me give up the work of research in medical biology.

My point of view and my status in society changed, and I found myself in a blurred field of similarities between the social and political organizations of science and dance. I felt like a fugitive who actually never escaped what he thought he was.

I had a need to change the way of changing.

I had a need for more critical work and, at the same time, I realized that the content of a piece was not enough for a critical position.

During the same period, around 1996, I had the luck to be invited to join the Quatuor Albrecht Knust, a French dance company working on the re-creation of dance pieces that have played an important role in our modernity.
The project was to work on the re-creation of *Satisfyin' Lovers*, a piece by Steve Paxton, and *Continuous Project—Altered Daily*, a piece by Yvonne Rainer created in 1970.

This project was very important for me, and it still has a very big influence on my work.

It was more than a way to access the history of dance through the practice of it, which was already a great experience. It proposed a lot of answers to my questions, because the project was very aware of all the aspects implied in the production of a dance piece.

For example, the practice of dance questions the body and the process of work, as well as the composition methods, and everything is related to social or political questions and criticisms. Like, for example, individual responsibility and group conscience take over power and hierarchy during the work process as well as during the performance.

It was a lot of fun to do. I will now demonstrate two parts of it, the first called *Running*. The second part is called *Chair and Pillow Dance*.

11. I leave the microphone, run around the stage for a time that changes with each performance. Then I take a pillow and a chair goes at the position of the chair where it was at the beginning of the performance and I do the Chair and Pillow Dance from Continuous Project—Altered Daily.

These experiences had for example, a lot of influence on a project realized in 1997 in collaboration with Alexander Birntraum (composer-musicologist). The project was called *Das To.Be. Projekt* and was about exploring different types of relationships between dance and music or sound and movement. The whole project was presented as a series of speculative experiments trying to give different ways of perception to the audience, where listening was as important as watching.

After this experience, it became more difficult than ever to think in terms of the production of a dance piece. Sometimes I even thought that it's impossible to do anything else.

But I still had the feeling that it's a field where the questions about bodies and their representations could be explored.

Since then, I have tried to work on questions such as the following:

Can the production of a dance piece become the process and the production in itself, without becoming a product in terms of performance and representation? What kind of organization for which body? For which process of work? For which performance? Is it possible to work on all these parameters at the same time?

What is performance? What is representation?

Is the human body an extension of the environment or/and the environment an extension of the body?

As Elizabeth Grosz suggests in her book *Volatile Bodies*, the human body is not a stable system or a centered organization neither at the biological level nor at the historical, psychological, or cultural levels. She also suggests that any body-image is a continuous process of production and transformation.

Considering this, a perspective of work in the choreography field could be to look for ways to change the predetermined organization of the body in order to transform the form of performance and representation.

I am looking for ways to explore the performance of human and non-human bodies in a process of transformation and mediation. This research is based on ideas about the body as multi-centered and able to be every-body and no-body within the diversity of its affectations.

12. *I do sound and movement from the beginning of* Self-Unfinished, *going a few steps away from the microphone and then breaking off and coming back.*

That was the beginning of a piece called *Self-Unfinished* that I was working on in 1998 when I was invited by Marten Spangberg, Christophe Wavelet, and Hortensia Völckers to participate in an event about performance and theory called *Body Currency*. I was invited because as a dancer or choreographer, my currency in the "society of the spectacle" is to be an atypical dancer or a dancer-biologist.
For this event I was asked to think about possible theoretical pathways between biology and performance.

It was a very interesting challenge to try to make something out of this.

But it was impossible for me to get to an abstract and theoretical level. I could not generalize or conceptualize. I could not write a “real” paper, lecture, or discussion. So I decided to stay at a personal level and give some information about possibilities of exchange I experienced as a support for different thoughts. I was afraid, but I took the risk of being maybe too egocentric, hoping that I could provoke some questions.

This is how I came to produce what I just presented to you this evening.

Now, to end this lecture, I would like to suggest that this performance was about a contaminated body in its weavings of historical, social, cultural, and biological levels, being the place and time for a pathway of different thoughts unable to transform themselves into abstraction and theory.

And maybe theory is biography, presenting it is a lecture, and doing a lecture is performing.

Thank you for your attention. I’d be glad to answer any questions you might have.

References:

Debord, Guy. *Comments on the Society of the Spectacle*. London. New York: Verso Books, 1991.

Grosz, Elizabeth. *Volatile Bodies: Towards a Corporeal Feminism*. Bloomington: Indiana Unversity Press, 1994.

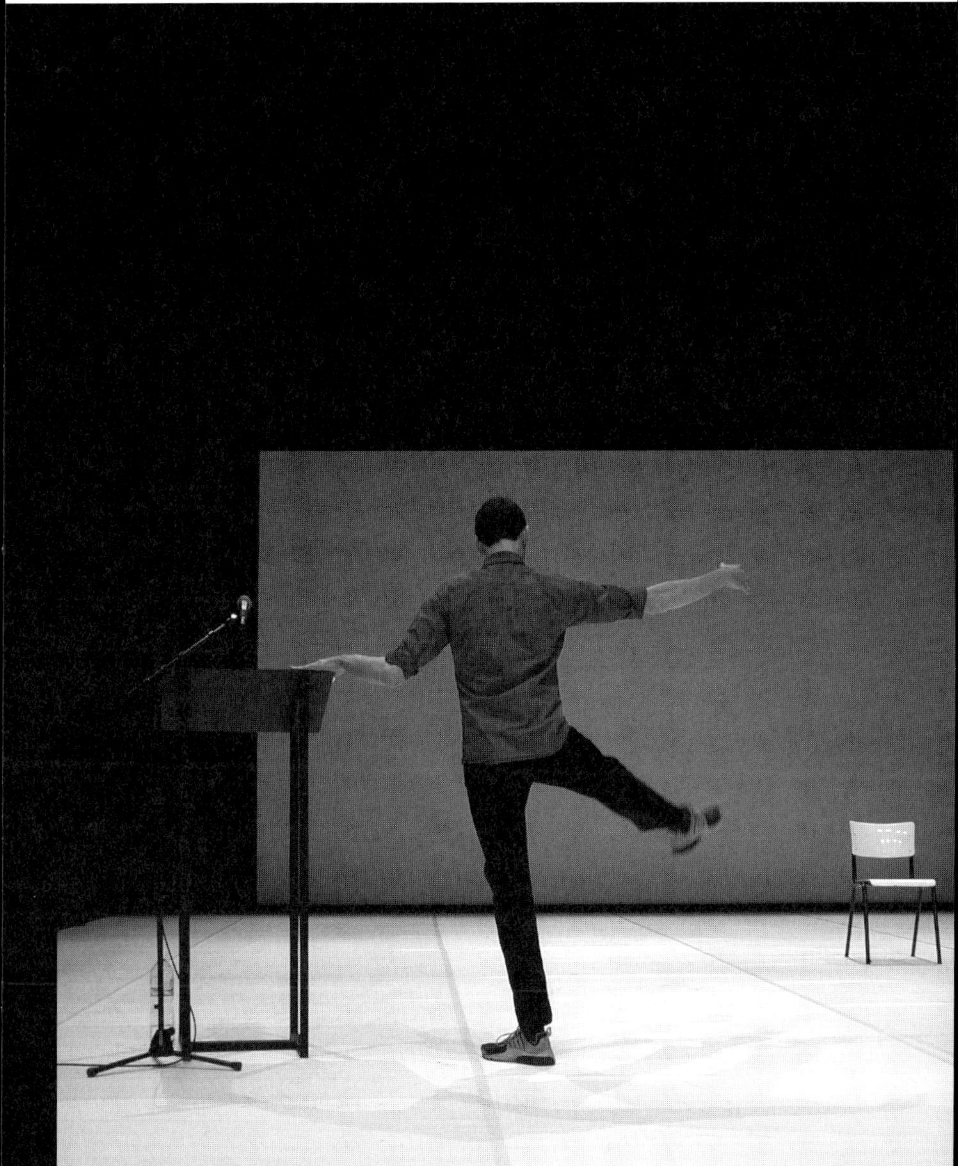

No. 6 - **NEW GHOST**

ENTERTAINMENT—ENTITLED

PAMPHLET FÜR EINEN GEISTERFILM

PAMPHLET FOR A GHOST FILM

PANFLETO PARA UNA PELÍCULA DE FANTASMAS

No. 7 Nosotras tambien nos sentimos obligadas a sumar,

Auch wir also fühlen uns dazu verpflichtet

☆ ☆ We, too, feel obliged ☆ ☆

a la transmisión mundial de información en vivo

Der weltweiten Übertragung von

To add to the worldwide transmission of

live Information

☆ weitere live Information hinzuzufügen ☆

otro tipo de información en vivo

another type of live information

No. 8 Por eso nosotras anunciamos

Aus diesem Grunde geben wir bekannt

Therefore we announce

que nos unimos a la historia de los que han trabajado

☆ uns in die Geschichte derer einzureihen, die über ☆

that we are joining the history of those who worked

on the concept of ☆ el concepto

FantasmasGeister

☆ Ghosts ☆

as an impossible possibilty of live tv

como una imposibilidad posible de la tv en vivo

als mögliche Unmöglichkeit live zu sein gearbeitet haben

No. 9 ★ En este moment ★ at this point ★ zu diesem Zeitpunkt ★ podemos comprobar ★ we can ascertain ★ können wir mit Sicherheit feststellen ★ que lo que recibimos como tv en vivo es realmente un fantasma ★ that what we recieve as live tv is actually a ghost ★ dass es Geister sind, die wir als live emfangen

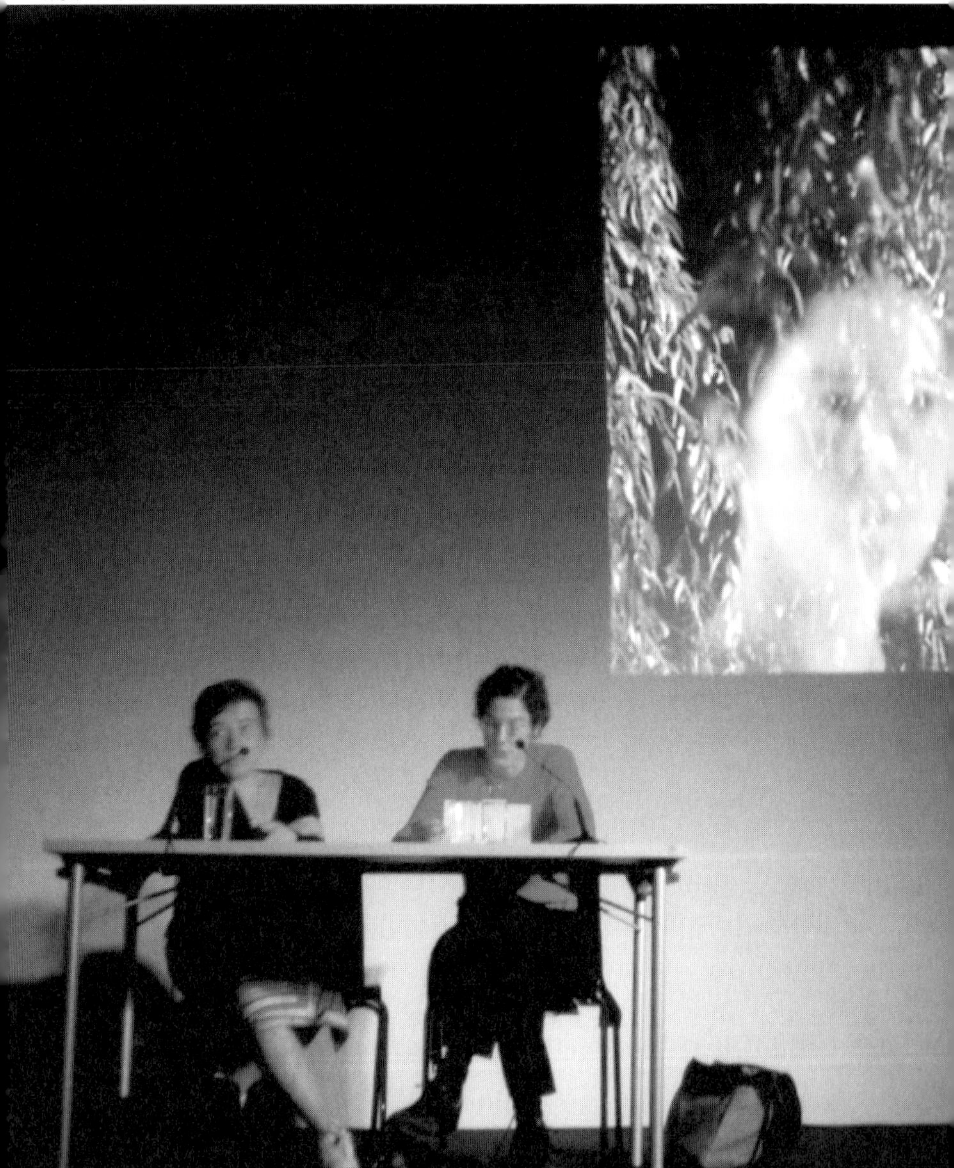

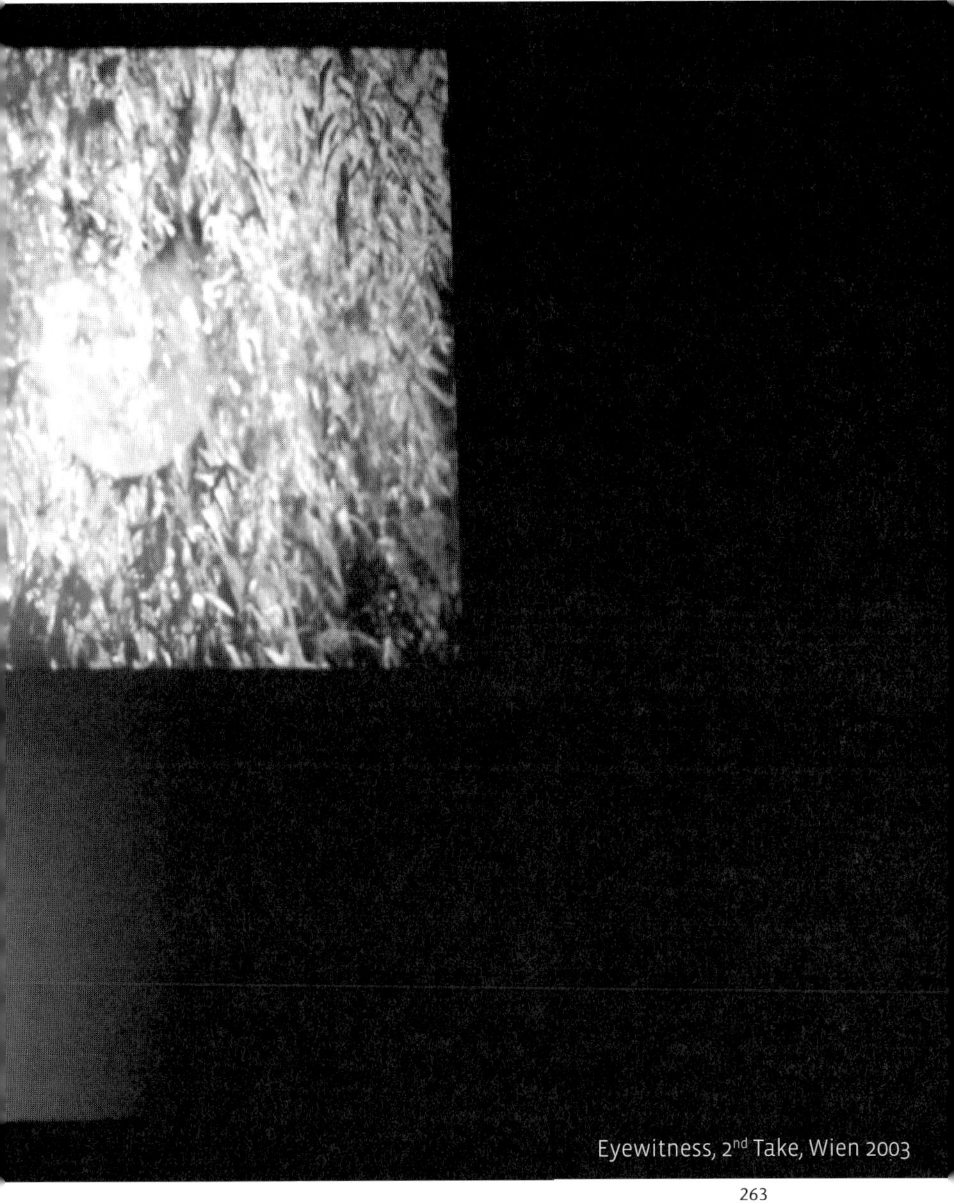

Eyewitness, 2nd Take, Wien 2003

the tables began to dance
when the rest of the world appeared to be
standing still

als die Tische zu tanzen anfingen

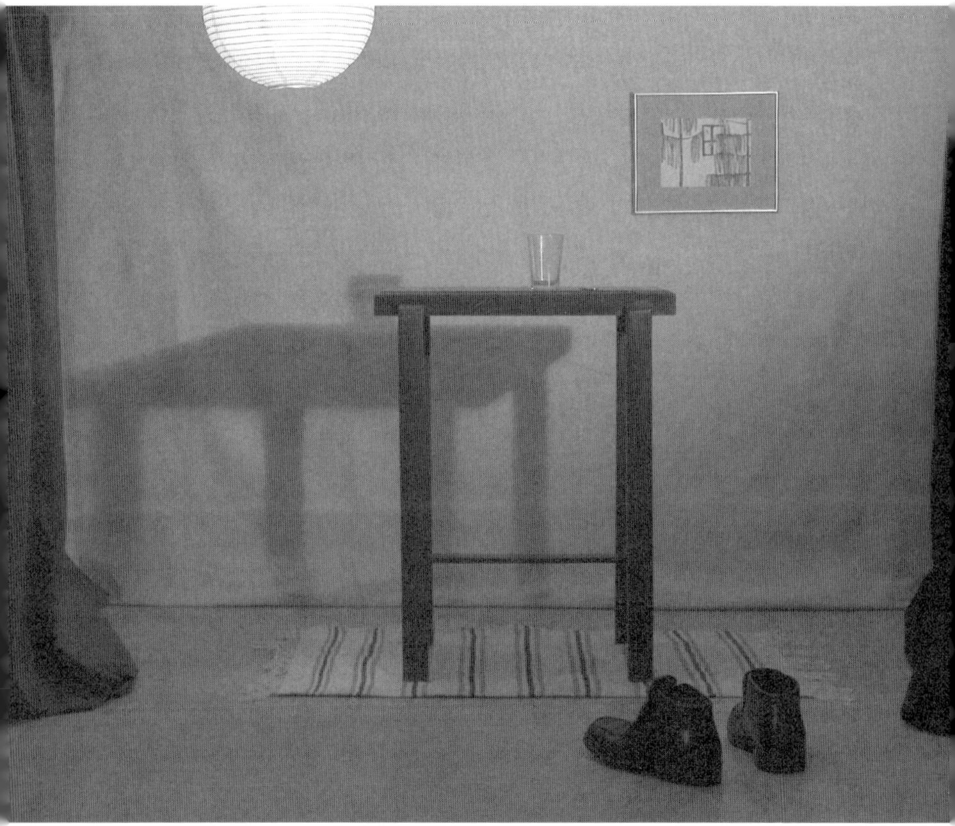

pour encourager les autres

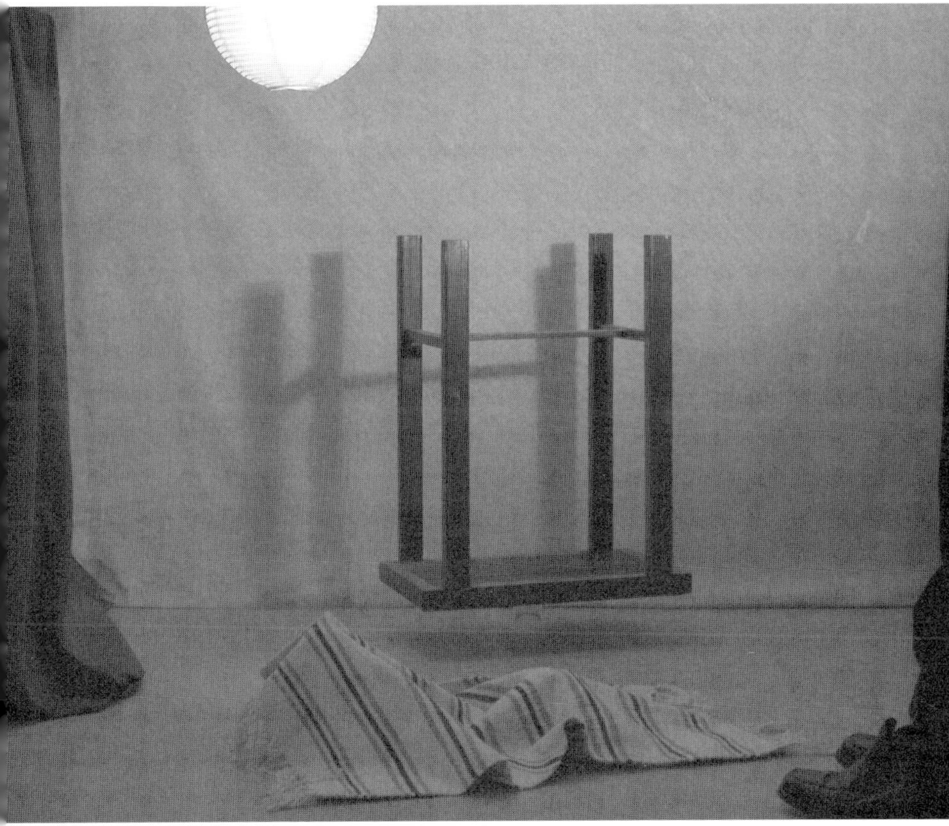

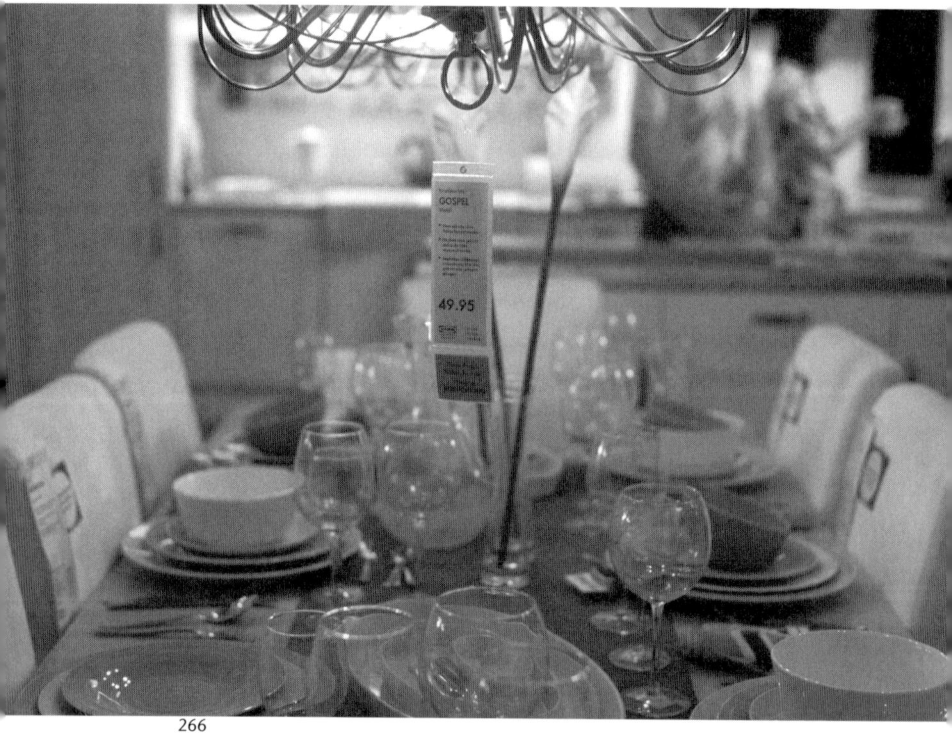
GOSPEL
49.95

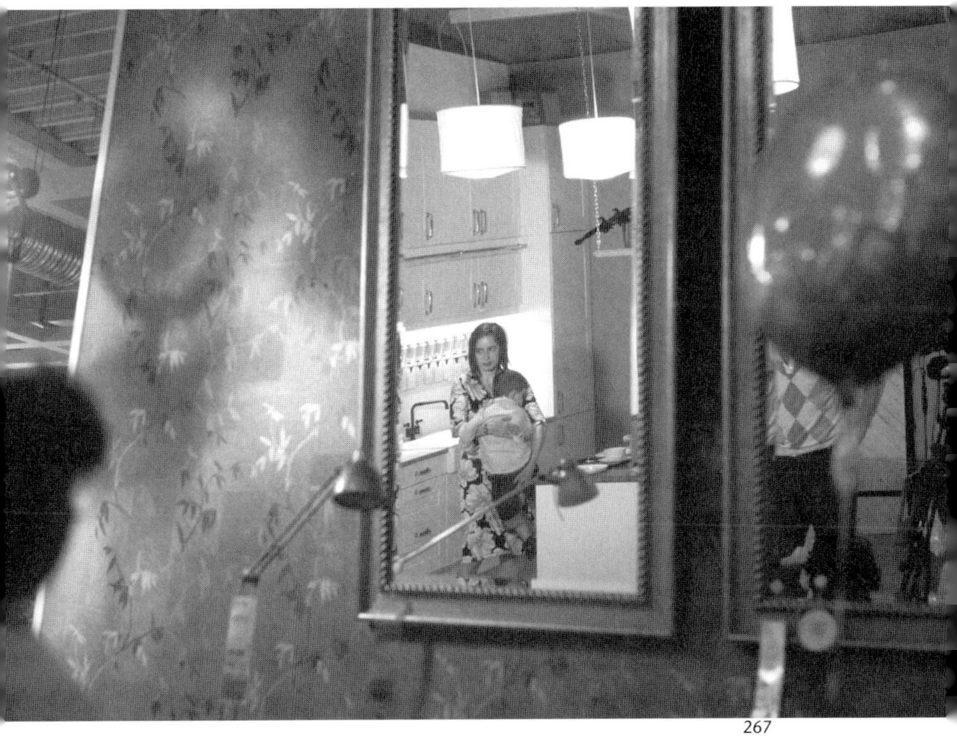

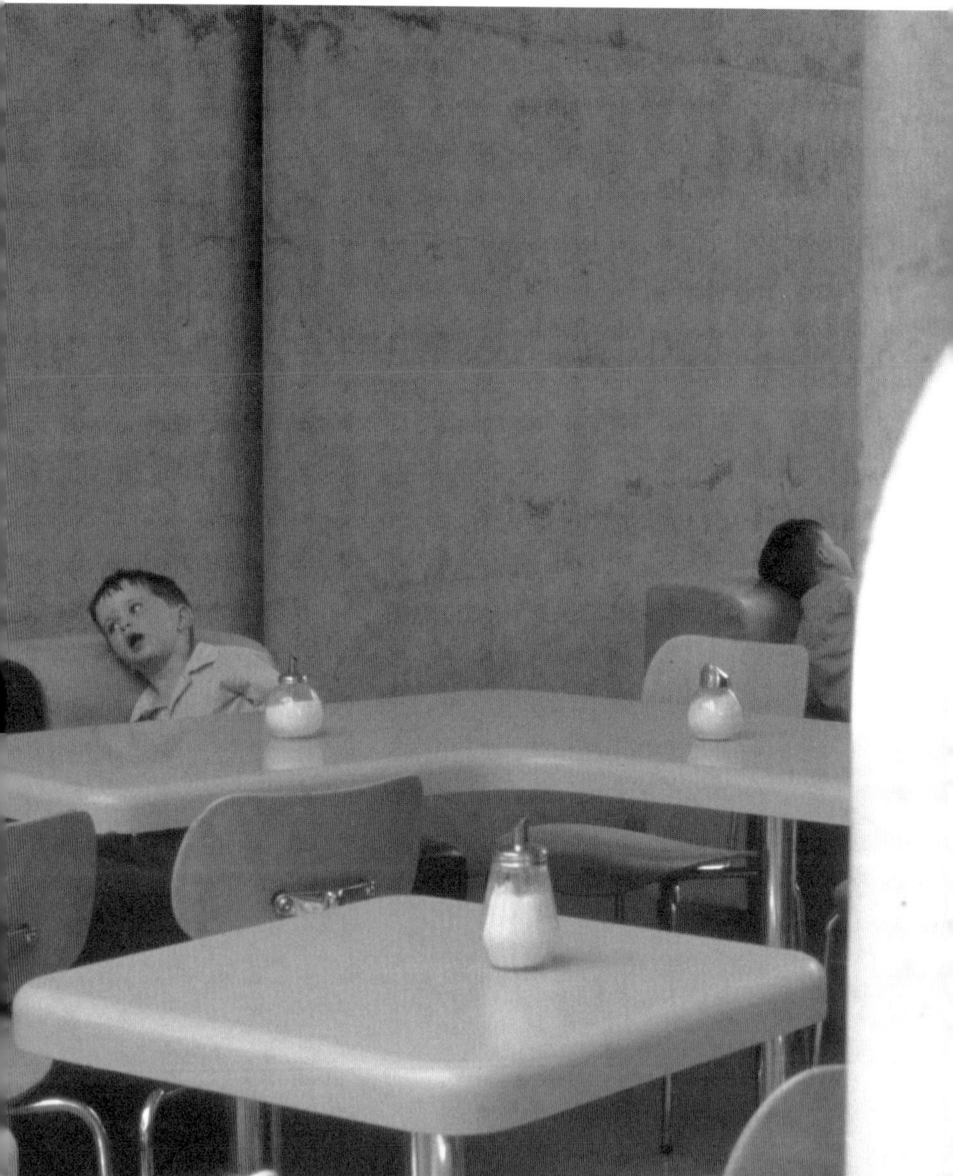

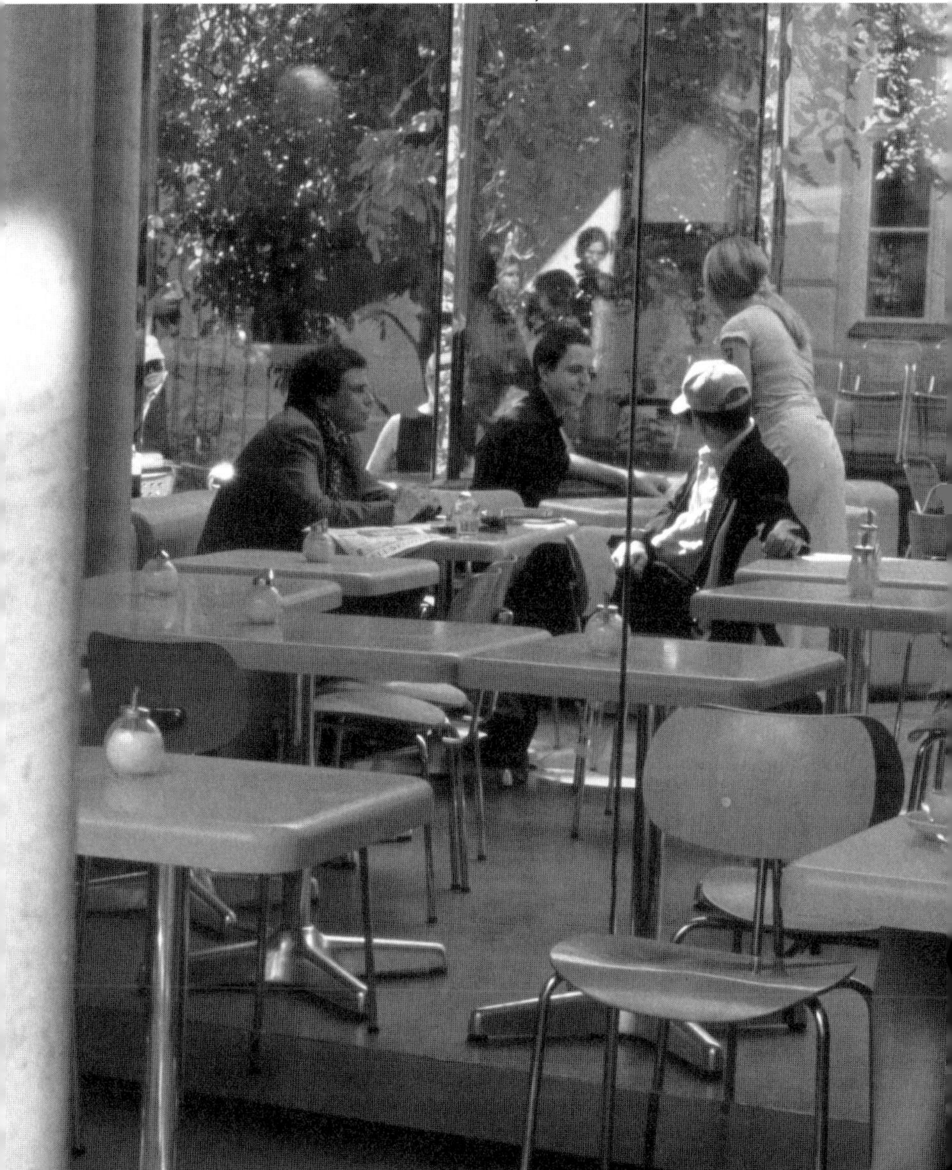

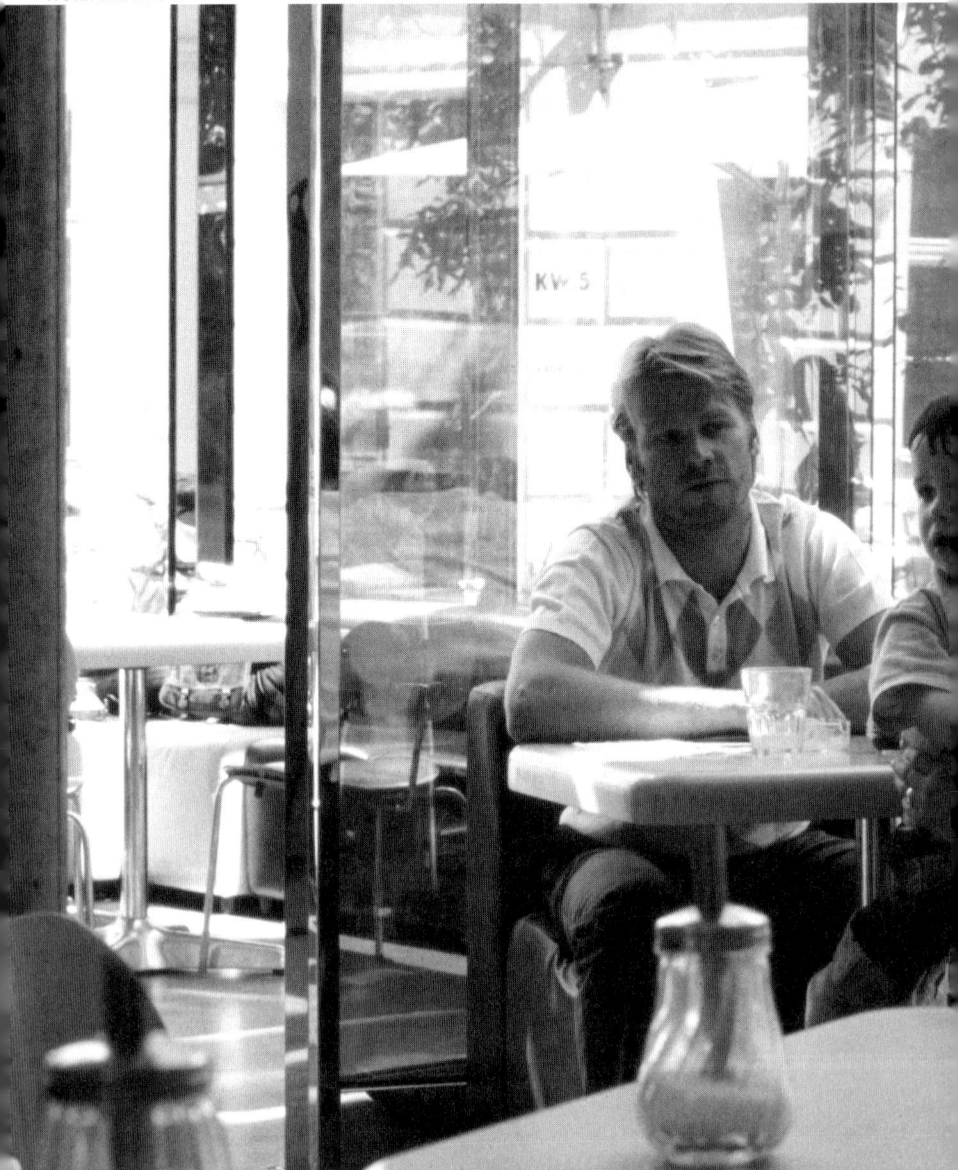
KW 5

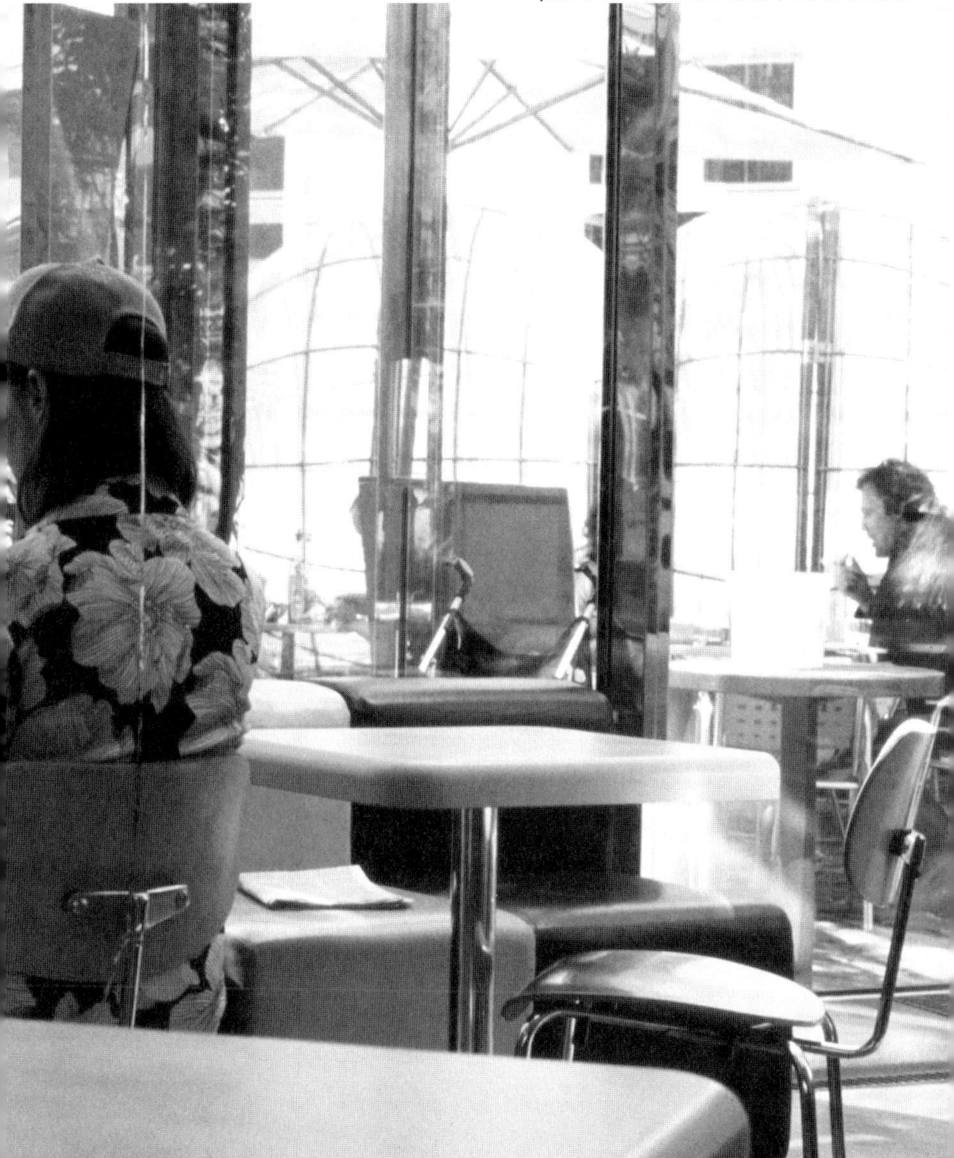

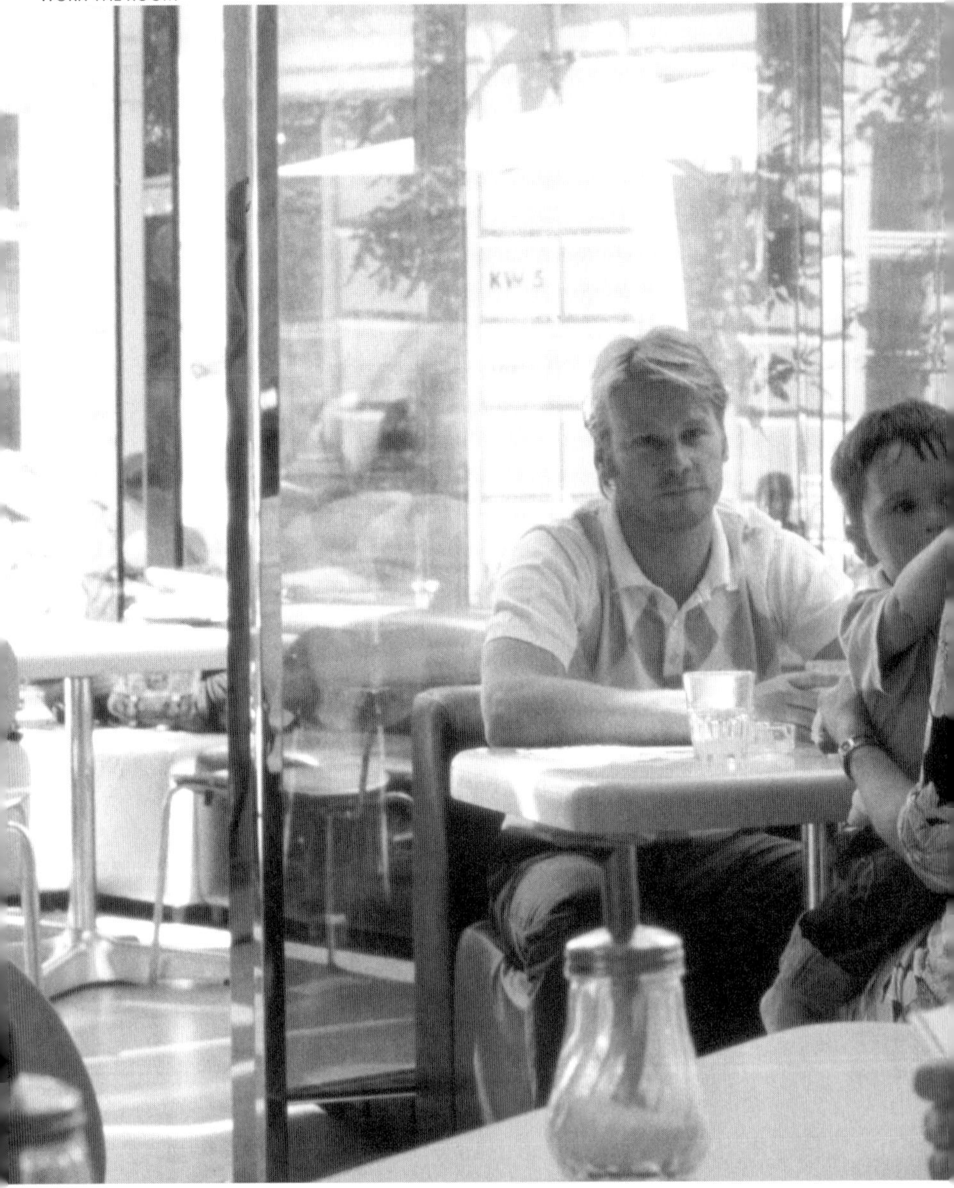

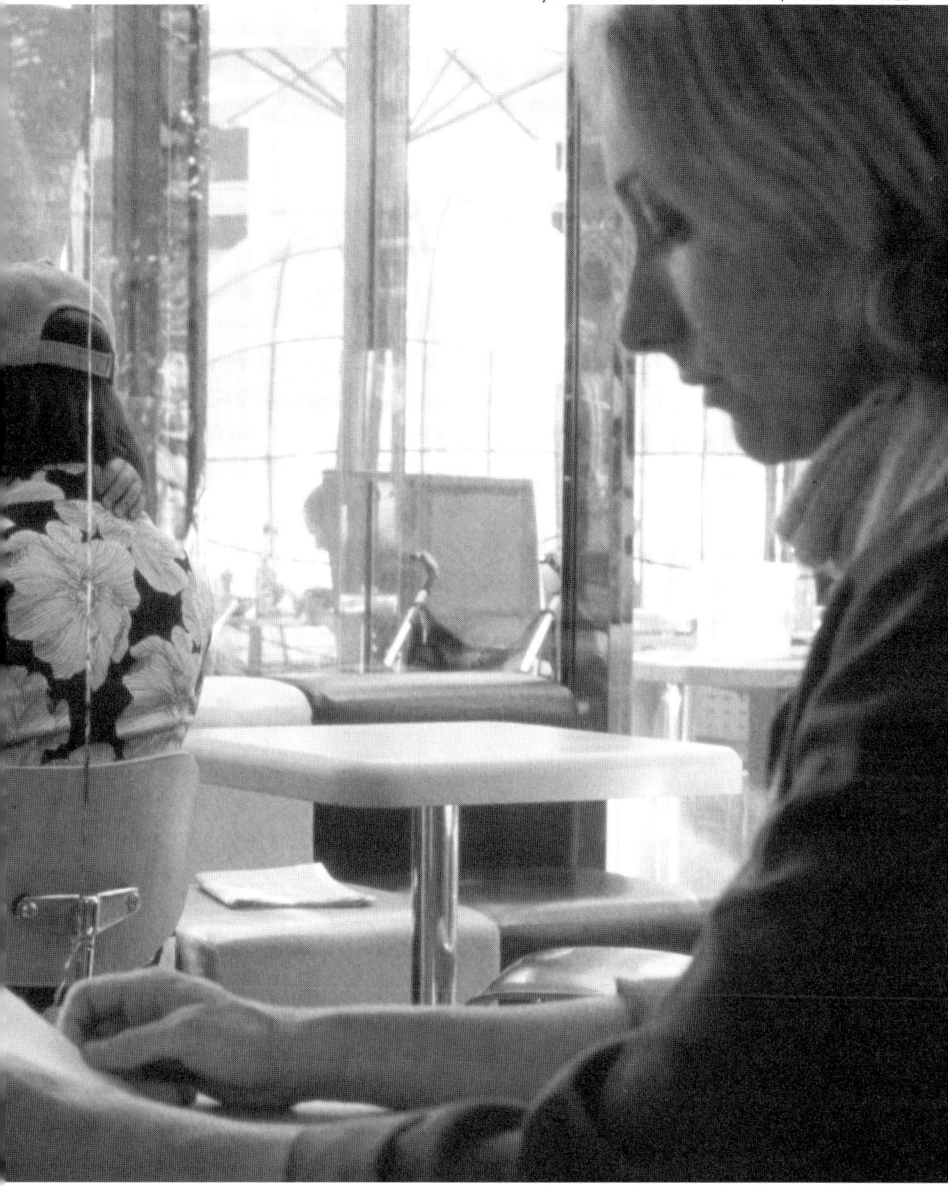

the apparition (an actress)

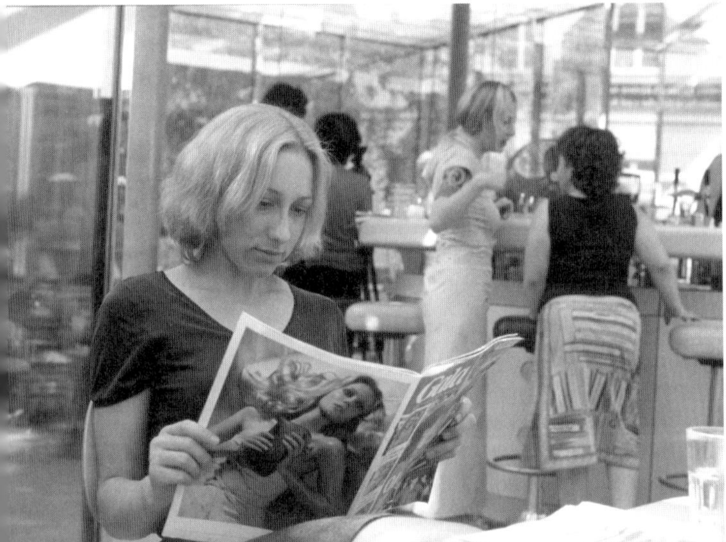

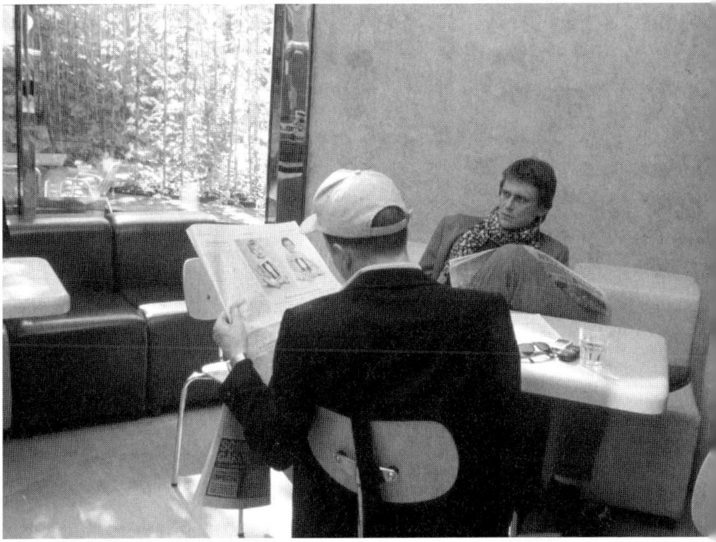

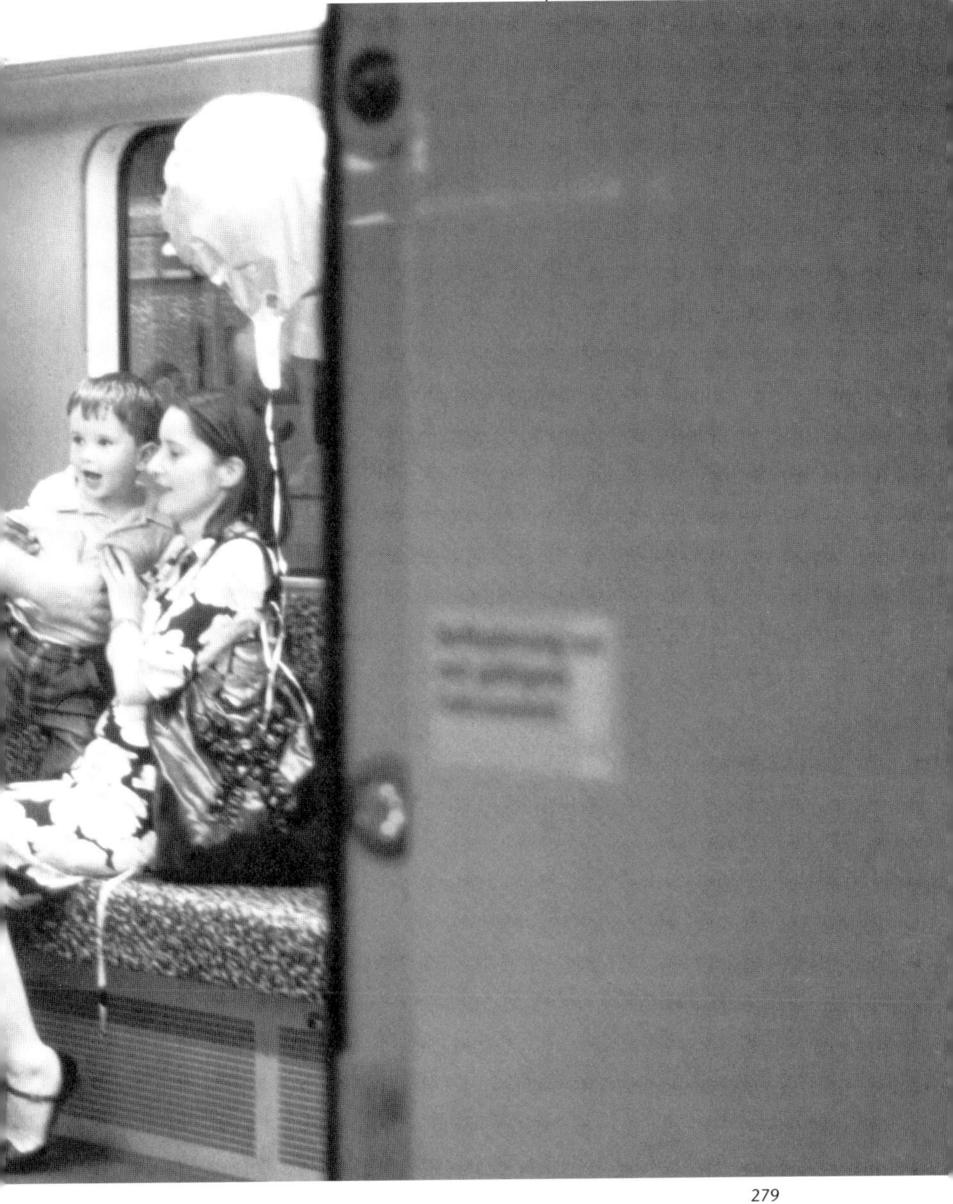

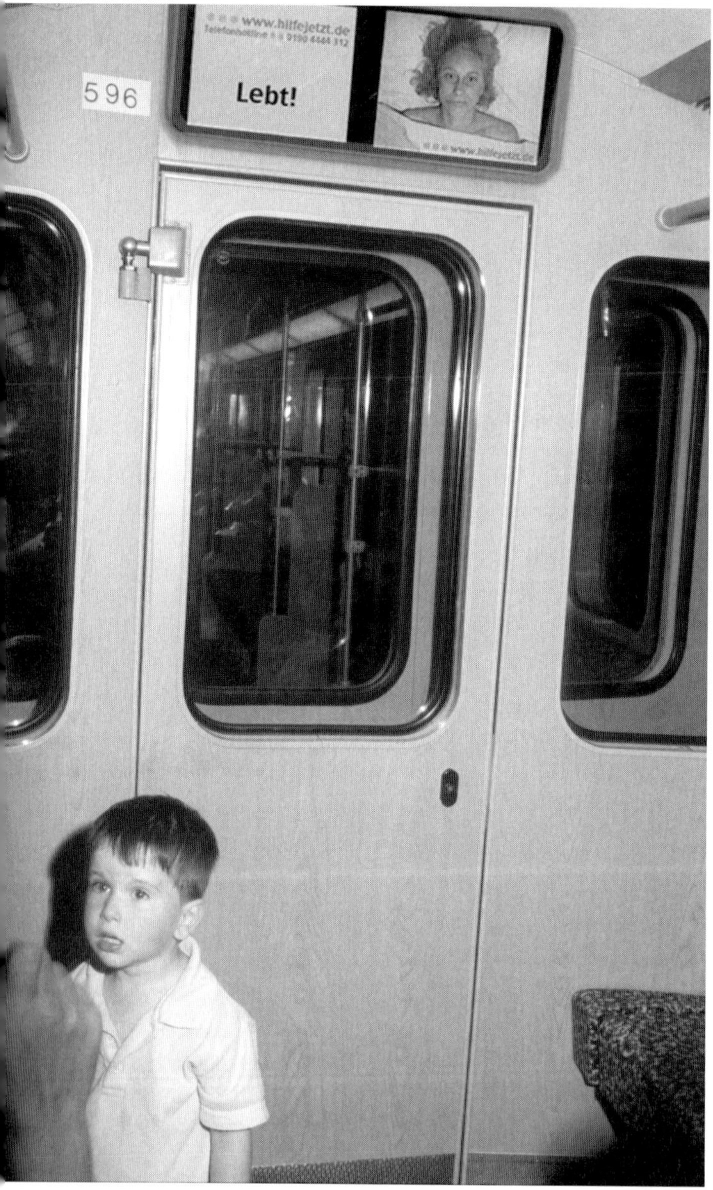
www.hilfejetzt.de
596
Lebt!

The tables dance, and society is closing in

The performance *Eyewitness 2nd Take/Lecture for Two Ghosts* came about within the context of preparations for a film project in which we used ghosts as a model of thought for current social events and their representation in the media. This approach evolved from the question of how information—in the context of war coverage, for instance—is broadcast daily into the private and public spheres and how it is subsequently perceived by a (secondary) eyewitness. Starting from the idea that the representation of events has an uncanny feel to it, we decided to consider mediumistic practices and ghost stories as specific kinds of news transmissions. Ghosts stand here as a trope for the embodiment and the staging of a gap within what is speakable, a gap between the perception of an event and its representation, i.e., the possibility to speak about it.

In the performance we associatively presented some basing points about the historical origins of spiritualist practices by using various kinds of medial devices. The wave of spiritualism in Europe and America in the second half of the nineteenth century can be seen in direct relation to modern reproduction and communication technologies such as photography, telegraphy and wireless radio. Looked at from today's point of view, a phenomenon like spirit photography shows the overlap between questions of being a witness and photographic documentation. In its own time modern spiritualism was recognized as both an experimental science and a popular religious movement, with close links to political reform movements in the United States such as abolitionism and the early women's rights movement. The first women speakers to attract a large public audience in America were spiritualist trance speakers, and spiritualism became a major vehicle to spread feminist ideas. The radical social agenda of spiritualists spans from their commitment to the emancipation of women to their critique of the norms imposed by society and religion as constituting unequal structures of relations between human beings. Thus they denounced not only the authority of men over women, but of churches over believers, governments over citizens, doctors over patients, and masters over slaves.

Around the same time as "the tables begin to dance," Marx borrowed from the mediumistic vocabulary for his economic analysis of the social relations between men and objects to describe how products of human labor become commodities, "changed into something transcendent."

The ghost film *The Uninvited* takes place in various locations in the ghostly world of the "New Center" in Berlin at the beginning of twenty-first century—a setting that needs to be kept under surveillance and secured constantly. The film is structured by tableaux-like sets in which the gaze relationships of the actors are staged. The camera follows the family on an ordinary day through different places of transmission—places that serve the mediation of news or so-called information—and observes the particular perspectives and technologies of the gaze.

In this environment two ghosts appear who can be seen as personifications of social unease. One is the arrival ghost, whose characteristic is to always arrive twice (most likely he is a journalist). The other apparition disappears as quickly as she appears: the ghost of an actress, who appeared as an Oded girl in a public service announcement in the subway.

Society is closing in and the ghosts show themselves directly in its center.

Die Tische tanzen, und die Gesellschaft rückt näher

Die Performance *Eyewitness 2nd Take/Vortrag für zwei Geister* entstand im Rahmen der Vorbereitung zu einem Filmprojekt, in dem wir Geister als Denkmodell für aktuelle gesellschaftliche Ereignisse und deren mediale Repräsentation benutzen. Dieser Ansatz entwickelte sich aus der Untersuchung, wie Information – zum Beispiel im Rahmen der Kriegsberichterstattung – täglich in den privaten und öffentlichen Raum übertragen wird. Insbesondere interessierten uns die Formen sekundärer AugenzeugInnenschaft, die dabei entstehen. Da der Repräsentation von Ereignissen etwas Gespenstisches innewohnt, beschlossen wir, mediumistische Praktiken und Geistergeschichten als spezifische Formen der Nachrichtenübertragung zu betrachten. Geister stehen dabei als Gedankenmodell für die Verkörperung und Inszenierung einer Lücke im Aussprechbaren, einer Lücke, die zwischen der Wahrnehmung von übertragenen Ereignissen und der Möglichkeit entsteht, diese Ereignisse zu besprechen oder darzustellen.

In der Performance legten wir zunächst unter Einbeziehung verschiedener Medien assoziativ einige Referenzpunkte über die historischen Entstehungsbedingungen spiritualistischer Praktiken dar. Die Spiritualismuswelle in Europa und Amerika in der zweiten Hälfte des 19. Jahrhunderts kann in direktem Bezug zu modernen Reproduktions- und Kommunikationstechnologien wie Fotografie, Telegrafie und Radiofunk gesehen werden. Aus heutiger Sicht betrachtet, überschneiden sich im Phänomen der Geisterfotografie Fragen von ZeugInnenschaft und fotografischer Dokumentation. Bereits zu seiner Zeit wurde moderner Spiritualismus sowohl als experimentelle Wissenschaft als auch als religiöse Bewegung verstanden und stand häufig in enger Verbindung mit reformpolitischen oder feministischen Anliegen, wie zum Beispiel der Bewegung zur Abschaffung der Sklaverei und der frühen Frauenbewegung. Die ersten öffentlichen Rednerinnen, die ein großes Publikum auf sich ziehen konnten, waren in Amerika spiritualistische Sprecherinnen, „trance speakers“, und Spiritualismus wurde ein wichtiges Mittel zur Verbreitung feministischer Ideen. Die radikale soziale Agenda des Spiritualismus reichte vom Engagement für die Emanzipation der Frau bis zur Kritik an den von Gesellschaft und Kirche gesetzten Normen, die ungleiche Beziehungsstrukturen zwischen Menschen konstituieren. Daher verurteilten sie nicht nur die Autorität von Männern über Frauen, sondern genauso von Kirchen über Gläubigen, Regierungen über BürgerInnen und HerrInnen über DienerInnen. Etwa zur selben Zeit, als „die Tische zu tanzen begannen", bedient sich Marx in seiner ökonomischen Analyse über die gesellschaftlichen Verhältnisse von Menschen und Gegenständen des Vokabulars jener mediumistischen Konjunktur und beschreibt, wie Produkte menschlicher Arbeit zu Waren werden, „sinnlich übersinnliche" oder gesellschaftliche Dinge.

Der Geisterfilm *The Uninvited* spielt an verschiedenen Schauplätzen in der gespenstisch dinglichen Welt in der „Neuen Mitte" Berlins zu Beginn des 21. Jahrhunderts – eine Kulisse, die ständig überwacht und gesichert werden muss. Der Film wird von tableauartigen Szenenbildern strukturiert, in denen die Blickbeziehungen der AkteurInnen inszeniert werden. Die Kamera folgt einer Familie an einem gewöhnlichen Tag durch verschiedene Orte der Übertragung – Orte, die der Vermittlung von Nachrichten oder so genannter Information dienen – und beobachtet die jeweiligen Blickperspektiven und -technologien. In diesem Umfeld treten zwei geisterhafte Erscheinungen auf, die als Personifizierungen gesellschaftlichen Unbehagens angesehen werden können: der Ankunftsgeist, dessen Merkmal es ist, immer zweimal anzukommen (er ist wahrscheinlich ein Journalist); die andere Erscheinung taucht so unmittelbar auf, wie sie verschwindet: der Geist einer Schauspielerin, die als Drogentote auf einem Plakat in der U-Bahn zu sehen ist.

Die Gesellschaft rückt näher, und die Geister zeigen sich direkt in ihrem Zentrum.

Contributors

Christa Benzer is an art critic living and working in Vienna. She is an assistant editor for *springerin—Hefte für Gegenwartskunst* (www.springerin.at) and has published numerous texts and essays in art magazines and catalogs. Since April 2004 she has also been a freelance contributor to the Austrian daily newspaper *Der Standard*.

Linda Bilda is a Vienna-based visual artist, inventor, political activist, and co-editor of *Die weisse Blatt. Zeitschrift für Kunst und Politik* (www.dieweisseblatt.org). She is currently working on a large comics project, „Homo hominis lupus non est," which will be published in 2008. Her work, which has been shown internationally, focuses on projects with formative social effects.

Gregg Bordowitz writes and makes films and videos. *Fast Trip Long Drop* (1993), *A Cloud in Trousers* (1995), *The Suicide* (1996), and *Habit* (2001) have been shown internationally in festivals, museums, and cinemas as well as broadcast on television. *The AIDS Crisis Is Ridiculous and Other Writings 1986-2003*, a collection of his essays, was published by MIT Press in 2004.

Stephan Dillemuth, in his artistic research, proposes the stage as an apparatus for reflection, as an experimental space, and as a term for "exhibition." He aims at encouraging artists to see themselves as positioned on a (social) stage and to become active participants in the "game." In this project, entertaining aspects are used rather than rejected. For further information see www.societyofcontrol.com.

Discoteca Flaming Star is a project started by the artists Cristina Gomez Barrio and Wolfgang Mayer in 1998. Both live and work in Berlin. They also collaborated on the project space *innocence & mystery* (Berlin 2002-2003). Individual video work and drawings. For further information see www.discotecaflamingstar.com (E-mail: flamingstar@snafu.de).

Marie-Thérèse Escribano was born in Paris and grew up in Madrid. She received her education as a classical concert and opera singer in Madrid, Brussels, and Vienna, where she won the Belcanto Award in 1956. Numerous concerts in Europe and the US followed, including performances with Pierre Boulez, Lorin Maazel, Paul Sacher, and Friedrich Cerha. In the mid 1960s, she co-founded the early music ensemble Les Ménestrels, which she left ten years later to work on her own feminist music-theater performances. She lives and works in Vienna. Her recordings include German popular songs of the 1920s and 1930s, Sephardic songs, and most recently Spanish folk songs, *Canciones de seda verde*. For further information see www.escribano.at.

Andrea Fraser is a New York-based artist whose work has been identified with performance, context art, and institutional critique. Since the mid-80s she has produced site-specific performances, videos, installations, and publications with museums, galleries, and foundations throughout the United States, Europe, and Latin America. Major performances include *Museum Highlights: A Gallery Talk* (Philadelphia Museum of Art, 1989), *May I Help You?* (American Fine Arts Co., New York, 1991), *Inaugural Speech* (inSITE97, San Diego, 1997), *Kunst Muss Hängen* (Galerie Christian Nagel, 2001) and *Official Welcome* (MICA Foundation, New York 2001). Between 1986 and 1996 she was also a member of the feminist performance group The V-Girls. *Andrea Fraser: Works 1985-2003*, a retrospective of her work, was organized by the Kunstverein in Hamburg in 2003 with a catalog by DuMont. In 2005, MIT Press released *Museum Highlights: The Writings of Andrea Fraser*, a collection of her essays and performance scripts (edited by Alexander Alberro and with a foreword by Pierre Bourdieu).

Sharon Hayes is a New York based artist. Her work moves among multiple mediums in an ongoing investigation into the interrelation of history, politics, and speech. Her installation, video, and performance work has been shown in New York at P.S.1 Contemporary Art Center, Andrew Kreps Gallery, Parlour Projects, the Whitney Museum of American Art's Indepedent Study Program, Dance Theater Workshop, Dixon Place, HERE, Performance Space 122, the Joseph Papp Public Theater, the WOW Cafe, and the New Museum of Contemporary Art; and in Los Angeles at LACE, Track 16, Gallery 2102, and The Project.

Achim Hochdörfer has been a curator at the Museum of Modern Art Ludwig Foundation Vienna (MUMOK) since 2002. Exhibition projects include *Jeff Wall. Photographs* (2003); *Mike Kelley. The Uncanny* (2004); *John Cage* (2004). Publications on contemporary art include, most recently, "Louise Lawler. Preliminary Remarks on a "'Phenomenology of Cuts'" (*Camera Austria*, December 2005). Since 2000, he has been teaching in the art history department of the University of Vienna.

Judith Hopf is an artist and video-maker living and working in Berlin. From 2002 to 2005 she was visiting professor for video and sculpture at the School of Art and Design Berlin Weissensee. She is engaged in collective video projects like *A-clip* (www.aclip.net) and *Ping Pong d'Amour*. Her writings have appeared in *Starship* (starship-magazine.org) and other publications. Recent exhibitions include *100 Radiodays* (De Appel Museum, Amsterdam, 2005) and *Universal Experience: Art, Life and the Tourist's Eye* (Museum of Contemporary Art Chicago, 2005).

Christof Kurzmann currently lives in Berlin. Musician working between electropop, improvisation, and "new music," sometimes as a soloist but preferably part of a collective or cooperative setting. Concerts on all continents except Australia. Organizer of various events in the field of music and film. Runs the independent record label charhizma (www.charhizma.com). A conscientious objector to both the military and alternative civilian services, he continues to be politically active and interested. Likes to travel, to go to movies and concerts, to read. E-mail to charhizma@charhizma.com (however, he frequently doesn't respond).

Xavier Le Roy studied molecular and cellular biology. While working on his Ph.D. he started to study dance. Since 1991 he has worked as a dancer and choreographer. For more information see www.insituproductions.net.

Matthew Lyons studied art history at Vassar College and the Modern Art and Curatorial Studies Program at Columbia University. He is currently the Curatorial Associate at The Kitchen in New York City. E-mail: matthew@thekitchen.org.

Sabine Marte lives in Vienna. Since 1993 her work has been mainly in the fields of video, video performance, and music. She is a member of the bands SV Damenkraft and Pendler, and has participated in performances, conferences, and exhibitions in Berlin, Bangkok, Chicago, Feldkirch, London, Mexico City, Nickelsdorf, Osnabrück, Paris, Rotterdam, Tábor, Vienna, and Zürich. For more information see sabinemarte.klingt.org; klingt.org/~oliver/prb (on "*Step behind the ropes please! no.2*"); www.sixpackfilm.com (on further video pieces); and www.no-racism.net (on the Publix Theatre Caravan).

Mattin is a proletarian of noise, understanding noise as the underclass, rejected, marginalized and beyond music. His main mode of production is improvisation—mostly using computer feedback on a GNU/Linux operating system. An ongoing collaboration with Radu Malfatti led to their CD, *Whitenoise* (released on Mattin's label w.m.o/r). A second CD of the duo, *Going Fragile*, came out in spring 2006 on Formed Records (www.formedrecords.com). Mattin lives and works in London. For more information see www.mattin.org. E-mail: mattin@mattin.org.

Ulrike Müller is an artist currently living and working in New York. Since 2005 she has been an editor for the queer feminist art journal *LTTR* (www.lttr.org). Exhibitions, performances and and video screenings include *Diagonale, Festival of Austrian Film* (Graz, 2005), *LTTR Explosion* (with Marie-Thérèse Escribano) (New York, 2004); and *Mothers of Invention—Where is Performance Coming From* (MUMOK, Vienna, 2003). The artist's book *Every little bit helps—Ulrike Müller: Two Audio Works* (2005, with essays by Gregg Bordowitz, Barbara Schröder, Lanka Tattersall, and Walter Johnston), is distributed by Revolver (www.revolver-books.de). E-mail: ulrike@lttr.org.

Katrin Pesch received an MFA from School of Art and Design Berlin Weissensee in 1999. In 2000 she participated in the Whitney Museum of American Art Independent Study Program in New York. In 2004-2005 she was a visiting artist at the Art Center College of Design in Pasadena. Her work explores, reenacts and develops modes of cultural production that employ narrative strategies as a form of political storytelling. She is currently organizing the exhibition project *New Ghost Entertainment Entitled* (OR Gallery in Vancouver, Canada, fall 2006). E-mail: katrinpesch@gmx.net.

Yvonne Rainer is a filmmaker and choreographer. Further information about her work can be found in *Work 1961-73* (Nova Scotia College of Art and Design and New York University Press, 1974), *The Films of Yvonne Rainer* (Indiana University Press, 1989), and *A Woman Who...: Essays, Interviews, Scripts* (Johns Hopkins University Press, 1999). Her memoir *Feelings Are Facts: A Life* was published by MIT Press in 2006.

Britta Scholze studied German literature, philosophy, and political science in Freiburg im Breisgau and in Berlin. A scientific associate at the FU Berlin, she wrote her dissertation on *Art as Criticism: Adorno's Step Beyond Dialectics*. From 2000-2005 she worked as a consultant for art and culture for the Heinrich-Böll-Stiftung Berlin, and was also a consultant for cultural politics for the Green Party in the German parliament in 2005. At the end of 2005 she moved to Switzerland, where she is currently studying at the Zürich University to become a teacher. She has published on art and politics.

AutorInnen

Christa Benzer ist Kunstkritikerin und lebt in Wien. Sie ist redaktionelle Mitarbeiterin der *springerin – Hefte für Gegenwartskunst* (www.springerin.at). Zahlreiche Veröffentlichungen in Kunstzeitschriften und Katalogen; seit April 2004 freie Mitarbeiterin der österreichischen Tageszeitung *Der Standard*.

Linda Bilda lebt in Wien, sie ist bildende Künstlerin, Erfinderin, politische Aktivistin und Mitherausgeberin von *Die weisse Blatt. Zeitschrift für Kunst und Politik* (www.dieweisseblatt.org). Derzeit arbeitet sie an einem umfangreichen Comicprojekt, „Homo hominis lupus non est", das 2008 erscheinen wird. Schwerpunkt ihrer Arbeit sind Projekte, die gesellschaftskonstituierend wirken. Internationale Ausstellungstätigkeit.

Gregg Bordowitz schreibt und macht Filme und Videos. *Fast Trip Long Drop* (1993), *A Cloud in Trousers* (1995), *The Suicide* (1996) und *Habit* (2001) wurden international auf Festivals, in Museen sowie im Kino und im Fernsehen gezeigt. Seine gesammelten Schriften sind 2004 unter dem Titel *The AIDS Crisis Is Ridiculous and Other Writings 1986–2003* bei MIT Press erschienen.

Stephan Dillemuth schlägt in seinen Forschungsprojekten die Bühne als einen Apparat für Reflexion, als experimentellen Ort und Terminus für „Ausstellung" vor. KünstlerInnen sollen dazu ermutigt werden, sich auf einer (sozialen) Bühne positioniert zu sehen und als aktive TeilnehmerInnen in das „Spiel" einzugreifen. Dabei wird der unterhaltsame Aspekt nicht geleugnet, sondern benutzt. Weitere Informationen unter www.societyofcontrol.com.

Discoteca Flaming Star wurde 1998 von den KünstlerInnen Cristina Gomez Barrio und Wolfgang Mayer gegründet. Beide wohnen und arbeiten in Berlin. Der Projektraum *innocence & mystery* (Berlin 2002–2003) war ebenfalls ein gemeinsames Projekt. Individuelle Arbeiten im Bereich Zeichnung und Video. Weitere Informationen unter www.discotecaflamingstar.com (E-Mail: flamingstar@snafu.de).

Marie-Thérèse Escribano wurde in Paris geboren und wuchs in Madrid auf. Ihre Ausbildung als klassische Opern- und Konzertsängerin erhielt sie in Madrid, Brüssel und Wien, wo sie 1956 mit dem Belcanto-Preis des Österreichischen Rundfunks ausgezeichnet wurde. Zahlreiche Konzerte in Europa und den USA, unter anderen mit Pierre Boulez, Lorin Maazel, Paul Sacher und Friedrich Cerha. Mitte der 1960er-Jahre Mitbegründerin des Ensembles für alte Musik, Les Ménestrels, das sie zehn Jahre später verließ, um ihre eigenen feministischen Musik- und Theaterperformances aufzuführen. Sie lebt und arbeitet in Wien. Auf CDs sind Aufnahmen ihrer Programme, deutsche Schlager der 1920er- und 1930er-Jahre, sephardische Lieder und seit kurzem auch spanische Volkslieder, *Canciones de seda verde*, erhältlich. Weitere Informationen unter www.escribano.at.

Andrea Fraser ist eine in New York lebende Künstlerin, deren Arbeit als Performance, Kontextkunst und Institutionskritik beschrieben wurde. Seit Mitte der 1980er-Jahre produziert sie ortsspezifische Performances, Videos, Installationen und Publikationen mit Museen, Galerien und Stiftungen in den USA, Europa und Lateinamerika. Zahlreiche Performances, etwa *Museum Highlights: A Gallery Talk* (Philadelphia Museum of Art, 1989), *May I Help You?* (American Fine Arts, Co., New York, 1991), *Inaugural Speech* (inSITE97, San Diego, 1997), *Kunst muss hängen* (Galerie Christian Nagel, 2001) oder *Official Welcome* (MICA Foundation, New York, 2001). Von 1986 bis 1996 war sie Mitglied der feministischen Performancegruppe The V-Girls. Die Retrospektive *Andrea Fraser: Works 1985-2003* wurde 2003 vom Kunstverein in Hamburg organisiert, der Katalog zur Ausstellung ist bei DuMont erschienen. 2005 publizierte MIT Press *Museum Highlights: The Writings of Andrea Fraser*, eine Sammlung ihrer Aufsätze und Performanceskripte (herausgegeben von Alexander Alberro und mit einem Vorwort von Pierre Bourdieu).

Sharon Hayes lebt und arbeitet in New York. Ihre Arbeit, eine fortwährende Untersuchung der Zusammenhänge von Geschichte, Politik und Sprechweisen, ist zwischen mehreren Medien angesiedelt. Ihre Installationen, Video- und Performancearbeiten wurden im P.S.1 Contemporary Art Center, in der Galerie Andrew Kreps, bei Parlour Projects, im Whitney Museum of American Art Independent Study Program sowie bei Dance Theater Workshop, im Dixon Place, HERE, Performance Space 122, Joseph Papp Public Theater, WOW Café und New Museum of Contemporary Art in New York und in Los Angeles bei LACE, Track 16, Gallery 2102 und The Project gezeigt.

Achim Hochdörfer ist seit 2002 Kurator am Museum Moderner Kunst Stiftung Ludwig Wien (MUMOK). Ausstellungsprojekte umfassen unter anderem *Jeff Wall. Photographs* (2003), *Mike Kelley. Das Unheimliche* (2004) oder *John Cage* (2004). Publikationen zur Kunst der Gegenwart, zuletzt „Louise Lawler. Vorbemerkungen zu einer ‚Phänomenologie der Schnitte'" (*Camera Austria*, Dezember 2005). Seit 2000 Lehraufträge am Institut für Kunstgeschichte der Universität Wien.

Judith Hopf lebt als Künstlerin und Videomacherin in Berlin. Von 2002 bis 2005 war sie Gastprofessorin für Video und Skulptur and der Kunsthochschule Berlin Weißensee. Beteiligung an kollektiven Videoprojekten wie *A-clip* (www.aclip.net) und *Ping Pong d'Amour*. Ihre Texte sind in *Starship* (starship-magazine.org) und anderen Publikationen erschienen. Ihre Arbeiten waren in letzter Zeit unter anderem in den Ausstellungen *100 Radiodays* (De Appel, Amsterdam, 2005) und *Universal Experience: Art, Life and the Tourist's Eye* (Museum of Contemporary Art Chicago, 2005) zu sehen.

Christof Kurzmann lebt derzeit in Berlin. Musiker zwischen Elektropop, Improvisation und „neuer Musik", manchmal Solist, lieber aber Teil eines Kollektivs oder einer Arbeitsgemeinschaft. Konzerte in allen Kontinenten außer Australien. Veranstalter diverser Events im Musik- und Filmbereich. Betreiber des Kleinlabels charhizma (www.charhizma.com). Wehr- und Zivildienstverweigerer, weiterhin politisch aktiv und interessiert. Reist gerne, geht gerne ins Kino und zu Konzerten, liest gerne, auch E-Mails an charhizma@charhizma.com (antwortet aber oftmals nicht).

Xavier Le Roy studierte Molekular- und Zellbiologie. Während der Arbeit an seiner Dissertation begann er, Tanzworkshops zu besuchen. Seit 1991 arbeitet er als Tänzer und Choreograf. Mehr Information unter www.insituproductions.net.

Matthew Lyons studierte Kunstgeschichte am Vassar College und besuchte das Modern Art and Curatorial Studies Program der Columbia University. Er ist derzeit kuratorischer Mitarbeiter bei The Kitchen in New York. E-Mail: matthew@thekitchen.org.

Sabine Marte lebt in Wien. Sie arbeitet seit 1993 schwerpunktmäßig in den Bereichen Video, Videoperformance und Musik und ist Mitglied der Bands SV Damenkraft und Pendler. Performances,

Auftritte, Konferenzen und Ausstellungen in Berlin, Bangkok, Chicago, Feldkirch, London, Mexiko-Stadt, Nickelsdorf, Osnabrück, Paris, Rotterdam, Tábor, Wien und Zürich. Mehr Informationen unter sabinemarte.klingt.org, klingt.org/~oliver/prb (zu *„Step behind the ropes please! nr. 2"*), www.sixpack-film.com (zu weiteren Videoarbeiten) und www.no-racism.net (zur Volxtheaterkarawane).

Mattin ist ein Noise-Proletarier, wobei er Noise als die Unterklasse versteht, jenseits von Musik, verworfen und marginalisiert. Sein hauptsächlicher Produktionsmodus ist Improvisation, er verwendet zumeist Computerfeedback auf einem GNU/Linux-Betriebssystem. Seine aktuelle Zusammenarbeit mit Radu Malfatti führte zu der CD *Whitenoise* (erschienen auf Mattins Label w.m.o/r), eine zweite CD des Duos, *Going Fragile*, wurde im Frühjahr 2006 auf Formed Records (www.formedrecords.com) veröffentlicht. Mattin lebt und arbeitet in London. Weitere Informationen unter www.mattin.org. E-Mail: mattin@mattin.org.

Ulrike Müller ist Künstlerin, sie lebt und arbeitet derzeit in New York. Seit 2005 ist sie Redakteurin und Mitherausgeberin der queer feministischen Kunstzeitschrift *LTTR* (www.lttr.org). Ausstellungen, Performances und Videoscreenings unter anderem bei der *Diagonale* (Graz, 2005), *LTTR Explosion* (mit Marie-Thérèse Escribano, New York, 2004); *Mothers of Invention – Where is Performance coming from* (MUMOK, Wien, 2003). Das Künstlerinnenbuch *Every little bit helps, – Ulrike Müller: Two Audio Works* (2005, mit Aufsätzen von Gregg Bordowitz, Barbara Schröder, Lanka Tattersall und Walter Johnston) ist bei Revolver erhältlich (www.revolver-books.de). E-Mail: ulrike@lttr.org.

Katrin Pesch studierte an der Kunsthochschule Berlin Weißensee. Von 2000 bis 2001 nahm sie am Whitney Museum of American Art Independent Study Program in New York teil. 2004/2005 war sie Visiting Artist am Art Center in Pasadena. Ihre Arbeiten untersuchen narrative Strategien kultureller Produktion, um daraus Formen des politischen Geschichtenerzählens zu entwickeln. Zurzeit organisiert sie das Ausstellungsprojekt *New Ghost Entertainment Entitled* (OR Gallery, Vancouver, Kanada, Herbst 2006). E-Mail: katrinpesch@gmx.net.

Yvonne Rainer ist Filmemacherin und Choreografin. Für weitere Information über ihre Arbeit siehe die Publikationen *Work 1961–73* (Nova Scotia College of Art and Design, New York University Press, 1974), *The Films of Yvonne Rainer* (Indiana University Press, 1989) und *A Woman Who...: Essays, Interviews, Scripts* (Johns Hopkins University Press, 1999). Ihre Memoiren sind 2006 unter dem Titel *Feelings Are Facts: A Life* bei MIT Press erschienen.

Britta Scholze studierte Germanistik, Philosophie und Politikwissenschaft in Freiburg im Breisgau und in Berlin. Wissenschaftliche Mitarbeiterin an der FU Berlin, Promotion über *Kunst als Kritik. Adornos Weg aus der Dialektik*. 2000 bis 2005 Referentin für Kunst und Kultur an der Heinrich-Böll-Stiftung Berlin. 2005 zusätzlich Referentin für Kulturpolitik bei der Bundestagsfraktion von Bündnis 90/Die Grünen. Ende 2005 Umsiedlung in die Schweiz und Aufnahme der LehrerInnenausbildung an der Universität Zürich. Publikationen zum Thema Kunst und Politik.

Image Index

p 29 Gregg Bordowitz and Andrea Fraser in the audience. *Public Affairs* symposium, MUMOK, Vienna, September 2003. (photograph: Lisa Rastl).

p 31 Sharon Hayes, *After/Before*, 2005. Kemba Bloodworth and Ewa Einhorn (video stills: Sharon Hayes).

p 32 Sharon Hayes, *After/Before: voiceover. Public Affairs*, MUMOK, Vienna, September 2003 (photograph: Lisa Rastl).

p 45, 47 and 48 Yvonne Rainer, *AG Indexical, with a little help from H.M.*, 2006 (rehearsal photographs: Andrea Geyer).

p 62-69, 71 and 76-79 drawings and photographs: Linda Bilda.

p 70, 74 and 82-83 Linda Bilda and Peter Döllmann in: *Linda in Action, or Business as Usual. Public Affairs*, MUMOK, Vienna, September 2003 (photographs: Lisa Rastl).

p 84 Linda Bilda and Gregg Bordowitz in *Linda in Action, or Business as Usual. Public Affairs*, MUMOK, Vienna, September 2003 (photograph: Lisa Rastl).

p 88 Gregg Bordowitz, *The Temperaments and Their Sway. Public Affairs*, MUMOK, Vienna, September 2003 (photograph: Lisa Rastl).

p 92 and 98 Marie-Thérèse Escribano, *Nostalgie. Public Affairs*, MUMOK, Vienna, September 2003 (photographs: Lisa Rastl).

p 104-105 Discoteca Flaming Star, *Black Banner*, 2003.

p 106 Discoteca Flaming Star, *Sexy Bloody Cat. Public Affairs*, MUMOK, Vienna, September 2003 (photograph: Lisa Rastl).

p 110-121 photographs and drawing: Discoteca Flaming Star.

p 130 and 134 Christof Kurzmann, *the air between. Public Affairs*, MUMOK, Vienna, September 2003 (photographs: Lisa Rastl).

p 152-161 video stills: Sabine Marte.

p 171 and 172 Andrea Fraser, *Starting where she's standing. Public Affairs*, MUMOK, Vienna, September 2003 (photograph: Lisa Rastl).

p 187 and 188 Andrea Fraser, *Official Welcome*, 2001. Still from video documenting performance at the Kunstverein in Hamburg, 2003.

p 204 and 206 Ulrike Müller as Hans-Dieter in Werner von Delmont, *Corporate Rokoko. Public Affairs*, MUMOK, Vienna, September 2003 (photograph: Lisa Rastl).

p 219 and 220 Stephan Dillemuth and Ulrike Müller in Werner von Delmont, *Corporate Rokoko. Public Affairs*, MUMOK, Vienna, September 2003 (photograph: Lisa Rastl).

p 234, 246, 249, and 259 Xavier Le Roy, *Product of Circumstances* (photographs: Katrin Schoof).

p 260-261 Judith Hopf und Katrin Pesch, *Pamphlet*, 2003.

p 262-263 Judith Hopf and Katrin Pesch, *Eyewitness, 2nd Take. Public Affairs*, MUMOK, Vienna, September 2003 (photograph: Lisa Rastl).

p 264 and 265 photographs: Judith Hopf und Katrin Pesch

p 266-280 Judith Hopf and Katrin Pesch, *The Uninvited, 2004*. Film production stills: Christina Zück.

Abbildungsverzeichnis

oe – organizational excess

oe is a series of critical readers into contemporary visual cultures; their emergences, contingencies and possibilities. The series is edited by Katya Sander and Simon Sheikh, artist and theorist. We are committed to theory, but not to discipline, and every reader thus revolves around a specific notion or event, seen and discussed from various vantage points or positions. Through an analysis of visual cultures – art, film, tv, the net, the street and so on – different regimes of visuality can be located. The circulation, production, reproduction and interpretation of images is seen as crucial to an understanding of contemporary politics, not just of representation, but also of the imaginary. Analysis is therefore not only to be understood as reflective, but also as active or activating. It is proposition(s).

#1: The Meaning of Site

Notions of space analyzed through practices of site-specificity

Edited by Katya Sander, Simon Sheikh and Cecilie Høgsbro Østergaard. Texts by Katya Sander, Marion von Osten, Jochen Becker, Simon Sheikh, Poyin Auyoung and Cecilie Høgsbro Østergaard.

#2: Death Drive

Art and Film Beyond the Pleasure Principle

Edited by Gertrud Sandqvist. Texts by Gertrud Sandqvist, Laura Mulvey, Friederich Meschede, Matts Leiderstam / Peggy Phelan and Denise Robinson.

#3: Rent

About the temporary relation many people have to things around them

Edited by Stuart Koop. Texts by Rex Butler, Edward Colless, Stuart Koop, Gary Foley, Philip Brophy, Elizabeth Grosz and John Leigh.

#4: I said I love. That is the Promise.

The tvideo politics of Jean-Luc Godard

Edited by Gareth James and Florian Zeyfang. Texts by Dave Beech, Elisabeth Büttner, Manthia Diawara, Simon Sheikh, Jason Simon, Stephan Geene, Kaja Silverman and Michael Eng.

#5: In the Place of the Public Sphere?

On the establishment of publics and counter-publics

Edited by Simon Sheikh. Texts by Miwon Kwon, Nils Norman, Valerie Tevere, Bojana Pejic, Frans Jacobi, Stephan Dillemuth, Charles Esche, Marion von Osten, Gunnar Krantz, Copenhagen Free University, Stephan Geene, Ultra Red and Pauline van der Mourik Broekman.

#7: Capital (It Fails Us Now)

Edited by Simon Sheikh. Contributions from Brian Holmes, Oleg Kireev, Stephan Geene, Isabell Lorey, Katja Diefenbach, Gerald Raunig, Trude Iversen, Fia-Stina Sandlund, Elin Wikström, Natascha Sadr Haghighian, Olafur Gislason, Michael Blum, Jason Simon, Knut Åsdam, Regina Dold, Katia Foquet, Florian Gass, Marietta Kesting, Katya Sander, Ashley Hunt, Oliver Ressler, Copenhagen Free University, Maria Eichhorn, Andrea Creutz, Chto Delat?, Susan Kelly, and Stephen Morton.

Forthcoming:

#6: Here and Elsewhere

Routings, Relationalities and Imaginings between places

Reader & DVD. Edited by Katya Sander and Simon Sheikh. Texts & videos by An Architektur, François Bucher, Zach Formwalt, Andrea Geyer, Sharon Hayes, Brian Holmes, Janna Holmstedt, Ashley Hunt, Anders Michelsen, Yates McKee, Gerald Raunig, Georg Schöllhammer, Hito Steyerl, Alex Villar, Ulf Wuggenig, among others.